W9-BBH-171

# GERMAN CLASSICAL DRAMA

This book is a historical and critical survey of the great tradition of German drama in the eighteenth and nineteenth centuries, and provides an introduction to its major authors and works from Lessing, through Goethe, Schiller and Weimar classicism, to Kleist, Grillparzer and Hebbel. F. J. Lamport traces the rise and development in the German-speaking world of the last form of 'classical' poetic drama to appear in European literature. This development is seen as reflecting the intellectual and political ferment of the age: the great flowering of German philosophical thought, the rising aspirations of Germans to national unity, and the waves of revolution and counter-revolution which mark the European history of the period.

# GERMAN CLASSICAL DRAMA

## Theatre, humanity and nation
### 1750–1870

### F. J. LAMPORT

*Fellow of Worcester College, Oxford, and*
*University Lecturer in German*

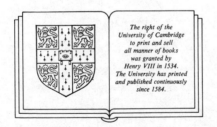

The right of the
University of Cambridge
to print and sell
all manner of books
was granted by
Henry VIII in 1534.
The University has printed
and published continuously
since 1584.

## CAMBRIDGE UNIVERSITY PRESS

*Cambridge*
*New York   Port Chester*
*Melbourne   Sydney*

Published by the Press Syndicate of the University of Cambridge
The Pitt Building, Trumpington Street, Cambridge CB2 1RP
40 West 20th Street, New York, NY 10011, USA
10 Stamford Road, Oakleigh, Melbourne 3166, Australia

First published 1990

Printed in Great Britain at the University Press, Cambridge

*British Library cataloguing in publication data*
Lamport, F. J. (Francis John)
German classical drama
1. Drama in German, 1750–1870 – Critical studies
1. Title
832'.6'09

*Library of Congress cataloguing in publication data*
Lamport, F. J. (Francis John)
German classical drama/F. J. Lamport.
p.     cm.
Bibliography.
Includes index.
ISBN 0-521-36270-9
1. German drama – 18th century – History and criticism.
2. German drama – 19th century – History and criticism.
3. Classicism in literature.
1. Title.     II. Series.
PT643.L34     1989
832'.609'142 – dc20     89-31435     CIP

ISBN 0 521 36270 9

*For Nanna*

# Contents

# Contents

# Illustrations

# *Preface*

The subject of this book is the drama of the so-called classical age of German literature, from its beginnings in the middle of the eighteenth century to the achievements of Goethe and Schiller at the century's end, and the subsequent attempts of Kleist, Grillparzer and Hebbel to prove themselves the true heirs to the tradition which Goethe and Schiller had established.

The term 'classical' has many meanings. Some definition will be attempted in Chapter I, but it is impossible to be absolutely precise or consistent. I hope though that the reader will gain some sense of a coherent tradition, evolving against the background of a particularly momentous period of European history.

The time seems ripe for such an undertaking, as the German drama of this period is beginning to find increasing acceptance in the theatre in Britain. In recent years plays by Lessing, Goethe, Schiller, Kleist and Grillparzer have been performed on British stages. The work of Robert David MacDonald and the Glasgow Citizens' Theatre is deserving of special mention. Audiences in Manchester, Edinburgh and London have been able to appreciate Schiller's power as an historical dramatist in *Don Carlos* and *Mary Stuart*. And 1988 has seen the triumph on the stage of the Lyric Theatre, Hammersmith, of the first performance in England of both parts of Goethe's *Faust*. I hope that in these circumstances this book will be of interest not only to the specialist student of German literature.

My approach is, however, basically a literary one, though I have taken some account of theatrical history and of the circumstances in which the plays were actually staged in their own time. The history of the theatre is a subject of its own – and one in which Goethe, in particular, occupies an important position. But classical drama (however defined) is essentially a literary form, its indispensable basis an author's text, which will demand, and survive, interpretation in a variety of theatrical styles to suit the requirements of ages other than its own. This is not necessarily to agree with Dr Johnson that 'a play read affects the mind like a play acted' or that 'a dramatic exhibition is a book recited with concomitants'. But it is to insist on the author's text as the prime repository of discoverable dramatic, or even theatrical, meaning. Such an approach seems above all appropriate in the case of German classical drama, whose relationship to the living theatre of its age is, as we shall see, a particularly tense and problematic one. All the major figures dealt with in this book were at some time or other actively involved with the theatre (apart from Kleist, who never saw any of his plays performed). But they came to the theatre as writers, poets and thinkers, rather than as practitioners of the stage like Shakespeare or Molière.

I have given all quotations in my own English versions, though with a few samples of the original German where this appeared particularly significant. It seemed to me important, however, to attempt to give some impression of the verbal flavour of such pre-eminently verbal art, and I have therefore (although, like Lessing, I make no claims to be either an actor or a poet) kept the original metres in all verse examples. References are by act and/or scene number, or by line number in verse plays where scenes are not numbered. I am grateful to Penguin Books for permission to reprint (sometimes in modified form) extracts from *Five German Tragedies* and from Schiller's *The Robbers* and *Wallenstein*, which have appeared in the Penguin Classics. Thanks are also due to the museums, libraries and individuals noted in the List of Illustrations for permission to reproduce material in their possession.

This book presents a personal view of its subject, but it is one which has grown and changed (as it will no doubt continue to do) in the course of many years of discussion with my Oxford pupils and colleagues. Among the latter I should particularly like to mention Ray Ockenden, Kenneth Segar, Jim Reed and my former tutor Gilbert McKay. I should also like to thank Giles Barber, librarian of the Taylor Institution, and all his staff for their unfailing helpfulness.

*Preface*

Michael Black, Barry Nisbet, John Williams and John Wilders have read the work, or parts of it, at various stages of its gestation and offered much-appreciated advice and encouragement. So too, last but not least, has my wife, to whom it is gratefully dedicated.

# CHAPTER I

# Classicism and neo-classicism: Germany and the European tradition

In Nestroy's farce *Einen Jux will er sich machen* (rendered by Tom Stoppard in his adaptation as *On The Razzle*) the newly engaged servant Melchior is challenged by his employer, Zangler, as to the meaning of his constantly repeated catch-phrase, 'That's classic':

ZANGLER Why do you keep using that stupid word 'classic'?
MELCHIOR It's not a stupid word. People just often use it stupidly.

The words 'classic' and 'classical' (in German, 'klassisch' does duty for both) are indeed not easy to define. Their basic etymological meaning is simply 'first class' or 'exemplary'. It is, of course, in this sense that Melchior uses it; and it is in this sense that Nestroy's plays can be called classics of the stage, or Nestroy himself a classic playwright. But he is hardly a classical one. The term 'classical' is generally applied to the civilisations of ancient Greece and Rome; to their art and literature, which the scholars and artists of the European Renaissance perceived as exemplary; and to works of modern European art which seek in some way to emulate these models from classical antiquity. The 'classical' drama of the modern European languages claims direct descent from the comedy of Aristophanes, Plautus and Terence, and especially from the tragedy – traditionally regarded by scholars as the more serious form – of Aeschylus, Sophocles, Euripides and Seneca; and its practitioners frequently seek to explain or justify their work by reference to the critical authority of Aristotle or Horace, as expounded by the scholars of the Renaissance.

Much modern European drama has also drawn its subject-matter from classical antiquity, from Greek or Roman mythology or history; but where such subject-matter is treated in a deliberately modern style, as with Lessing's modern-dress Medea or Virginia tragedies or with the adaptation of ancient legend by twentieth-century French dramatists such as Anouilh or Sartre, the term 'classical drama' is of more doubtful applicability. Style, rather than subject-matter, is the deciding factor. But the classical style itself is generally held to imply or necessitate a degree of distance rather than familiarity between the audience and the characters and events portrayed on stage, so that the choice of historical or legendary subject-matter, whether of classical Greek or Roman or of other provenance, is a characteristic feature.

With regard to style too, however, the term may be applied in a broader or in a narrower sense. More broadly, it has come to signify, particularly in relation to German literature, any form of serious poetic drama which observes principles of formal order and discipline analogous to those underlying the work of Greek or Roman playwrights. More narrowly, it is used to indicate the direct emulation, or supposed imitation, of the Graeco-Roman style, such as was carried to its furthest lengths in the *tragédie classique* of seventeenth-century France. Here elaborate 'rules' of the drama were set out, based allegedly on ancient precedent and precept. The most famous, or notorious, of these was the rule of the Three Unities of action, place and time: a tragedy had to portray a single action, without subplots or subsidiary interests, unfolding in a period not exceeding twenty-four hours and in a single unchanging location. There was much controversy in the seventeenth century about the Unities, particularly that of place (in observing which, incidentally, the serious, literary drama was deliberately denying itself many of the spectacular scenic effects, such as transformations, which the advancing stage technology of the period could offer, and which were accordingly banished to the realms of opera and other, more popular forms of theatrical entertainment). Of the two great tragic dramatists of seventeenth-century France, Corneille found the Unities irksome, but did his best to comply with them, sometimes to the detriment of dramatic probability; with Racine, whose drama is essentially one of concentration and of inward rather than outward action, observance of the rules has become second nature.

Scarcely less important than the rule of the Unities was that of *bienséance*, propriety or decorum, which lay down what was not appropriate or seemly for dramatic representation – forbidding, for example, the direct portrayal of violent action or the use of coarse or violent language on the stage, thus imposing there an etiquette as rigid as that which prevailed at the court of Louis XIV. Another aspect of the rule of decorum was the strict separation of the dramatic genres: tragedy and comedy went their separate ways, and the introduction of comic or 'low' characters into tragedy was unthinkable. Again this reflected the rigorous segregation of the social classes which characterised France under the rule of Bourbon absolutism. Tragedy concerned itself with the misfortunes of the great, of kings and princes and similar characters drawn from the most part from ancient history and myth – though Racine argued in the preface to his modern Oriental tragedy *Bajazet* that geographical distance (*éloignement*) could serve as well as historical distance to ensure the dignity which he saw as essential to the genre. Drama which conforms more or less closely to these rules is sometimes described as 'neo-classic', or (with more derogatory undertones) as 'pseudo-classical' or 'classicistic'.

French neo-classic tragedy is a courtly and highly sophisticated form of drama, which makes no concession to the tastes of the unlettered. Its comic counterpart, the work of Molière, presents a wider social range of characters, of obviously contemporary prove-nance (though generally disguised with vaguely antique-sounding names, such as Oronte and Alceste), and draws upon traditions of popular drama, of farce and the Italian *commedia dell'arte*; but these elements are firmly contained within a framework of metropolitan sophistication. Here too the absolutist centralisation of seventeenth-century French society is clearly reflected.

Elsewhere in Europe, however, forms of drama arose in which the new learning of the Renaissance was more freely assimilated to existing theatrical tradition and practice, and in which less attention was paid to the 'rules' elaborated by the scholars. This was the case in Elizabethan England, where Shakespeare 'warbled his native woodnotes wild', as Milton later from his more learned and orthodox neo-classic viewpoint was to put it – though Shakespeare was far from ignorant of classical learning, and was well acquainted with the plays of Plautus and Seneca in particular. But Elizabethan drama undoubtedly had strong roots in popular forms of dramatic entertainment, in pre-Reformation religious drama and in the improvised performances of strolling players. It is a robust natural growth, rather than a carefully tended hothouse plant. Shakespeare rarely observes the Unities to the letter, and more often disregards them completely; death and even mutilation take place upon the stage before our eyes; tragedy and comedy are frequently mixed, though it will be observed that Shakespeare generally treats his characters seriously in direct proportion to their social rank; and verse and prose are similarly alternated, though again 'low' characters are rarely allowed the dignity of verse. The mixture of characters, styles and registers in Shakespearian drama, compared with the stylistic segregation of French neo-classicism, may well reflect the broader social mixture of Elizabethan theatre audiences – though whether Elizabethan society as such was very much freer or more 'democratic' than that of France under the Bourbons is doubtful. Certainly this was not the case in seventeenth-century Spain, but here too, in the hands of Lope de Vega and Calderón, a national form of poetic drama evolved which owed more to indigenous (and in the case of Spain, particularly to religious) tradition than to Renaissance learning and Aristotelian critical authority, and in which the 'rules' are applied more liberally, if at all. Some critics have described these forms of drama as 'romantic' rather than 'classical' – another much-disputed term.

Both the drama of Elizabethan England and, subsequently, the Spanish drama of the Golden Age were, however, to exercise a powerful influence on those later German dramatists who were seeking to establish a national drama on what they explicitly saw as 'classical' principles. Both forms are essentially poetic rather than naturalistic, and their adoption of a stylised manner betokens their concern with the general rather than the particular – with the higher and 'more philosophical' truth of poetry, as Aristotle put it, 'not with what has happened but with the kind of thing that might happen'. This is true even when, for example, Shakespeare treats subject-matter from English history, of real and particular concern to him and to his contemporaries. On the one hand, the histories assimilate the stories of English kings to the universal pattern of tragedy; on the other, they are concerned not simply to chronicle the deeds of particular kings, but to dramatise ideas, even ideals, of monarchy and nation. Though they are far removed in externals from neo-classical tragedy, forms such as these nevertheless have something of its representative and universal character.

The national element in English and Spanish drama was itself undoubtedly a powerful factor in its appeal to German writers. From the turmoil of the fifteenth and sixteenth centuries, the collapse of feudalism and of medieval Christendom of which the Renaissance had been the cultural counterpart, France, England and Spain had all emerged, in their different ways, as centralised nation-states with effective monarchical systems of government and unity (albeit enforced) of religious belief. In Germany, this had failed to happen. Into the eighteenth century and indeed beyond it, the 'Holy Roman Empire of the German Nation' (Heiliges Römisches Reich Deutscher Nation) retained its cumbrous medieval constitution, with a multitude of principalities large and small, ecclesiastical territories and Imperial Free Cities, all owing a scarcely more than nominal allegiance to the Emperor in Vienna. As was later observed, it was in fact neither holy, nor Roman, nor in any real sense an empire. The German nation was real enough, in the sense of the people who spoke the German language; but it had no political identity[1]. The Empire indeed included other nationalities, such as the Czechs of Bohemia, while excluding the German-speaking population of eastern Prussia. Attempts to consolidate and centralise the Imperial power under the Emperor Maximilian I at the beginning of the sixteenth century had failed; the Reformation and counter-Reformation created religious divisions which strengthened the resistance of the individual territories to centralisation, and which were confirmed by the fearfully destructive, but ultimately indecisive Thirty Years' War of the seventeenth century. The Peace of Westphalia in 1648 restored the patchwork map of 1618; similarly, the post-Napoleonic settlement of 1815 restored in essence the state of affairs of 1789, even though the Empire itself had been formally dissolved in 1806. Bismarck's Second Reich or German Empire of 1871 deliberately excluded Austria; Hitler's Third Reich at last came close to achieving complete political unification of the German-speaking lands with the incorporation of Austria and the

Sudetenland, but ended, of course, in the present division between West and East Germany.

As Germany had failed to achieve national unity, so it is unsurprising that no major German national dramatist had emerged before the eighteenth century. A few names are, however, deserving of mention. Hans Sachs (1494–1576), the shoemaker-poet of Nuremberg, idealised in Wagner's *Meistersinger* as the exemplary German artist, was the dramatist in whom the traditions and forms of the medieval world met the first influence of the Renaissance in Germany. His Shrovetide plays ('Fastnachtsspiele'), by-products of an ancient ritual such as still survive, in the Catholic areas of Germany, in the entertainments of the Carnival, are sometimes earthy and crude, sometimes moralising in tone, but always familiar and homely. The same is true, to their detriment, of his fifty-odd tragedies, written on a variety of historical, biblical and legendary subjects: the rape of Lucretia, King Saul, Alexander the Great, Tristram and Iseult. His stories are simple, his characters are flat, his four-stressed rhymed couplets (known as 'Knittelverse') are lacking in dignity and sophistication. Sachs's work has a certain rough vigour and assurance, and he undoubtedly speaks for his society, for the emergent middle classes of the Free Imperial City of Nuremberg; but it was a provincial society, and Sachs's work remains essentially provincial. The same is true even of the most ambitious German playwrights of the seventeenth century – the Silesians Andreas Greif, usually Latinised as Gryphius (1616–64) and Daniel Casper von Lohenstein (1635–83). Gryphius, though he also wrote a number of enjoyable comedies, chose as his characteristic tragic themes the vanity, misery and corruption of earthly life (also, and more memorably, treated in his two collections of sonnets, of 1637 and 1657, which are reminiscent of the contemporary 'metaphysical' style in England) and the steadfastness of the virtuous stoic or Christian martyr. Examples of the latter are furnished by history both ancient (*Katharina von Georgien*, *Leo Arminius*) and very modern (*Carolus Stuardus*, written or at least begun in 1649, the very year of King Charles's execution). If Gryphius's tone is best described as elegiac, Lohenstein is a more cynical observer of the violence and brutality of human affairs, of power politics and sexual jealousy, fascinated like the English Jacobean dramatists by self-

6

ishness and cruelty. Gryphius and Lohenstein are the two major exponents of what has come to be called the Baroque style in German drama:[2] stately, tortuous, and (as it has seemed to most subsequent generations) frigidly rhetorical. Their chosen verse form is no longer the homely German 'Knittelvers', but the stately twelve-syllable alexandrine, imported from France, where it had established itself as the almost universal standard form of serious verse: it was to enjoy a similar prestige in Germany for the next hundred years, though its character is in many ways alien to the rhythms of the German language.

In the eighteenth century, the sense of a frustrated national identity was gaining in intensity throughout the German-speaking lands. As the German language was their only unifying factor, it was natural for them to look to literature, and in particular to the drama – which by virtue of its public performance is the most social of the literary arts – to create a national culture which would in the first instance substitute for, but perhaps in the future help to bring about, national unity in the political sense. As Lessing observed after the failure of the Hamburg National Theatre in 1768, it was a strange idea to try to establish a German national theatre when the Germans were not a nation: it was putting the cart before the horse. But throughout the century, in many parts of Germany, not only German writers and critics, but public-spirited German citizens and even rulers had sought to foster the growth of a national literature and in particular of a national drama. Theatres were founded or re-founded with the ambitious designation 'Deutsches National-theater': in Hamburg by private civic enterprise, in Vienna in 1776 under the patronage of the enlightened Emperor Joseph II, in Mannheim in 1778 under that of the Elector Palatine. In Goethe's novel *Wilhelm Meisters theatralische Sendung* (*Wilhelm Meister's Theatrical Mission*), begun in the mid-1770s, the idealistic young hero dreams of becoming 'the creator of a great National Theatre, something which he had heard so many people sighing for'. Twenty years later, in one of the *Xenien* or satirical epigrams which they published jointly in 1797, Goethe and Schiller were to mock the 'national' ideal and to urge their countrymen to look to more cosmopolitan goals:

Germans! in vain you aspire to form yourselves into a nation;
Seek, for you can, all the more freely to make yourselves men.

Zur Nation euch zu bilden, ihr hoffet es, Deutsche, vergebens;
Bildet, ihr könnt es, dafür freier zu Menschen euch aus.

Yet it was they who, in the years immediately following, were at
last to create the longed-for national theatre and the exemplary
national literary culture which we now know under the name of
Weimar classicism.[3]

The first major pioneer of literary and theatrical reform in
eighteenth-century Germany was the critic Johann Christoph
Gottsched (1700–66). Gottsched was a native of East Prussia who
had made his home in Leipzig, in the kingdom of Saxony. (It is
noteworthy that Gottsched spent his working life in a different
political division of Germany from that to which he owed allegiance
by birth; similarly, Lessing was to move from Saxony to Prussia and
subsequently to the Free City of Hamburg and to the Duchy of
Brunswick, and Goethe was to move from the Free City of
Frankfurt, and Schiller from the Duchy of Württemberg, to the
Duchy of Weimar in Thuringia. In Gottsched's case, the move was
prompted at least in part by his desire to escape conscription into the
Prussian army.) Gottsched decided that the only way to create a
serious German drama which could stand comparison with those of
classical antiquity and of its legitimate modern descendants was to
make a clean break with the past and to build anew on a foundation
of reason, good taste and sound critical principles – which he saw
embodied and perfected in the drama of seventeenth-century
France. In his *Versuch einer kritischen Dichtkunst für die Deutschen*
(*Essay in Critical Poetics for the Germans*) of 1730 he lays down rules
for all the literary and dramatic genres in the strictest neo-classical
spirit, and in his 'model tragedy' *Der sterbende Cato* (*The Death of
Cato*) of the following year he sought to demonstrate how they
might be applied in practice. In the preface to *Cato* he admits that he
has perhaps applied the rules with excessive stringency, but, he says,
'I did not wish to give the impression that a piece negligent thereof
might also have merit.'

Gottsched also took steps to put his programme into practice in
the living theatre.[4] This was no easy business. The permanent

theatres in eighteenth-century Germany were mostly attached to princely courts and devoted to the performance of opera and other forms of stage entertainment than literary drama. The needs of the common people were catered for by travelling troupes of actors, performing on temporary stages, their repertory and style (and, no doubt, their standards) not unlike those of the players in *Hamlet*. As Gottsched put it in the preface to *Cato*, what the German theatre had to offer was 'nothing but bombastic main and state actions ('Haupt-und Staatsaktionen')[5] spiced with harlequinades, nothing but un-natural fantastic adventures and amorous confusions, nothing but vulgar caricature and obscenity'. This was no basis for the theatre as a respectable social institution, capable of appealing to the growing educated middle-class public of such towns as Leipzig. Gottsched succeeded, however, in finding a troupe of actors, led by Johann Neuber and largely inspired by his highly talented wife Caroline, who were willing to adopt his programme of reform. Frau Neuber was not willing to go all the way with Gottsched: she thought his desire for authentic Roman costume in *Cato* ridiculous, and so Cato duly appeared in the traditional tragic fancy dress of the hero of the 'Haupt- und Staatsaktion', a mixture of classical armour and baroque court dress, much as one sees on statues and funerary monuments of the period, with a full-bottomed wig and a kind of turban with a plume of feathers – principally designed, no doubt, like the 'buskins' of Greek tragic actors, to make him look taller than ordinary mortals. She agreed to the separation of the genres and to the banishment from the respectable stage of the clown or Harle-quin, usually known in Germany as Hans Wurst or 'Jack Sausage'; hand in hand with this went the abolition of extemporisation (the mainstay of many a popular theatrical performance) in favour of fidelity to a literary text. Even here there had to be compromises: *Cato* was performed as part of a traditional mixed bill with a comic after-piece, and the mixed bill indeed remained standard practice throughout the century.

In 1759 Lessing, in the seventeenth of his so-called *Literaturbriefe* (*Briefe, die neueste Literatur betreffend*, or *Letters concerning the latest Literature*), launched a scathing denunciation of Gottsched's pro-gramme for the German theatre:

Nicht alles, so da gleist,      als wahres Gold sich weist.

C. Pr. S. C. Maj.

1    The German theatre before Gottsched's reform: the hero of the 'Haupt-und Staatsaktion' in his traditional finery. In the background: left, a scene from a Turkish drama; right, Dr Faust and the devil. Engraving by Martin Engelbrecht, Augsburg, *c.* 1730, from a series of cautionary illustrations of 'frivolous livelihoods'. The caption informs us that 'All that glisters is not gold.'

No one, we are told. . .will deny that the German stage owes a great deal of its initial improvement to Professor Gottsched. I am this No-one; I deny it outright. One might wish that Professor Gottsched had never meddled with the theatre at all. His supposed improvements either concern matters of trivial superfluity, or are positively harmful. . . His desire was not so much to improve our former theatre as to create a completely new one. And of what kind? A Frenchified one (eines französierenden); without inquiring whether or not this Frenchified theatre was appropriate to the German way of thought.

Lessing's mockery of Gottsched has been largely echoed by subsequent generations, unfair though it is in many ways: Lessing himself admits the sorry state of the German theatre before Gottsched's reform – in words which closely echo those of Gottsched's preface to *Cato* – and recognises that Gottsched was the first man to have the courage to do anything about it. But his criticism that Gottsched paid too little regard to the actual requirements of the German public is largely justified. And after this destructive beginning, he goes on to make positive recommendations which were to have a decisive influence on the development of classical drama in Germany. First, he draws the attention of his German readership to the English drama, which, he argues, appeals much more naturally to the German character than does that of France. In particular he points to the example of Shakespeare, and argues that Shakespeare, condemned by Gottsched as a barbarian, is in fact a more truly 'classical' dramatist than Gottsched's dramatic idol, Corneille:

Even to judge the issue by the example of the ancients, Shakespeare is a far greater tragic dramatist than Corneille, although the latter knew the ancients very well, and the former scarcely at all. Corneille approaches them more closely in mechanical technicalities, and Shakespeare in essentials. The Englishman achieves the object of tragedy almost without fail, whatever strange and individual paths he may choose to follow; and the Frenchman hardly ever achieves it, even though he follows closely in the footsteps of the ancients.

Lessing's championship of Shakespeare was to prove momentous, though in his own work he makes little or no attempt to imitate him. It was undoubtedly Lessing's advocacy, backed by his formidable critical prestige, which encouraged the rising generation of German writers to look more closely at Shakespeare (most of the plays were translated, albeit into prose, by Wieland in the 1760s). And if at first the Germans saw Shakespeare as exemplifying a drama completely free of neo-classic restraint, by the end of the century it was rather Lessing's assertion of Shakespeare's 'essential' classicism that remained influential, so that Shakespeare could still serve as a model for Goethe and Schiller after they had moved beyond their early phase of iconoclastic rebellion.

Lessing also suggests that German dramatists should be less scornful of the popular heritage of the German stage, the repertory of the travelling players. Here again he points to an example singled out for particular opprobrium by Gottsched, the 'fairy-tale of Doctor Faust', as the latter had called it. The story of Doctor Faust, his pact with the devil, and his eventual damnation was the great national legend of modern Germany, and was the subject of numerous plays performed by travelling actors and even puppet theatres. No authentic text of any of these plays has survived, though scholars have attempted to reconstruct them. Some or all of them may well have descended not from any original German play but from Marlowe's *Tragical History of Doctor Faustus* (itself of course based on a German chapbook source), which featured in the repertory of the troupes of English actors who were a familiar sight in seventeenth-century Germany – proof indeed of a genuine historical affinity between the popular theatres of Germany and England, though one of which Lessing seems not to have been aware. The Faust plays belong very much to the world of popular entertainment rather than to literary drama. In the seventeenth *Literaturbrief*, however, Lessing argues that the Faust legend has a potential which is only awaiting the touch of some 'Shakespearian genius' to bring it to serious dramatic life. He did in this case himself make a number of attempts to follow his own suggestion by writing a Faust drama, but none was ever completed (though there is a persistent legend that a finished or almost finished *Doctor Faust* was lost in Lessing's baggage on one of his numerous journeys). To his younger contemporaries, however, the suggestion proved irresistible. Several Faust dramas, finished and unfinished, were written in Germany from the second half of the eighteenth century onwards. The greatest of them is, of course, Goethe's: the work which was to occupy him throughout his long creative life, and which crowns not only his career but also the edifice of German classical drama – even if it is, rather like the Holy Roman Empire, neither classical nor drama within the usual senses of those terms.

By the time Lessing wrote his momentous *Literaturbrief*, Gottsched's star had in fact already waned. He had been attacked from various quarters, and the most talented even of his own allies and disciples had rebelled against his dogmatism and his dictatorial spirit. Frau Neuber had after a few years fallen out with her former patron and begun to lampoon him. The young playwright and critic Johann Elias Schlegel (1719–49) had already argued that national drama must take account of differences in national taste; and as early as 1740, in a comparison of Shakespeare's *Julius Caesar* and Gryphius's *Leo Armenius* which can be called the first piece of serious Shakespeare criticism in German (*Vergleichung Shakespeares und Andreas Gryphs*), he had praised the English playwright for his powers of characterisation, though in true neo-classical spirit he finds him even more guilty of rhetorical bombast than the German Baroque playwright. Schlegel's own plays, both comedies and tragedies, show a considerable dramatic talent, albeit corseted in the Gottschedian style, and enjoyed some success on the German stage at least into the 1770s. His tragedies explore a variety of subject-matter, classical and national, historical and legendary. *Orest und Pylades* is based on the Euripidean model later adapted by Goethe in *Iphigenie auf Tauris*. *Canut*, probably his best tragedy, celebrates the magnanimity of the great Danish king (Schlegel lived and worked for a number of years in Denmark, and this play was written – albeit in German! – for the Danish court theatre in Copenhagen). And with his *Hermann* (1743), Schlegel initiated a series of attempts by German writers of the period to dramatise the story of the fabled German national hero Hermann or Arminius, who defeated the Roman legions in a battle in the Teutoburg Forest in AD 9. Schlegel's output is quite substantial, despite his early death; it illustrates the merits, but also the limitations, of the neo-classic style. Even if he had lived longer, it is doubtful whether German drama would have developed further on these lines. And with the plays of Lessing it moved in a radically different direction from any we have yet mentioned: away from classicism altogether – or so it might seem – towards another and in this case a completely new style which was evolving in the European drama of the eighteenth century, that of contemporary realism.

# CHAPTER II

# Classicism in modern dress: Lessing and the beginnings of realism

Gotthold Ephraim Lessing was born in 1729 in the small Saxon provincial town of Kamenz, near what is now the border between East Germany and Poland. He had begun his dramatic career while a student at the University of Leipzig, writing a number of comedies which explore a range of styles within the tradition of Molière and his successors; one of them, *Der junge Gelehrte* (*The Young Scholar*), was successfully performed by the Neuber troupe in January 1748. They are accomplished pieces of apprentice-work, rarely straying far from the conventional, though two of them, *Die Juden* (*The Jews*) and *Der Freigeist* (*The Freethinker*), do touch upon important contemporary issues – of prejudice and religious toleration – which were to concern Lessing intensely throughout his life. He also began, but did not finish, two tragedies in the conventional neo-classic manner. Moving to Berlin in 1750, he soon made himself a reputation as a professional critic, journalist and essayist, publishing articles and reviews on a wide range of subjects. He established and wrote for two periodicals devoted to theatrical and dramatic criticism, *Beiträge zur Historie und Aufnahme des Theaters* (*Contributions to the History and Improvement of the Theatre*, 1750) and *Theatralische Bibliothek* (*Theatrical Library*, 1754–8) in which he began to draw his compatriots' attention both to the dramatic repertory of classical antiquity – Plautus, Seneca, Euripides – and to the latest developments in modern European theatre, and to encourage German dramatists to experiment and to break free from their exclusive dependence on the models of French neo-classicism. In an essay in the *Bibliothek* of 1754 he notes that English dramatists had begun to choose heroes from the middle ranks of society for their 'domestic tragedies' – he is plainly thinking of such works as George Lillo's immensely popular *George Barnwell, or the Merchant of London* (1731), which had already been successfully translated into German – and in his first completed tragedy, *Miss Sara Sampson*, written early in 1755, he follows their example, emphasising the English influence by the English setting and characters of his play and by its subtitle 'bürgerliches Trauerspiel', with which it initiates a new dramatic genre.[1] It was a play calculated to appeal directly to a new kind of theatre-going public – the largely middle-class Protestant North German public of towns like Leipzig, Berlin and Hamburg (or Frankfurt-on-Oder, where *Miss Sara Sampson* was first performed). It was the same public which Gottsched had also sought to appeal to, but had largely failed to reach because he had continued to practise and to advocate what was essentially a courtly, aristocratic form of drama. Lessing is the first German playwright and dramatic theorist to argue that the spectator will be most deeply moved by the fortunes and misfortunes of characters like himself, and that 'the names of princes and heroes may furnish a play with pomp and majesty, but they do nothing to touch our emotions' (*Hamburgische Dramaturgie*, No 14).

His second tragedy, the brief one-acter *Philotas* (1759), is set in ancient Greece, but in it Lessing voices a very contemporary concern, using some of the trappings of classicism to attack the misguided patriotism and the waste of human life engendered by the Seven Years' War (in which Saxony, the land of his birth, and Prussia, his adopted homeland at the time, stood on opposite sides). His most successful play, the comedy *Minna von Barnhelm*, is set in Berlin, the Prussian capital, in the immediate aftermath of the war, and represents, among other things, a plea for reconciliation between the German states. And his last tragedy, *Emilia Galotti* (1772), treats with a high degree of realism the potential conflict between the social classes, the ultimate defencelessness of a self-respecting and would-be self-reliant middle class in the face of princely power and its abuses, in a pocket-sized despotic state which, for all its Italian guise, bears a considerable resemblance to its contemporary German equivalents, such as Brunswick–Wolfen-büttel, the principality where Lessing was employed as court librarian at the time of the play's completion, and where he died in 1781.

*Miss Sara Sampson*, though it has been revived on the German stage a number of times in recent years, is likely to strike a modern audience as sentimental and lachrymose. In the very first scene the old English country gentleman Sir William Sampson weeps to discover his daughter, who has eloped with her lover Mellefont, staying in a wretched inn. Sara, the landlord tells us, spends her time locked in her room, weeping. Mellefont weeps tears of repentance: 'See there, running down my cheek, the first tear that I have shed since boyhood!' (I,v). In Act III the faithful servant Waitwell weeps on bringing Sara her father's offer of forgiveness and reconciliation. Even the villain of the piece weeps – Marwood, Mellefont's former mistress, who, on finding that her hopes of regaining his affections and persuading him to restore her good name in society by marrying her are in vain, exacts her revenge by poisoning Sara, leaving a letter boasting of her crimes. (The characters' names bear witness to Lessing's close acquaintance not so much with England as with English drama, notably the plays of Congreve.) But generally it is the virtuous characters in the play who weep, bearing witness by their tears to the depth of their moral and emotional sincerity and encouraging in this the spectators' compassionate identification. In the year after the completion of *Miss Sara Sampson*, in the preface to a German translation of the tragedies of James Thomson, Lessing wrote that 'these tears of compassion and of the feeling of common humanity are the only object of tragedy, and it can have no other'. Tears are the badge of human solidarity.

Lachrymosity is not the only weakness of the play. It is excessively long, unusually so even by the standards of the day: the playbill for the Hamburg performance of 1767 announces that 'on account of the length of the piece, Madame Hensel will sing an Italian aria' – instead, that is, of the usual comic after-piece. It is often verbose and excessively rhetorical; though the choice of prose rather than verse for a tragedy was itself at the time a revolutionary step in the direction of dramatic realism, the elliptical simplicity of Sir William's opening question – 'My daughter here? Here in this miserable inn?' – soon gives way to more elaborate confrontational set-pieces, and Lessing himself recognised that some of the speeches were 'undeclaimable'. Its characters seem flat and passive, drawn too simply in moral black and white, lacking in psychological complexity. There is not much action, and a great deal of moral attitudinising. But all this, which can today seem tedious, was exactly what Lessing's original audiences found so moving. The passivity of the other characters tends to throw the real dramatic interest onto the relationship between Mellefont and Marwood. From this point of view the play can be read as a modern-dress version of the classical story of Jason and Medea, which had been treated by many dramatists including Euripides, Seneca and Corneille, and in the nineteenth century was to be dramatised again by Grillparzer. Indeed Marwood, blackmailing Mellefont by threatening to kill the child she has had by him, invites him to 'see in me a new Medea' (II, vii). Lessing appears, however, to have tried to shift the centre of tragic gravity from the figure of Medea to that of Jason's new love, King Creon's daughter, who in the other dramatisations of the legend is a minor figure, and in Euripides' version does not actually appear in the play at all; in this he has not entirely succeeded. But in divesting his tragedy of the trappings of state, the pomp and majesty of kings and mythological heroes, Lessing has undoubtedly laid bare a simple, moving, purely human situation. A father and his daughter are estranged; the weakening of the family bond lays them open to a hostile, alien intervention, and forgiveness and reconciliation take place too late to prevent the fatal consequences.

Estrangement and reconciliation (whether successful or frustrated) between the generations was to remain one of Lessing's favourite dramatic formulae. The play also embodies one of his most characteristic themes, in which his humanitarianism and that of the age are repeatedly voiced: the danger of fanaticism, the threat posed to human relationships, and hence to society, by rigid insistence on principle – whether it be Sir William Sampson's initial refusal to approve his daughter's match with Mellefont, or Sara's almost masochistic refusal to accept his forgiveness, her morbid dwelling on her own guilt and unworthiness. Sara dies like a martyr, forgiving her enemies, but her martyrdom is self-inflicted.

These themes and motifs, which in *Miss Sara Sampson* are treated in a modern setting at perhaps excessive length, reappear in *Philotas*, where they are presented with laconic brevity in a setting of classical antiquity. Lessing was not unaware of the faults of *Sara* and may well have been trying specifically to remedy them by the imposition of a classical discipline. But the result is again of doubtful success. The play was undoubtedly prompted in part by the wave of patriotic enthusiasm which swept over Prussia during the Seven Years' War. Indeed, some of Lessing's contemporaries (and many of the more patriotically minded of subsequent German critics) saw in this brief tale of the young captive prince, who kills himself in order to spare his father the humiliation of suing for peace to secure his return, a glorification of patriotism and heroic self-sacrifice. In this they were mistaken. Lessing was no Prussian patriot, even though he, a Saxon by birth, spent the later years of the war as secretary to a Prussian general. He wrote to the poet Gleim, author of patriotic verses glorifying the exploits of Frederick the Great and the Prussian army, that he had no sense of patriotism whatever, and regarded it as 'at best a heroic weakness, which I am very happy not to share'. And in order to attack this mistaken ideal, Lessing writes a kind of satirical inversion of the sort of heroic tragedy which had traditionally extolled such sentiments and held them up for admiration. In a lengthy correspondence on tragedy with his friends Moses Mendelssohn and Friedrich Nicolai, in the wake of the writing of *Miss Sara Sampson*, he had argued strongly against heroic tragedy and had urged that the dramatist should in no way seek to arouse admiration for superhuman qualities in his protagonist (as was clearly the intention in the tragedies of Corneille, for example, or in Gottsched's *Cato*), as this could only weaken the true tragic effect of compassion. In fact the young fanatic Philotas seems to arouse in us, as he does in the other characters of the play, a mixture of admiration for his undoubted courage and for the promise of his budding manhood, and exasperation at his unreasonableness; and his death provokes not so much compassion as a shock of horror and disbelief. The Prince's captor, King Aridäus, tells him that his capture is a heaven-sent opportunity for a negotiated peace: 'The gods – I am convinced of it – keep watch upon our virtue as they do upon our lives. To preserve both for as long as possible is their secret, eternal concern' (Scene iii). But Philotas will have none of this. Like Sara Sampson, who insists that her sin has made her unworthy of her father's forgiveness, he regards himself as disgraced by his capture and insists upon judging himself more severely than either his father or even the gods, whom he describes as 'too kindly'. Thus to refuse the chance of continued life and happiness is a blasphemous rejection of the benevolence of the divine plan, and it is in this sense that Aridäus in the final scene describes Philotas' eventual self-immolation (with a sword which he has tricked his captors into giving him) as an act of 'raging melancholy' ('wütende Schwermut').

*Philotas* is a curious experiment, which has generally met with incomprehension, misinterpretation or simply critical rejection. Lessing did not make his meaning clearer by the choice of a classical setting. Partly at least this is because the story is not a well-known historical or legendary one: the names are Greek, but the characters and the situation are of Lessing's own invention. This gives the work a rather abstract air. It has found little favour on the stage, but is of interest in showing Lessing trying to combine modern concerns with the settings and some of the formal discipline of Greek tragedy.

Lessing was on much surer ground with his next play, *Minna von Barnhelm*, which is commonly accounted his most wholly successful dramatic work and the first of the few serious 'classical' comedies of the German stage. It was conceived in 1763 in the immediate aftermath of the Seven Years' War, and depicts a characteristic post-war situation. The Prussian Major von Tellheim has been not only discharged as redundant at the end of the war, but also refused payment on the grounds of a false charge of financial impropriety arising out of the occupation of Saxony, where his nobility and generosity have won him the love of the Saxon heiress Minna von Barnhelm. The play was completed in 1767 when Lessing took up his post in Hamburg as resident playwright and critic to the newly established National Theatre, and it was plainly intended as a 'national' play, with its theme of reconciliation between the German states and its apolitical German, rather than warlike Prussian or Saxon, patriotism. Goethe in his autobiography, looking back fifty years later on the rise of a German national literature and stressing the 'national' character of *Minna von Barnhelm*, attributes Lessing's success to Frederick the Great and his victories in the war. Though there is undoubtedly some truth in this, Lessing's portrait of Prussia and its king – who does not actually appear in the play, but looms large in the background – is not uncritical. Indeed, the Prussian authorities even tried to prevent the first performance in Hamburg (which as a Free Imperial City was not actually within Prussian jurisdiction), and some more recent critics have seen the play as essentially a satire on the despotism and corruption of Frederick's Prussia, and the happy ending, in which a royal intervention helps to disentangle the confusion, as bitingly ironic. But this seems an exaggerated and anachronistic view of what is essentially a cheerful rather than a satirical comedy.

*Minna von Barnhelm* admirably exemplifies Lessing's blending of traditional and modern elements in the drama. Its plot is based upon the familiar comic formula of a lovers' tiff and reconciliation, but the lovers are representatives of two nations, or rather of two political entities within the German nation, which had very recently been at war, and so their relationship takes on important political under-tones. The play observes the classical unities of time and place, its action unfolding within a single inn; but the inn is a real inn (or closely based on one) in a real city, the Prussian capital of Berlin, and outside its windows all the characteristic noise and bustle of the capital is going on, keeping the heroine's maid Franziska awake at night: 'The carriages, the night-watchmen, the drums, the cats, the corporals – they never stop their rattling, their shouting, their rolling, their miaowing, their cursing' (II, i). The characters we meet within this setting are almost without exception stock comic types (and could readily be typecast by the typical theatrical company of the times): a pair of lovers; a guardian or father-figure opposed, or believed to be opposed, to their marriage; a pert lady's-maid and a curmudgeonly but almost excessively loyal manservant; a breezy friend, a creditor, a foreign braggart who maltreats the language. But these characters are all given real contemporary names and identities. We meet Prussians and Saxons, officers and other ranks within the Prussian army, a war widow, a French adventurer whose boasting and dishonesty and mangled German are plainly a satire on the Francophilia of eighteenth-century Germany, Prussia in particular. Money, or the lack of it, as a determining factor in human affairs, is also a traditional comic motif; but Tellheim's financial difficulties are related precisely to the circumstances of the war, to the levying of contributions by Prussia upon occupied Saxony. We are in a familiar, timeless world of comedy, but we are also unmistakably in Germany in the 1760s.

The play has other serious aspects, however, which were probably nearer to Lessing's heart than the national and contemporary theme. The motif of fanaticism, of excessively rigid adherence to principle, is an important one here too. Tellheim's humanity and generosity, as a Prussian in occupied Saxony, have won him Minna's love. But the same high standards of conduct lead him, now that he has no money and his honour has been impugned, to believe that he must not allow himself to return her love, despite the promptings of his own heart. At their first, unexpected meeting in the play, his true feelings reveal themselves, but he immediately represses them:

VON TELLHEIM (*enters, and as he sees her, rushes towards her*). Ah! my Minna!
MINNA (*rushing to meet him*) Ah! my Tellheim!
VON TELLHEIM (*suddenly hesitates, and draws back again*) I beg your pardon, my dear lady – to find Fräulein von Barnhelm here –
MINNA Can surely not have been a complete surprise to you?

(II, viii)

But Tellheim continues to draw back. Proud and obsessively self-reliant, he refuses, like Philotas and Sara Sampson, to accept the opportunity for reconciliation which Providence – through the apparent chance of Minna's arrival in the very same inn – has offered him. Indeed, his pride has already led him into pessimistic gloom – in the first act he tells his former colleague Captain Marloff's widow that 'You come upon me at a moment when I might easily be tempted to complain at the decrees of Providence' – and in the course of the play he sinks ever deeper into misanthropy and despair. The efforts of Minna and of his loyal friend Sergeant-Major Werner seem of no avail: he bursts out into a bitter laughter at the cruelty of his situation, prompting Minna to cry out: 'Oh, stifle that laughter, Tellheim! It is the terrible laughter of misanthropy. If you believe in virtue and in Providence, do not laugh like that!' (IV, vi). Tellheim has to be taught a lesson: not to set pride and principle above the promptings of his own heart, but to accept the love and generosity of his friends and, by implication, of divine Providence.

2 Classical tragedy in modern dress: the death of Emilia Galotti. The frontispiece from Benjamin Thompson's *German Theatre*, though dating from thirty years later, captures well the atmosphere of Lessing's 'bürgerliche Virginia'.

And after a good deal of confusion, leading as in so many comedies to the very brink of disaster, that lesson is finally learnt. In its humanity and optimism the play already breathes the spirit of German classicism as it was to emerge at the end of the next decade.

In 1772 Lessing completed his last and, despite its puzzling imperfections, probably his greatest prose drama, the tragedy *Emilia Galotti*. Once again it is an attempt to combine classicism with contemporary realism. It was an old project, dating back to 1758; it was intended as a modern-dress version of the Roman story of Virginia, whose father Virginius killed her rather than allow her to become the slave and concubine of a tyrant. Lessing claimed that it was his intention to eliminate the political element and to write a purely 'bürgerliche Virginia', the purely human tragedy of a girl killed by her father 'to whom her virtue is dearer than her life'. His Emilia is the victim not so much of the lust and tyranny of the Prince, who is portrayed (just as Sir William Sampson had described Mellefont) as weak rather than wicked, but rather of the high-minded moral impetuosity of her own father, another of Lessing's characters who put principle before natural human affection. But she herself also plays an active part in her own death. When Odoardo, her father, seems for all his moral bluster totally incapable of resolute action, and about to abandon her to the Prince, it is she who prompts him to strike the fatal blow by reminding him of the Roman Virginius: 'Once there was a father who, to save his daughter from disgrace, took steel, the nearest he could find to hand, and thrust it into her heart – gave her life a second time. But such deeds are all of long ago! Such fathers are no more!' (v, vii).

The conclusion jars: it is as if Lessing feels it necessary to remind us, through the mouth of his heroine, of the classical pedigree of his modern tragedy. The relationship between father and daughter is invested with considerable psychological depth and complexity, but the ultimate significance of Emilia's death remains unclear, like that of Philotas': is it a heroic sacrifice, or is it an act of 'raging melancholy' – a fulfilment, or a frustration, of the design of Providence? Odoardo Galotti calls upon Providence to save his daughter, but not in the spirit of faith which Minna enjoins on Tellheim: 'Let Him who hurled her innocent into this abyss draw her out again!' (v, vi). Emilia herself despairs at her father's failure to save her, but despairs also of her own moral strength and of her ability to resist the seductive charms of the very man who has just had her fiancé, Count Appiani, assassinated before her very eyes: 'I have blood too, my father, blood as youthful and as warm as any. My senses too are senses. I can answer for nothing. I am worth nothing' (v, vii). In the original Roman story, Virginius' killing of his daughter had been an act not merely of despair but also of political defiance, leading directly to an uprising of the people and the overthrow of the tyrant. By playing down this dimension of the story – in which evil is identified as political in origin and therefore remediable by political action – Lessing has turned it into an expression of something more like pessimistic resignation, strangely inconsistent with the general tenor of his work and thought.

In fact many commentators have read the play, despite Lessing's declared intention, as essentially political in its message: some of Lessing's younger contemporaries were already arguing that Odoardo should have killed the Prince rather than his own daughter. For if *Emilia Galotti* is, despite the artificiality of its ending, the first really successful German tragedy (much to Lessing's annoyance, Goethe made Werther commit suicide with a copy of *Emilia Galotti* open on his desk), it is also, perhaps more importantly, the first successful German or even European realistic social drama. It presents us with a complete social panorama of a typical petty eighteenth-century principality, with its ruler, its courtiers, its respectable middle class, its servants and even the criminal classes on its fringe. Even if Lessing is not concerned to present class conflict as such, the psychology of the characters and their relationships is plainly influenced to a high degree by their social positions and by the social system under which they live. Particularly interesting in this connection is the contrast which Lessing draws between two aristocratic figures, Emilia's fiancé Count Appiani and the Prince's favourite Marinelli. Appiani is an aristocrat of progressive, bourgeois sympathies – turning his back on his own class by making, as Marinelli observes (I, vi), a *mésalliance* with 'a girl of no fortune or rank', which will 'close society's doors to him', and taking her off to his country estate to live in Rousseauistic seclusion, away from the court and its corruptions. Marinelli is the completely amoral, scheming courtier of the *ancien régime*, who for that very reason hates Appiani and all that he stands for. Social relationships typical of Lessing's day are also epitomised in the roles of Countess Orsina and of such minor figures as the court painter Conti and the minister Camillo Rota.

Their social realism, their immediate, contemporary relevance and their articulation of the values of a rising middle class are what made Lessing's plays such an important new departure in their own day, and what ensures their continuing stage success in ours – for these are the first German literary dramas which are still regularly performed today (*Minna von Barnhelm* and *Emilia Galotti* in par-

ticular are frequently revived).[2] In them Lessing appears as deliberately forward-looking, a socially and even politically progressive
figure, the conscious and resolute spokesman of the middle class to
which he belonged. This is probably an anachronistic impression.
Though Lessing's extensive critical and theoretical writings range
widely over the common concerns of the European Enlightenment
– philosophical and theological questions, art and aesthetics, and the
heritage of classical antiquity – he seems to have had little interest in
social or political issues. Even the term 'bürgerliches Trauerspiel',
which seems to proclaim a class allegiance, has for Lessing no
necessary political implications: it denotes a play portraying the
misfortunes of ordinary 'private citizens' – a 'tale of private woe', as
Lillo had described his *London Merchant* – and not concerned, like a
'Haupt- und Staatsaktion' – or indeed, like tragedy as it had
generally been conceived hitherto – with rulers and affairs of state.
Social class is a mere accidental (in fact, Lessing's protagonists tend
to be drawn from the lesser aristocracy rather than the middle classes
as such), and Lessing criticises Diderot, the French pioneer of social
realism in the drama from whom, by his own acknowledgement, he
had learnt so much, for arguing that social *condition*, as Diderot calls
it, rather than character, should be the mainspring of dramatic
motivation.

For it was not Lessing's aim to write dramas of social realism.
Though he wrote with a much keener awareness than Gottsched had
had of the specific needs of the contemporary German public, his
concern was to furnish the German theatre with works of timeless,
universal human appeal. Hence his repeated invocation of Aristotle,
his repeated attempts to establish the exact meaning of classical
authority, his implicit belief that the dramatist must follow faithfully the spirit, or even the letter, of Aristotelian precept if his work
is to achieve that timeless validity – even while in his own plays he is
actually doing something very different. He did not aim to portray
'Bürger', but 'Menschen'; not members of any particular class, but
human beings, stripped of the accidentals, as he saw them, of social
rank and political power. In his most systematic treatise on aesthetic
matters, *Laokoon, oder über die Grenzen der Malerei und Poesie*
(*Laocoon, or On the Limits of Painting and Poetry*, 1766), Lessing
defends the sculptor of the classical Greek *Laocoon* group for having

portrayed the priest and his sons, contrary to literal verisimilitude, in the nude: the sculptor, he argues, wished to portray not the trappings of priestly rank, but the unadorned spectacle of suffering humanity. There is a latent egalitarianism here, which remains an important undertone throughout the period of German classicism, even if its political implications are rarely brought to the surface.

Lessing's mature critical reflections on the drama are collected in the *Hamburgische Dramaturgie* (*Hamburg Dramaturgy*), originally a periodical review which he produced in his capacity as resident critic to the Hamburg National Theatre between 1767 and 1769.[3] The Hamburg enterprise was another attempt to unite serious literary drama with the living theatre. A group of idealistically motivated private citizens of the Free City had formed a consortium to take over the running of the theatre recently built by Konrad Ackermann – one of the first permanent theatres for spoken drama, as opposed to opera, to be built in Germany. Unhappily, idealism soon succumbed to commercial pressures, and the consortium was wound up within two years. Similarly, personal and professional jealousies soon forced Lessing to stop commenting on the actual performances (he had never had any say in the choice of plays to be performed), and the *Dramaturgie* becomes, as a result, more and more literary in character. But the early numbers, like the *Theatralische Bibliothek* of the 1750s, show a considerable interest on Lessing's part in the art of acting, as well as in such other theatrical matters as the use of incidental music. Then as now there were basically two approaches to acting: the one holding that it was largely a matter of learnable techniques, the other that an actor had to identify with his role and re-create the character he was portraying, as it were from the inside. Lessing favoured the latter view: in a letter to Moses Mendelssohn, for example, he defended the long speeches of *Miss Sara Sampson* by claiming that in writing at such length he was trying to help the players to feel their way into their roles. It is a pity that matters such as these are not more extensively discussed in the *Hamburgische Dramaturgie*: in the later numbers we often feel that serious drama and the stage are drawing apart again. But Lessing repeatedly insists that it is from living performance that drama gains its greater emotional impact, and thus its superiority to other literary forms such as 'cold' narration.

Lessing grounds the universal appeal of drama in universal human nature, as Aristotle had done: the dramatist must show us 'not what this or that particular man did, but what any and every man of a certain given character would do in certain given circumstances' (*Dramaturgie*, No. 19). The spectator must be able to identify completely with the dramatic protagonist, and so the latter must be shown to be cast in the same human mould as himself – 'vom gleichen Schrot und Korne' (No. 75). The 'pity and terror' (*eleos kai phobos*) of Aristotle's definition of tragedy are glossed by Lessing as 'compassion and fear' ('Mitleid und Furcht') – the latter further explained as the intensification of compassion by the recognition of common humanity in suffering, 'compassion turned upon ourselves'. Tragedy is defined with utter simplicity as 'a form of poetry which excites compassion' ('ein Gedicht, welches Mitleid erreget', *Dramaturgie*, No. 77) and in doing so achieves the highest possible goal of artistic communication: for, as Lessing had earlier declared in a letter to Moses Mendelssohn, 'the most compassionate man is the best man, the most disposed to social virtues', and 'the poet who makes us compassionate makes us better and more virtuous'. This doctrine is modified, perhaps over-ingeniously, in the *Dramaturgie* to bring it into line with the Aristotelian theory of 'catharsis' or 'purgation',[4] but Lessing still holds the arousal of compassion to be the prime task of the tragic poet.

These requirements are in many respects best met by a realistic form of drama: several of the traditional formal embellishments of tragedy, such as verse, Lessing regards as dispensable, and he was quite willing to depart from his neo-classic predecessors in what were for him superfluities, like Laocoon's priestly vestments. The use of prose, and of contemporary settings and costumes, also entailed an altogether more realistic style of acting than that of earlier drama, and such a style was indeed evolving in the theatre of Lessing's day, as exemplified in the work of Konrad Ekhof, the leading actor of the Hamburg troupe. Ekhof (1720–78) occupies a place in the history of the acting profession in Germany very much like that of Lessing in the history of the German drama. Even before his engagement in Hamburg, notably at the court of the Duke of Mecklenburg at Schwerin in the 1750s, he had already done much to raise the general standard of acting and the status of the acting profession. His style of performance owed much to that of Garrick in England, and in commending Ekhof in the *Dramaturgie* Lessing also commends the realism of Garrick. He recalls (*Dramaturgie*, No. 7) the visit of Tom Jones and Partridge to Garrick's *Hamlet* in Book 16, Chapter 6 of Fielding's novel – where, it may be recalled, Partridge found nothing remarkable in Garrick's reactions upon seeing the ghost, and preferred the performance of the king on the grounds that 'anybody may see he is an actor' – a reminder that in the mid-eighteenth century the preference for the 'natural' was an advanced and sophisticated taste. But Ekhof's style was soon surpassed in realism by that of the next generation of actors such as Friedrich Ludwig Schröder (1744–1816). Ekhof resisted, for example, the increasing demand for authenticity of historical costume, and was mocked by Schröder for still playing Schlegel's Canute in court dress and full-bottomed wig in the 1770s.

Like Ekhof's acting, the style of drama Lessing envisaged was not what Goethe later called 'naturalistic': it was not designed to reproduce literally the surface appearance of reality. As it is intended to portray universal humanity, so it is intended to reveal universal truth. Here Lessing enlists the drama more directly in the service of the optimistic philosophy of the Enlightenment – the Leibnizian doctrine of the 'best of all possible worlds', memorably if unfairly caricatured by Voltaire in *Candide*. This philosophy held that individual misfortune and suffering have their places in an overall scheme of things devised by an all-wise, omnipotent and ultimately benevolent divine Providence. The dramatist is, in Lessing's words, a 'mortal creator' and the world he creates in his play must be a model of the world made by the Creator himself, a perfected whole in which every detail is seen to play its part and none is left uncomprehended (*Dramaturgie*, No. 79). In comedy, all can be brought to a happy conclusion; in tragedy, all can be explained, all shown to be inevitable and even for the best, despite appearances. Tragedy is a form of 'theodicy' – a word Leibniz had coined to describe his own philosophy, a vindication of divine justice. This means that the dramatist must pay careful attention to the formal organisation of his work: all discords must be resolved, and no loose ends left hanging. It also provides a new justification for the neo-classic doctrine of the separation of the genres (which originated, as we have seen, in social divisions). Wieland, the novelist and essayist, who in the 1760s had produced the first major translation of Shakespeare's plays into German, had defended Shakespeare's mixture of the genres on the grounds of its truthfulness to real life, in which laughter and tears, serious and trivial matters, are often inextricably mixed. But Lessing argues that by thus imitating the surface appearance of life, with its inconsistencies and inconsequentialities, the dramatist is being false to the higher truth in which these contradictions are resolved (*Dramaturgie*, No. 70). Similarly Diderot, in his essays of 1757–8 which Lessing had translated into German, had advocated the creation of a form of drama which would be neither tragedy nor comedy, but simply *drame*, as he called it, a form which would aim not at the distinct *effects* of the traditional genres – tears or laughter – but simply at the faithful representation of ordinary life. Again, despite his admiration of Diderot's work, Lessing criticises this radicalism. His own dramatic theory thus contains, beside those elements which point in the direction of realism, others which justify at any rate some measure of the stylisation which is an essential feature of classical drama.

Realism and classicism are similarly blended in Lessing's plays. Their content – the characters, situations and problems they depict – is essentially modern, but their form is traditional. Until his last play, which we shall discuss in a later chapter, he maintains the traditional generic distinction of tragedy and comedy, even though he tends to draw the genres closer together by the increased realism of both forms, by his introduction of ordinary 'private citizens' into tragedy and by his insistence that comedy must no less than tragedy seek to arouse sympathetic identification between audience and stage figures. And although he was prepared, in his polemic against Gottsched's slavish adherence to the French style, to invoke the examples not only of Shakespeare but also of the popular German plays such as *Doctor Faust*, he was not willing himself to imitate their freedom of form. All his prose plays are planned with classical concision and economy. The unity of place is relaxed slightly in *Miss Sara Sampson* and in *Minna von Barnhelm*, and more significantly in *Emilia Galotti*, where the social conflict of the play is emphasised by the contrasted settings of the Prince's palace and the (albeit well-to-do) middle-class Galottis' house. But in all three plays the unity of time is retained, indeed insisted upon as an essential determining factor in the action, whether retarding or precipitating. Minna von Barnhelm assures the landlord that her uncle, whose arrival will solve all the problems and complications of the situation, is confidently to be expected within twenty-four hours; but Sir William Sampson arrives just too late to save his daughter from the machinations of her wicked rival, and in *Emilia Galotti* the hasty intrigues of Marinelli are set in motion by the Prince's agitation on discovering that Emilia is to be married that very day. (All three plays also begin early in the morning, in order that the action may be completed within the allotted time.) In one of Lessing's plans for a Faust drama, Faust was to be tempted, compacted with the devil, and led to salvation or damnation, all in the space of twenty-four hours. But in general his observance of the unities is not pedantic: they provide a firm base of theatrical practicality, which is undoubtedly one of the reasons for the plays' continued success. The Germans had never followed the French rule forbidding all violent action, and in particular death, on stage (Gryphius had even staged the execution of King Charles in full view of the audience!), and all Lessing's tragic protagonists die before our eyes; but again in general the proprieties are observed – which, if it appears of less concern to us today, was another factor in ensuring the general acceptance of these plays in their own time. Of Sophie Hensel's performance as Sara Sampson in the Hamburg production of 1767 Lessing observed, it appears unironically, 'Madame Hensel died with exceptional propriety' ('ungemein anständig', *Dramaturgie*, No. 13). Some of Lessing's relaxations occasioned adverse comment: the actor playing the servant Just in the first performance of *Minna* refused to speak the word 'whore', but was condemned by Lessing for his prudery.

The combination of modern and classical elements occasionally causes problems. This is particularly the case in tragedy. Lessing was plainly seeking, in both theory and practice, to establish the continuing relevance of this, traditionally the most prestigious of literary forms, to the concerns and sensibilities of a modern audience. But the very vehemence of his efforts has led many critics to wonder whether the implicit meanings of tragedy in its traditional form were not perhaps essentially alien to Lessing and his age. In this light Marwood's self-stylisation as a 'new Medea' and Emilia Galotti's evocation of Virginius and his daughter appear incongruous, ill-suited to the character and situation of eighteenth-century personages. Some modern critics have seen these references as *deliberately* incongruous, as proto-Brechtian 'alienating' devices, designed to cast into question the whole notion of 'tragedy' and the audience responses associated with it. But Lessing's aim, even in *Philotas*, was to revitalise tragedy rather than to subvert it.

Lessing's prose plays occupy a crucial, but ambiguous, place in the history of German and of European drama.[5] By precept and example, Lessing had sought to create what he regarded as a true classicism, purged of the aberrations of the French and their German imitators. His realism was designed to contribute to the psychological immediacy which he regarded as timelessly essential to all drama, rather than inspired by self-conscious modernity or by the desire to criticise social or political institutions. What his immediate successors saw was that in throwing off such appurtenances of neo-classicism as the exclusive employment of noble and elevated characters, the use of verse, the slavish and artificial observance of the unities, he had made serious drama available for the depiction of the affairs of ordinary people of the same social character as the majority of those who made up the theatre audiences. This would lead naturally to the presentation of issues of particular concern to the social groups from whom those audiences were drawn. The tradition of the 'bürgerliches Trauerspiel' instituted by Lessing runs through the 'Sturm und Drang' to Hebbel's *Maria Magdalena* and the social tragedies of Ibsen and Strindberg, Hauptmann and Schnitzler; and through the more radical strain represented by Lenz and Büchner to Wedekind and the more innovatory social dramatists of the twentieth century. In this sense Lessing can be called the founder not merely of modern German but of modern European drama. The creation of German classical drama proper – a form less realistic, more overtly poetic, concerned with contemporary reality only indirectly or in symbolic reflection – involved a turning-back from some of Lessing's innovations. Lessing himself contributed to this development with his last play, *Nathan der Weise*. But the young dramatists of the 1770s, the immediate inheritors of Lessing's work of emancipation, regarded the disciplines of the classical style as dead, and saw the drama as the appropriate medium for the expression of a rebellious urge to freedom.

# CHAPTER III

## *The revolt of Prometheus (i): Goethe and the 'Sturm und Drang'*

Alongside the work of Lessing, many other attempts were being made, in the 1750s and 1760s, to create a serious German drama. The experimenters included men distinguished in other branches of literature – Klopstock, the great pioneer in lyric poetry; Wieland, the father of the modern German novel – as well as many who are now forgotten. They essayed a variety of forms and of subject-matter: they wrote in prose and in verse, in neo-classical and in freer styles, on historical, mythical, biblical and modern subjects. Klopstock dramatised both Hermann's defeat of Varus and the Roman legions and Cain's murder of his brother Abel.[1] But none of these experiments met with more than passing success. The next stage in the awakening of German drama comes in the 1770s, sometimes called by German literary historians the Age of Genius or, more commonly, the age of 'Sturm und Drang' (Storm and Stress), after the title of one of its most characteristic dramatic products, a play by F. M. Klinger, dating from 1776.

The German 'Sturm und Drang' is the first major outburst of the European Romantic movement. Suddenly the most culturally backward of the European peoples sprang into the limelight and created a new style in which to embody the attitudes and feelings character-istic of a new generation. Above all, the movement was the work of one man of extraordinary genius, Johann Wolfgang Goethe, who, born in 1749, had the good fortune to be coming to manhood at a time when in all the literary genres the pioneering work had been done, and lyric, drama and novel only awaited the 'golden touch'[2] to bring them fully to life. But the pioneers had had to do their work first. And it is not surprising that the new movement should thus break out in backward, disunited, frustrated Germany, for it was a movement born of frustration: born of a generation of young men's passionate desire for self-expression, and of their often angry impatience with the existing norms – literary, cultural, social, and even, at least implicitly, political – which seemed to exist only to deny them what they desired. Sometimes, it is true, they seem to have little to express save the burning desire to express themselves. Typical is the description of the hero, Wild (his very name is of course characteristic), in Klinger's *Sturm und Drang* itself: 'He uttered a curse and looked up to Heaven, as if possessed by some deep, genuine feeling' (I, iv). But at their best they were genuine idealists, longing for a better world in which men could enjoy what the founding fathers of the American republic proclaimed in that same year of 1776 to be their self-evident and inalienable rights to 'life, liberty and the pursuit of happiness'. Klinger's play is actually set in America: his characters have crossed the seas in pursuit of their ideals.

Literary historians often date the epoch of Storm and Stress from 1767, when the great theorist of the movement, Johann Gottfried Herder, published his *Fragmente über die neuere deutsche Literatur* (*Fragments on Modern German Literature*); and Heinrich Wilhelm von Gerstenberg's *Ugolino* of 1767–8 is sometimes claimed as the first Storm and Stress play. It is a dramatisation of an episode from Canto 33 of Dante's *Inferno*, depicting the starving to death of Ugolino and his sons, who have been imprisoned by their enemies' intrigues. It is a strange but characteristic piece, strictly classical in external form but very unclassical in substance and effect. A conventional dramatist might have chosen to portray something of the intrigues which have led to Ugolino's imprisonment, but Gerstenberg ignores this possibility and concentrates exclusively on the slow agony of his death. The process is inevitable, lacking in all tension and therefore, as Lessing argued in a letter to Gerstenberg, quite undramatic; Gerstenberg, however, was not concerned with dramatic tension in the conventional sense, but only with the evocation and progressive intensification of a mood of claustrophobic horror. To this end the observation of the unities – the action takes place in the course of a single stormy night in a dimly lit prison cell – makes its own contribution, and mood and setting were to be profoundly characteristic of the new movement. Passionately committed as they were to the ideal of freedom, the 'Stürmer und Dränger' came again and again to dwell upon its antithesis, the image of the prison.

Gerstenberg (1737–1823) also wrote critical essays in which, in the mid–1760s, he was already advancing some of the theories which were to typify the movement. But the real beginnings, especially as regards the drama, are to be sought in Strasbourg in 1770–1. Here Goethe, who had come to Strasbourg University in the course of his legal studies, met Herder, who had come for a series of eye operations, and subsequently J. M. R. Lenz, who was employed there as a private tutor. Herder was five years older than Goethe, Lenz two years younger. Essays by these three writers, all dating from 1771–2, sum up the dramatic creed of the 'Stürmer und Dränger': Herder's 'Shakespeare', published in 1773 in the collection *Von deutscher Art und Kunst* (*Of German Character and Art*), which may be called the manifesto of the movement; Goethe's *Rede zum Shakespeares-Tag* (*Address for Shakespeare's Name-day*), composed in October 1771; and Lenz's *Anmerkungen übers Theater* (*Notes on the Theatre*), published in 1774 as the preface to a translation of *Love's Labour's Lost*. Around their adulation of Shakespeare the three young men build up a reasonably coherent theory of drama for their own age. There are some variations, in Lenz in particular, but a great deal of common ground. Goethe's Shakespeare address echoes indeed not only Herder's ideas but also Herder's characteristic rhapsodic, ejaculatory and enthusiastic prose style.

The theory of these young writers differs fundamentally from that of earlier ages. First and foremost, they see writing, like all forms of art, as a matter not primarily of communication but of expression: whereas Gottsched and Lessing alike had been much concerned with the effect a piece of writing had or was intended to have upon its audience – the inculcation of a moral lesson, the arousal of compassion – the 'Stürmer und Dränger' lay a new emphasis upon individual genius and its powerful creative force or energy ('Kraft'). And as a natural corollary of this, they are no longer interested in the classification of works of literature into genres by the application of what seem to them merely external rules. Gerstenberg had already demanded 'Away with the classification of drama!' To Herder and Goethe, such divisions as that between tragedy and comedy, whether determined by social considerations or by the difference in their presumed or intended effect, are irrelevant to the dramatist's true aim, which is simply to portray his experience of the world; and Shakespeare's mixture of the genres seems to them therefore exemplary rather than reprehensible. The further restrictions of the neo-classic style are similarly rejected as a falsification of life and as unnecessary limitations on the free expression of genius. When Goethe read Shakespeare, he declares: 'I hesitated not a moment in renouncing the regular theatre. The unity of place seemed to me timid and narrow like a prison, the unities of action and time irksome fetters upon our imagination.' The rejection of the French style also takes on a new note of nationalistic intensity. Here Lessing had shown the way, but in Herder's eulogies of Shakespeare there are intimations of deeper affinities of blood between the Germans and the English. Finally there comes a point of a rather different, but also related kind. The drama, above all the tragedy, of earlier ages was concerned with actions and events: tragedy, Aristotle tells us, is an imitation not of persons but of action, and a tragedy without character portrayal, though it might not be very good, was nevertheless perfectly possible, while a tragedy without a plot was inconceivable.[3] But modern drama, for the 'Stürmer und Dränger', is a drama of character. This development in dramatic theory is already prefigured in Lessing, who despite his almost unquestioning reverence for Aristotle lays great emphasis on psychological motivation and on the self-identification of the spectator with the stage figures. But in the 'Stürmer und Dränger' the shift of emphasis is complete, and Lenz makes the point in flat contradiction of Aristotelian precept. Here too Shakespeare is seen as exemplary, as a creator above all of characters, of human beings ('Menschen'). As Goethe puts it: 'He vied with Prometheus, copied his human creatures feature by feature, but made them of colossal greatness; . . . then he breathed life into them all with the breath of *his* spirit, he speaks through all of them, and we recognise their kinship.' Twenty-five years later Schiller was to argue very differently, that Shakespeare, the 'naive' poet, presents his characters to us in pure objectivity, and that his own personality is completely inaccessible to us. But Goethe, at all events in his

Storm and Stress period, is concerned to emphasise the expressive nature of Shakespeare's character portrayal.

Goethe also declares that all Shakespeare's plays (though he is presumably thinking primarily of the tragedies) have the same theme: 'All his plays turn upon the secret point, which no philosopher has yet seen or defined, where the vaunted freedom of our will collides with the inexorable course of the whole.' The critic Gundolf observed that this is a truer description of Goethe's own Storm and Stress plays than of the plays of Shakespeare.[4] In fact Goethe has defined a theme which is common in some form to all tragic drama, but is perhaps particularly characteristic of the drama of emergent German classicism: the struggle of individual human beings – their individuality recognised and valued at this period more strongly than ever before – to assert their autonomy in the face of seemingly all-powerful, hostile, indifferent or uncomprehended alien forces. These forces may be identified as gods or as fate; as the impersonal forces of mechanical causality or of historical necessity; as the inherent limitations of the human mind in its understanding, and hence in its control, of external reality; or finally as some kind of world-spirit or immanent Idea. And the philosophers of German idealism did indeed seek to define that 'secret point', in a variety of ways, so that the history of the German classical drama runs parallel to that of the great age of German philosophy which was also just beginning. Many connections and parallels can be observed, sometimes conscious, sometimes subconscious, sometimes apparently merely coincidental: Schiller and Kleist with Kant and Fichte, Hebbel with Hegel, Grillparzer with Schopenhauer.

The dramatic theory of Storm and Stress may thus be said to have set the German drama of the period on a philosophical kind of course. It is from the start a self-conscious drama, even, as has been argued, a drama of self-consciousness.[5] This makes it from the start essentially a drama of sophisticated, rather than popular, appeal. And for all the enthusiasm of the 'Stürmer und Dränger' for popular culture, for ballad and folk-song, for all their imaginative sympathy with the lives of the common people, this tendency finds support in other elements of their thought. Their emphasis on individual genius and creativity, and their view of writing, even dramatic writing, as primarily an expression of individuality, lead to a neglect of the public, social aspect of drama, of which Gottsched and Lessing had both in their different ways been so keenly aware. In Herder the genius seems no longer to speak *to* his fellow-men, even if by some mysterious, almost mystical embodiment of the collective identity of the 'Volk' he may be seen as speaking *for* them.

This neglect of the public dimension is compounded by a considerable indifference to the practical exigencies of the theatre. In their enthusiasm for Shakespearian freedom of form – and in their general ignorance of the conditions under which Shakespeare's plays were designed to be performed, for the apron stage was unknown in Germany and even the travelling players used a picture stage with a front curtain – they assumed that Shakespeare had disregarded these matters and that in imitating him they might do likewise: hence the fifty-six scene-changes of Goethe's *Götz von Berlichingen* and the fifty-three of Klinger's *Otto*, or Lenz's scenes consisting of only five or six words. A certain amount of rapid scene-changing would, however, have been well within the technical capacities of a reasonably well equipped eighteenth-century German theatre, which would have a variety of painted backdrops and movable wings. Moreover, the young writers' literary discovery of Shakespeare is indeed paralleled by a theatrical discovery: in the 1770s Shakespeare was brought, albeit in imperfect prose translations and often in drastically modified form, to the German stage as well as to the German reading public. Here the pioneer was Schröder, who took over the running of the theatre in Hamburg in 1771. Another important event of that memorable year 1776 was Schröder's production of *Hamlet*, the first significant performance of a Shakespeare play in Germany, and the model for the description of Wilhelm Meister's performance of *Hamlet* in Goethe's novel.

The Germans' discovery of Shakespeare was thus not purely a literary phenomenon, nor was the drama of the young Goethe and his associates. The 'Stürmer und Dränger' wrote plays which, albeit with a certain amount of difficulty, could be, and indeed were, performed upon the contemporary stage. The increased realism and immediacy of their dramatic style also reflects the ever-increasing realism of contemporary acting styles, as exemplified in that of Schröder when compared with Ekhof. But the young dramatists were undoubtedly as impatient of the limitations of the stage as of

*Sebt Ihr denn nichts hier?*
Hamlet 4ter Aufz: 11ter Auftr.
Herr Doebbelin als Geist Herr Brockmann als Hamlet
Madam Fencke als Koeniginn.

3 Shakespeare on the German stage: *Hamlet* in Berlin, 1778, with the title role played by Brockmann, who had created the part in Schröder's Hamburg production two years previously. A contemporary engraving by Chodowiecki. Note that little or no attempt is made at authenticity in costume or setting.

other 'irksome fetters upon the imagination', and they lacked the practical commitment to the theatre as a social institution which had impelled Gottsched and Lessing. The result of this is that in the 1770s the gap between literary drama and the stage begins to widen again. The theatre-going public had enthusiastically accepted the realistic middle-class domestic drama which Lessing had introduced, and for the next generation and beyond, plays of this type enjoyed far more box-office success than any other. The most successful stage dramatists around the turn of the century were not Goethe, nor any of the other 'Stürmer und Dränger', nor Schiller, nor even Lessing himself, but August Wilhelm Iffland (1759–1814) and August von Kotzebue (1761–1819). Both were prolific writers, largely in the mode of contemporary realism, though Kotzebue also wrote some historical plays. Iffland was also a distinguished actor-manager, noted for the moderated realism of his performances, in which he continued the tradition of Ekhof. But their dramatic works make plain the weaknesses of the eighteenth-century 'bürgerlich' manner. All too easily – as we see from the beginning in *Miss Sara Sampson* – it degenerates into melodrama and sentimentality. It also dates: as the society which produced it disappears, its contemporary concerns lose their relevance and appear trivial. It is in fact, if not in the same kind of way as the French neo-classic style which it had supplanted, an essentially limiting style, and the 'Stürmer und Dränger' were right to try to escape from its limitations.

The first great work in which the dramatic imagination of Storm and Stress burst from its fetters was Goethe's historical drama *Götz von Berlichingen*. Sprawling, disorganised, but with a basic unity of character and theme and a great deal of rough immediacy and vigour, it presents all the characteristics of a work of spontaneous creative genius such as the theory of the young Shakespeare-worshippers had called for. In fact the familiar version of 1773 is a fairly radical revision of the original of 1771, but the original does appear to have been written in a fairly rapid burst of inspiration. The title of this original version, *Geschichte Gottfriedens von Berlichingen mit der eisernen Hand, dramatisiert* (*The History of Gottfried von Berlichingen with the Iron Hand, dramatised*) indicates its loose, 'epic' character, its closeness to its historical source, and its lack of concern for the exigencies of the stage. Despite some tidying-up, all these qualities are still evident in the revised version, whose subtitle 'Schauspiel' (play) indicates not so much an increased regard for theatrical practicality as a continued disregard for the accepted generic subdivisions of the drama. However, though it is not designated a tragedy, *Götz* is the most unambiguously, and probably the most convincingly, tragic of all Goethe's major plays.

It is indeed a Shakespearian play, at any rate as Goethe and Herder had understood their idol's work: Herder's reported comment to Goethe that 'Shakespeare has been your ruin' was unfair, for it was very much Shakespeare seen through Herder's eyes. It is the first great example of drama as expressive utterance, revealing the creative personality of its author through the portrayal of a figure himself understood to be a 'creative' personality: strong, noble, magnanimous, straightforward, loyal and honest, devoted to the cause of freedom. One might even describe Götz as a genius, even if he is not himself a creative artist (though we do see him, in the course of Goethe's play, embarking upon the writing of the autobiography which was to be Goethe's source). The whole play is concerned, directly and indirectly, with the evocation of this character, loved and revered by his family, his friends and servants, and the common people – 'this man whom the princes hate and to whom the oppressed will always turn' (Brother Martin in Act I), 'the model of a true knight, brave and noble in his freedom, and calm and faithful in misfortune' (Götz's wife Elisabeth in Act IV). Götz finds himself increasingly at odds with an age of selfishness, dishonesty, disloyalty and political intrigue: history makes him a rebel against the Empire to which he unceasingly professes his loyalty. The watchword of 'freedom' echoes through the play from Götz's first speech to his last, when he dies in prison with the word on his lips. The expression of this theme reaches its grandest climax in Act III, where Götz and his few faithful, beleaguered friends drink a toast to freedom with their last bottle of wine, evoking a vision not simply of individual freedom and anarchy – for which Götz's aggressive forthrightness and self-reliance can easily be mistaken – but of a world in which under a benevolent patriarchy all men of good will can live together in harmony.

The theme of freedom is also of course reflected in the form of

4   The rediscovery of German history: Götz and Brother Martin in Act I of
*Götz von Berlichingen*. Frontispiece from the first collected edition of
Goethe's *Schriften*, II, 1787. This kind of authenticity now began to appear in
stage productions as well as in book illustrations.

Goethe's play – seemingly anarchic, ostentatiously defiant of all the neo-classical unities and proprieties. As has been mentioned, there are fifty-six changes of scene (in the original version there are sixty), ranging freely and evocatively over much of southern Germany. There is no precise time-scale, but the action evidently spans a good number of years: the historical events upon which the play is based took place between 1495 and 1562, the year in which the real Götz von Berlichingen died (not in prison, incidentally, but at home in his own bed). The stage is filled with violent action – battles, storms, burnings and plunderings – and with violent language: Götz's invitation in Act III to the Imperial officer, sent to demand his surrender, to 'lick my arse' has earned undying notoriety, even though Goethe himself deleted it from later editions of the play. The unity of action is abandoned in favour of a series of loosely connected episodes and subplots and a continuous switching of focus between contrasting groups of characters – Götz and his associates, courtiers, soldiers, peasants, gypsies. Whereas neo-classic drama aims at the heightened uniformity of the 'grand style', Goethe makes each of these groups of characters speak its own distinctive language, in the Shakespearian manner – though apart from some interpolated songs (another Shakespearian feature) the play is written entirely in prose. Some of the subplots attain an almost disproportionate importance, notably the story of Götz's weak and vacillating friend Weislingen, his defection to the court party, and his betrayal by the *femme fatale* Adelheid – herself a figure who plainly fascinated Goethe (particularly in the original version of the play) more than her role in the dramatic economy would strictly warrant.

In all these respects *Götz von Berlichingen* was a landmark. But Goethe's most momentous innovation was his completely new treatment of historical subject-matter. Dramatists had hitherto used history to illustrate general truths about life, in accordance with Aristotle's distinction between poetry and history: the names of historical characters had given the drama dignity, as Gottsched had stated, or had served as a convenient shorthand for certain types of character, as Lessing had suggested (*Dramaturgie*, No. 24). But Lessing had also argued that the dramatist would do just as well to invent his own characters and names – as he had indeed done in his own plays. Lessing was in fact not much interested in historical drama, seeing it largely as an encomium upon the doings of the great, which was not in his view a proper use of the dramatist's art. But in *Götz* Goethe was doing something different. He was not simply using the figure of Götz to express timeless, universal human truths – though they are undoubtedly there in the play. Nor was he simply celebrating a great individual, though this was very much part of his intention: as he wrote to one of his friends in November 1771, 'I am dramatising the story of one of the noblest of Germans, restoring the reputation of a fine man.' Nor was he simply writing a patriotic play, though this again is an important element. He was also evoking the characteristic spirit of a past age, and dramatising the process of historical change;[6] and with this discovery of history as a theme in itself he gave the German drama one of its most constant preoccupations. The view of history conveyed in *Götz* is of course a highly romantic one – though if we use that adjective it is because *Götz* is one of the works in and through which the romantic vision of history was created. Götz's ideals of liberty and fraternity are those of the young Goethe and his contemporaries. Goethe, however, presents them as qualities of life which did in the past exist, but have since been lost, and shows us in his play when and how he believes them to have been lost. Götz fights for the values of the 'good old days' against the encroachments of 'progress': if he is a rebel, he is a conservative or even a reactionary one. Goethe portrays what was indeed a crucial period of German history, the age of the Emperor Maximilian, of the religious Reformation (the name of the character Brother Martin hints strongly at Luther himself), of the Peasants' Revolt and of the attempts of political reformers to reshape the structures of German society and to create a greater sense of unity and nationhood. We have earlier suggested that the tragedy of German history in the sixteenth century was the failure of Germany to emerge from medieval feudalism into the modern world. But Goethe's hero is an unrepentant champion of feudal values, and his play is designed to show a natural way of life and a natural, organic society being supplanted by a corrupt and artificial one.

Whether we agree with this view or not, Goethe's portrayal of the way in which in the course of history one way of life, one society, one set of values gives way to another was profoundly influential. Nor was its influence confined to Germany. It was partly through reading *Götz von Berlichingen* (which he translated into English) that Scott was moved to explore the changing face of Scottish society, and to portray the disappearance of the old, tribal Scotland in *Waverley* and the novels which succeeded it; and Scott's work in turn inspired further generations of European writers, and Americans such as Fenimore Cooper – so that Götz von Berlichingen can be described as the direct literary ancestor of the Last of the Mohicans. This, of course, is not what Frederick the Great, still unwavering in his exclusive admiration of the French classical style, had in mind when he described *Götz* as 'digne des sauvages du Canada'. Nor was Lessing favourably impressed, for *Götz* seemed to him little more than a reversion to the old-style 'Haupt- und Staatsaktion'. And indeed the immediate theatrical progeny of Goethe's play was a host of 'Ritterstücke', or, as we might say, 'robber-baron plays', anticipating the style of Hollywood medievalism: swashbuckling historical costume melodramas, full of spectacle and violence but of very little literary merit. The proliferation of works of this kind has perhaps made it harder to appreciate the originality and power of *Götz* itself. But if Ronald Peacock, in the major English monograph on Goethe the dramatist, could describe *Götz* as a 'rather a tedious play for non-Germans' and 'of all Goethe's plays, the one that has to be appreciated essentially by historical evaluation',[7] the playwright John Arden evidently felt very differently, making his own adaptation of *Götz* (*Ironhand*, London 1965) as well as treating a similar historical subject himself in *Armstrong's Last Goodnight*.

A historical vision similar to that of *Götz* again inspires Goethe's next major play, *Egmont*, which was also begun about this time although it was not completed until 1787. Again it shows the destruction of a traditional, natural, harmonious society and its values by the imposition of an alien system – in this case, the suppression of the traditional liberties of the Netherlands by Philip II of Spain and his agent the Duke of Alba; and again, the traditional values are embodied and supremely exemplified in the play's hero, Egmont, who was trapped and executed by Alba's orders in 1568 (the period, we note, is the same as that of *Götz*: evidently in Goethe's view the lights were going out all over Europe in the mid-sixteenth century). Again the hero is presented as a noble, forthright character, innocent of guile, a natural leader beloved and respected by the common people, especially by his mistress Klärchen, a simple but equally forthright 'Bürgermädchen' in whose company Egmont feels blissfully free of the cares and responsibilities which go with his noble rank. In conversation with his secretary in Act II Egmont describes himself as a sleepwalker, a man instinctively treading a dangerous path who will fall if he wakes up; and as a charioteer, drawn on inexorably by the 'sun-horses of time', steering his course between boulder and precipice as best he may, but unable to check his pace. He is a cheerful fatalist, allowing himself willingly to be driven on by an irresistible personal destiny, a *daimon* as Goethe later described it. He insists on living dangerously, on taking no thought for the morrow, refusing to play the devious game of politics which is the chosen element both of Alba, his jealous enemy, and of William of Orange, his anxious, prudent friend. Natural ruler though he is, born (like Götz) to govern his people with light but firm, benevolent, patriarchal hand, he is no match for Alba, the ruthless totalitarian politician: he refuses to believe that King Philip will send Alba to the Netherlands, or that Alba will act against the native nobility, Orange and himself. Like *Götz von Berlichingen*, *Egmont* depicts, on the political plane, the extinction of traditional liberties by a 'modernising' despotism, and on the individual plane the defeat of an essentially unpolitical man by the alien force of modern politics itself. Egmont falls as a result of his own innocence, an innocence which others often see as mere irresponsibility. These others have included not only his friends and foes within the play, but also generations of critics, beginning with Schiller in 1788, who have found fault with Egmont as a tragic protagonist: the controversies on this point show no sign of abating. They also, inevitably, extend to the dramatic efficacy of Goethe's play, held together as it is almost solely by the personality of its hero. Many have found it wanting, while others have drawn attention to the originality and to the poetic, rather than conventionally dramatic, unity of its form.[8]

Unlike *Götz von Berlichingen*, *Egmont* has very little external action, and the kaleidoscopic procession of short scenes, which in the earlier play so effectively, if at times a little confusingly, conveys the complexity and turbulence of the historical period, here gives way to a more leisurely series of static tableaux. In a sense *Egmont* can be said to observe a unity of action: the first three acts are all exposition, and nothing actually happens until Egmont's arrest in Act IV, followed inevitably by his execution in Act V. But whereas a Racinian exposition is a complex web of stresses and strains, a tense system of interrelationships, the scenes of *Egmont* are self-contained and discontinuous – a series of portraits of the hero from different points of view, first through the eyes of others (he does not himself appear in the first act), then face to face. And as Egmont himself lives for the moment, refusing until it is too late to consider the consequences of his actions, so the scenes of the play do not really lead on consequentially, one into the other: major figures like the Princess Regent, Orange, even Alba, each make only one appearance, in a single scene in which their part in the action is, so to say, placed before us complete rather than developed in the usual way from scene to scene, from act to act. The unity of *Egmont* is thus not a unity of action in a classical sense, but reflects the 'Sturm und Drang' theory of drama as being above all expressive of character.

The ending of the play is particularly remarkable. Like Götz, Egmont is last seen in the fatal setting of the prison – 'the dungeon, image and foretaste of the grave, hateful alike to hero and to coward' (Act V). And like Götz too he goes to his death with the word 'freedom' on his lips. But Götz's last despairing cry is consistent both with the situation to which the action of the play has finally brought him, and with the pessimism of the historical vision which the play embodies. Egmont's last speech, delivered as the stage fills with Spanish soldiers who are to lead him to execution, takes the form of an ecstatic evocation of future liberation, inspired by a dream-vision, shared by the audience, in which we see Klärchen transfigured into an allegorical embodiment of Liberty, anticipating the spirit of Delacroix's famous painting celebrating the Paris revolution of 1830. Schiller objected to what he called the '*salto mortale* into the world of opera' by which Goethe transforms tragedy into triumph: the effect is brilliantly captured in the overture which Beethoven wrote for the play in 1810, but in terms of ordinary dramatic psychology it remains questionable. It seems that here, even in his Storm and Stress period when the play was conceived, Goethe was already aiming at a new and specifically poetic form of drama, to which such prosaic considerations would not apply. Certainly by 1787, when it was completed, poetic rather than realistic drama had become his ideal, and he sought to impose a measure of classical discipline on a work parts of which, as he then wrote, had come to seem to him too 'unbuttoned' in character. The texture and rhythm of the prose, less richly varied and less earthy than that of *Götz*, often take on a distinctly poetic quality: pervasive images, such as that of horse and rider, underpin the play's thematic unity, and the cadence of its speech often falls into that of blank verse. Memorable above all, even if frustrating in terms of conventional drama, are the great confrontation scenes between Egmont and Orange, Egmont and Alba; and Alba's powerful soliloquy in Act IV as he waits for Egmont to ride into his trap, culminating as from the window he watches Egmont dismount from his horse: 'Step down! – So, now you stand with one foot in the grave! and now with both!'

In his early years Goethe made a number of other plans for dramas on the Shakespearian model, as he conceived it, portraying 'human beings of colossal greatness': titanic, heaven-storming individuals like Prometheus and Faust, or prophets and leaders of men like Socrates, Julius Caesar, Mahomet. Shakespeare's Caesar did indeed 'bestride the narrow world / Like a Colossus'; in Goethe's version, he is described with earthy colloquialism as 'ein Sackermentskerl', which might be rendered 'a hell of a guy'. (The 'Stürmer und Dränger' were particularly fond of the colloquial word 'Kerl' for 'man', so much so that they themselves, as well as their heroes, are often referred to as 'Kraftkerls'.) In these fragments, Goethe experiments further in form and style, notably in the use of verse of different kinds. But fragments they remained. He salvaged excerpts from *Prometheus* and *Mahomet* and published them as separate lyric poems, in which form they remain some of the most familiar and important works of his early years. The 'Prometheus' ode is the supreme expression of defiance, in which the Titan issues his powerful challenge to the divine authority of Zeus:

> Hier sitz ich, forme Menschen
> Nach meinem Bilde,
> Ein Geschlecht, das mir gleich sei,
> Zu leiden, zu weinen,
> Zu genießen und zu freuen sich,

Und dein nicht zu achten,
Wie ich!

Here I sit, forming men
In my own image,
A generation to resemble me,
To suffer and to weep,
To delight and to rejoice,
And to ignore you,
As I do!

Artists of a later generation, such as Beethoven and Shelley, were again to use the figure of Prometheus to symbolise the struggle of the human spirit to break free from the fetters of the old order. And Goethe himself was to complete the tragedy of that other, more modern rebel against divine authority, Faust, but not until many years later.

*Götz von Berlichingen* was not, however, the only dramatic work which Goethe had managed to complete before his move to Weimar in 1775, which marks the beginning of the end of his 'Sturm und Drang' years. The two domestic dramas *Clavigo* and *Stella* continue the vein of contemporary middle-class realism which Lessing had initiated. *Clavigo* is basically a fairly conventional 'bürgerliches Trauerspiel', which, however (or perhaps for that very reason), has long maintained a place in the German repertory. It is based, albeit loosely, on a contemporary real-life source, the memoirs of Beaumarchais, already a well-known figure of the time, although he had yet to earn his greatest fame as the author of *Le Mariage de Figaro*; Beaumarchais was, it seems, not amused by Goethe's portrayal of him as a fire-eating 'Kraftkerl'. In *Stella*, subtitled 'a play for lovers' ('ein Schauspiel für Liebende'), Goethe modifies the convention in a daring and original way, producing something much more like a modern 'problem play', steeped though it is in the sentimentality of its period. The bigamous hero Fernando (another vacillating figure in the mould of Mellefont and Weislingen) and his two wives Cäcilie and Stella end the play resolved to attempt to live together in a *ménage à trois*. Schröder produced *Stella* in Hamburg in 1776 and it was well received by the public, but soon banned by the authorities as immoral. In 1806, for a production in Weimar, Goethe was to revise the ending, turning it into a tragedy: Fernando shoots himself and Stella takes poison, and traditional propriety, both moral and dramatic, is thus restored. The original, less conventional version was, however, translated into both French and English, and in more recent times has enjoyed a number of successful revivals.

Goethe also completed in the early 1770s a number of minor works which explore other theatrical possibilities. *Erwin und Elmire* and *Claudine von Villa Bella* are plays with musical numbers ('Singspiele'), a form which attracted a good deal of attention at this time and reached its apogee with the German operas of Mozart; the text of *Claudine* was subsequently set by a number of composers, including Schubert. Goethe also wrote a number of farces, burlesques and revue-like pieces, including *Götter, Helden und Wieland* (*Gods, Heroes and Wieland*), an affectionate satire (Wieland took it in good part) on the latter's Rococo travesty of the Greek world in his 'Singspiel' *Alceste* (1773), and *Das Jahrmarktsfest zu Plundersweilen* (*The Lumberton Fair*), a revival of the Sachsian 'Fastnachtsspiel'. These are vigorous and lively works, distinctly popular and, in the latter instance, specifically national in flavour, and showing a considerable interest on Goethe's part in forms of theatrical entertainment far removed from the 'serious' literary drama as it had come to be understood in his day, and as he himself conceived it in *Götz* and *Egmont*. But it was only in *Faust* that he was eventually to achieve a synthesis of these very disparate styles.[9]

The other 'Stürmer und Dränger' of the 1770s stand very much in Goethe's shadow: they were indeed often referred to as 'Goetheaner'. Lenz is undoubtedly the most original of them, even if his originality at times verges on perversity, betraying the pathological streak which mars his work and was to destroy his life. Lenz in both his theory and his plays manifests a much keener social awareness than most of his contemporaries, perhaps indeed than any European playwright or dramatic theorist before him. He argues that the 'rules' of Greek drama are intimately related to the Greek view of life and the world, and in particular that the Greeks regarded the individual human being as much less autonomous, much more a creature of the gods or of fate than is the modern view. Like Goethe, Lenz advocates that modern tragedy should portray great, towering, heroic characters, rather than 'actions' in the classical sense: we want, he says in the *Anmerkungen*, to see 'a whole series of actions, following one upon the other like thunderclaps', all issuing from the character of the protagonist, so that at the end we can cry out in wonder and admiration 'Das ist ein Kerl!' (which again we might render 'What a guy!'). But at the same time Lenz argues that the modern theatre-going public is not capable of appreciating tragedy, and that therefore comedy is for the moment, until 'the comic playwright creates the tragedian's public for him', the more appropriate form. By comedy, however, Lenz understands something much more like modern critical social drama than the traditional form. Articulating more precisely the feeling already voiced by Diderot that the traditional genres were no longer appropriate to the needs of a modern audience, he writes: 'Comedy is a depiction of human society, and when the state of society is serious, its depiction cannot be a laughing matter.' Although, in accordance with his theories, his play *Die Soldaten* (*The Soldiers*, 1776) was originally to have been designated a comedy, Lenz changed this before publication to the neutral 'Schauspiel'. This and the earlier *Der Hofmeister* (*The Private Tutor*, 1774) are his best and his most familiar plays (*Der Hofmeister* was adapted by Brecht for the Berliner Ensemble in the 1950s). In both of them potentially tragic elements, notably the theme of seduction and abandonment, are treated with a degree of intellectual detachment; but both plays also convey a keen sense of the suffering caused by social injustice and class divisions, which Lenz himself knew only too well at first hand. His work is a more radical development of Lessing's domestic realism: it does not really belong in the history of German classicism, but points forward, as we have already suggested, to later developments of a quite different character.

The other most important dramatist of the 1770s was Friedrich Maximilian Klinger, author of the play by which the whole movement came subsequently to be known. His best play, however, is undoubtedly not *Sturm und Drang* but *Die Zwillinge* (*The Twins*), yet another product of the *annus mirabilis* 1776, when it won a prize offered by Schröder in Hamburg. It is a practicable piece of theatrical writing, having a very small cast and keeping close to the classical unities in form, despite its explosive content and style. It depicts the fatal rivalry of twin brothers, the passionate and dynamic Guelfo and the gentle, melancholy and reflective Ferdinando. The motif of hostile brothers is one which Klinger made very much his own: a familiar tragic subject, but one to which he gave a new intensity and expressive force. The Promethean revolt of the 'Stürmer und Dränger' against the literary, cultural, moral and social values of earlier generations is here expressed through the revolt of a son against family ties and paternal authority. But even in *Die Zwillinge*, though Guelfo does kill Ferdinando and is himself killed by their father in punishment, the energy of the theme is drained through rhetoric rather than channelled into genuine dramatic conflict. Klinger is more interested in histrionic gesture – Guelfo smashing his reflection in the mirror (IV, iv) – than in action or even than in serious character portrayal. His heroes – Guelfo, Wild in *Sturm und Drang*, Otto in the play of that name – in their passionate desire for self-fulfilment and self-expression seem to epitomise the ideal of the 'Kraftkerl', but in reality they do very little but rant and strike attitudes. For the true realisation of the dramatic potential of the theme of rebellion, we have to wait for Schiller.

# CHAPTER IV

# The revolt of Prometheus (ii): Schiller's prose plays

Goethe, Lenz and Klinger were born within a span of three years and were close personal acquaintances during the crucial years of the 'Sturm und Drang' movement, from 1770 until the middle of the decade. Then in 1775 Goethe moved to Weimar, entered a different world from that of his youth, and became more and more estranged from his earlier friends. Lenz began to show increasing signs of mental disturbance, while Klinger (a robust and basically well-ordered personality, very unlike his frenetic heroes) entered upon what was to be a long and distinguished career in the Russian Imperial army, to which his literary activities had to take second place. But the spirit of 'Sturm und Drang' was still alive, and it was natural that it should still inspire the works of the young Friedrich Schiller.

Schiller was born in 1759, ten years after Goethe, in the small town of Marbach, near Stuttgart, capital of what was then the Duchy of Württemberg. The Duke, Karl Eugen, was another of the century's 'enlightened' despots. In Stuttgart he had established a ducal academy, known as the Karlsschule, in which talented youths from a variety of social backgrounds were educated for the service of the state. The young Schiller, son of a junior officer in the Duke's army, showed obvious academic promise and so into the Karlsschule he was forcibly drafted, against his own and his parents' wishes. It was an upbringing very different from either Goethe's comfortable middle-class childhood or the harsh struggles of the lower-class existences from which both Lenz and Klinger had emerged: in fact, despite a progressive curriculum and some able and enlightened teachers, the Karlsschule was much more literally like the prison in which that earlier generation had felt itself metaphorically confined. It is therefore not surprising that in the early dramas of Schiller the theme of the desire for freedom, of man's aspirations to self-determination, to 'life, liberty and the pursuit of happiness', sounds more insistently than ever before.

In 1827, in conversation with Johann Peter Eckermann, the principal companion and literary assistant of his last years, Goethe observed that the ideal of freedom runs through all Schiller's works, but that in the earlier ones he is concerned with 'physical', in the later with 'ideal' freedom. The distinction is a useful one. Whereas Schiller's early heroes seek to achieve freedom in the real world, freedom to be themselves and to live their own lives, his later plays tend increasingly to be concerned with the realisation that this goal is an illusory one and that true freedom is to be found in the acceptance of necessity and of moral responsibility. But this realisation is present from the very beginning; and all Schiller's plays do indeed 'turn upon that secret point' which Goethe had identified as the key to Shakespeare's, 'where the vaunted freedom of our will collides with the inexorable course of the whole'. The young Schiller naturally shared his forerunners' enthusiasm for Shakespeare, and many echoes of Shakespeare – of *Hamlet* and the Roman plays, of *Macbeth*, of *Richard III* and *King Lear* – can be heard in his work, as well as the more direct influence of his immediate predecessors in the 'Sturm und Drang' and of Lessing, especially *Emilia Galotti*. But he is also from the beginning a writer of powerful originality, with an unmistakable voice of his own.

Schiller's first three plays were all completed within the space of two or three years. The first, *Die Räuber* (*The Robbers*, or *Brigands*) was written while he was still a pupil (or prisoner) in the Karlsschule, and smuggled out to a publisher in Mannheim, capital of the Pfalz or Rhenish Palatinate. Here it appeared in print in 1781, and in the following year it was performed, albeit in a drastically revised version, at the Palatine court theatre, designated 'Nationaltheater' in 1778 (it still retains this name today). Baron Dalberg, the director of the theatre, had seen Schiller's manuscript and had realised that here was a work of real theatrical genius; one reviewer of the production declared that here at last was the long-awaited German Shakespeare.[1]

Like *Götz von Berlichingen*, *Die Räuber* is a huge, sprawling work which flagrantly, indeed flamboyantly defies all the rules of neo-classic drama. The unities of time and place are swept away, violent action takes place on the stage, and the dialogue, especially in the scenes featuring the hero Karl Moor's band of libertine-turned-brigand friends, is spiced with obscenities far more colourful than the homely earthiness of a Götz; in much of this the young Schiller is plainly and simply out to shock. And again as in *Götz*, the classical unity of action is abandoned in favour of a loose, episodic chronicle of events, held together by a unity of theme – the desire for freedom and self-realisation – and of character. Or rather we should speak of a duality of character, for this is the most striking and original formal feature of *Die Räuber*. The play is ostensibly a story of fraternal hatred like *Die Zwillinge*, with the contrast between the brothers even more stridently marked. The evil, ugly and vindictive Franz Moor persuades his father, through slander and treachery, to disinherit his noble, handsome and forthright brother Karl. Karl becomes an outcast, leader of a band of robbers, like Robin Hood (the English outlaw-hero is actually mentioned in the play) a friend of the oppressed and an enemy of the rich and powerful, while Franz shuts his father up in a subterranean dungeon to starve to death and rules as Count in his stead, a sadistic tyrant supplanting a benevolent patriarch. (The plot is, as will be seen, a complex of familiar 'Sturm und Drang' themes and motifs.) Karl returns to exact revenge, but Franz evades capture by killing himself, and Karl, realising that his violent rebellion has caused more evil than good, gives himself up to justice. But the rivalry between the brothers which motivates the plot is only a mechanism which enables Schiller to present to us a pair of character portraits, parallel and ultimately, for all the contrasts, profoundly similar. In terminology borrowed from Schiller's later essay *Über naive und sentimentalische Dichtung* (*On Naive and Reflective Poetry*), Karl is often described as an idealist and Franz his opponent as a realist.[2] But although it is true that Karl is spontaneous where Franz is calculating, and that Karl's ends, if not the means he employs to achieve them, are good where Franz's are evil, it is probably more accurate to describe both as perverted idealists. The characteristic theme of Schiller's early plays is not so much the conflict of realism and idealism as the pitfalls of idealism itself. Both Karl and Franz desire, above all else, freedom – freedom to be their own masters, to live their own lives, to spread their wings and fly like eagles far above the snail's pace of ordinary life – the contrasted images of 'Adlerflug' and 'Schneckengang' are invoked by each of them in turn. Both are rebels: Karl a rebel against society and the perversions of man-made institutions, Franz against nature itself and the deepest ties of blood and kinship. And both are brought to despair (the very word, 'Verzweifelung', sounds like a knell throughout the play) as they realise the failure of their rebellion, though Karl conquers his despair in his final act of submission and atonement, while Franz is left in his despair to die. Each of the brothers has, so to speak, his own half of the play, each his own location or series of locations. Franz remains at home in the family castle, while Karl roams about central and southern Germany, from Saxony to the Bohemian forest and the banks of the Danube, with his robber band, before returning home in Act IV to meet again his childhood sweetheart Amalia, his faithful old servant Daniel and at last his father, whom he releases from his prison on the point of death – but never actually encountering Franz, the true author of all his miseries. He sends his men to capture Franz and bring him to be judged, but they find only his corpse. So, in what is perhaps the most remarkable technical feature of the play, the two brothers never actually meet on stage.[3]

*Die Räuber* is thus a kind of double tragedy, with a 'hero' and a 'villain' of almost equal tragic status, martyrs both to the elusive ideal of human autonomy and freedom. Karl and Franz both cast themselves in roles of power and greatness; and the motif of role-playing is another that will recur throughout Schiller's dramatic work. Franz dreams of the triumph of mind over matter, believing himself – but himself only – superior to the 'Schneckengang der Materie', the 'snail's pace of material existence' (II, i), and to the filthy 'morass' of human life (IV, ii), which he describes with eloquent loathing in his lengthy monologues, strongly reminiscent (like much of his role) of Shakespeare's Richard III. Karl's first words in the play, 'This ink-splashing century disgusts me, when I read in my Plutarch of great men', his lament that the 'bright spark of Promethean fire is burnt out', his wish 'that the spirit of Hermann still glowed in the ashes' (I, ii), reveal a longing for a lost ideal of heroic greatness that recalls Goethe's nostalgia in *Götz* or *Egmont*; but here the nostalgia is Karl's and not Schiller's , for Schiller shows it to be deeply problematic. Despite the social concerns which Karl voices, and despite the grandiose denunciation of corruption which reaches its peak in the great harangue which he delivers to the priest sent to demand his surrender in Act II (again very different from Götz's brief and earthy dismissal of the Imperial officer!), his attempt to put his ideals into practice leads to crimes scarcely less horrendous in nature, and on a far larger scale, then those which Franz in his cynicism openly embraces. Within Karl's band this cynicism finds an advocate in Spiegelberg, Karl's brutal, boastful rival for the leadership; and even Spiegelberg is a kind of grotesque caricature of the idealist in his desire for freedom, a goal which he of course interprets with crude materialism as freedom from all restraints whether physical or moral. The world of Schiller's vision is not, it seems, the perfect creation of a benevolent Providence, as Lessing had argued, but the idealist who seeks to right its imperfections may himself be just as deeply flawed in his own character, and may thus bring upon himself and others evils as great as those he seeks to eradicate.

In *Die Räuber*, as in *Götz von Berlichingen*, and in full accord with the dramatic theory of the early 'Stürmer und Dränger', the articulation of a plot, the 'imitation of an action' in the Aristotelian sense, takes second place to the unfolding of character and the expression of a central idea or theme by the use of parallel and contrast and the deployment of secondary characters and episodes. In his preface, Schiller describes the work as a 'dramatised history' (the phrase recalls Goethe's designation of the original version of *Götz*, which Schiller, however, can hardly have known) in which the dramatic method is used to 'catch the secret operations of the soul'. The plot is arbitrarily constructed and the play is full of inconsistencies, improbabilities and crudely melodramatic devices, but this is of little consequence, for its real substance lies in its evocation of character, theme and mood. Here too there are crudities and excesses. Many of the scenes and speeches are too long;

Schiller's prose style is uneven, the mixture of registers often dissonant and less convincing than in *Götz*; sentimentality rears its head in the portrayal of old Count Moor, the brothers' father, and of Amalia, the only woman in a large and otherwise all-male cast. Schiller himself soon realised these faults, and in his two subsequent prose plays he is plainly trying, in different ways, to discipline his exuberant imagination. But *Die Räuber* is nevertheless a work of unmistakable genius, an extraordinary first achievement by a young man of twenty-two. For all its complexities it has a powerful basic simplicity; its principal characters, Karl, Franz and Spiegelberg, are striking and memorable; and its language has at its best a blazing intensity, notably in the evocation of that key emotion of despair – in Karl's great speech to the setting sun by the Danube in (III, ii) or in Franz's night of terror leading to his suicide (V, i). We can already see in it not only its author's characteristic themes and preoccupations, but also clear intimations of his talent for poetic drama.[4]

It is also a superbly theatrical work and achieved a tremendous success at Mannheim in 1782, even if in what we must regard as a travestied version. Not only had Schiller mutilated his text at Dalberg's insistence, but the Mannheim 'house style' was in general much more restrained than that which *Die Räuber* called for. Schiller's taste was for the flamboyant gesture, often carried to excess: in a production of Goethe's *Clavigo* by the students at the Karlsschule in 1780 Schiller, playing the title role, had reduced the audience to helpless laughter by his convulsively exaggerated performance, and in *Die Räuber* Old Moor tears his face and hair, Franz writhes in his chair in torment, and Karl in his despair charges into an oak-tree. In Mannheim the part of Franz was played by Iffland, who was much acclaimed for his performance, but he was much concerned to tone down Franz's daemonic will to evil, his radical egocentricity and his nihilism in favour of a characterisation more humanly comprehensible, 'more in keeping with the conduct of a son and a gentleman' – roles which Schiller's Franz explicitly repudiates.[5] But the compromises which Schiller was forced to make, however reluctantly, with Dalberg led to a period of fruitful collaboration between Schiller and the Mannheim theatre, even if it was inevitably accompanied by a good deal of continuing friction; and Schiller remained for the rest of his life on good terms with

5   The psychological realism of the 'Sturm und Drang'. Iffland as Franz
Moor in the original production of *Die Räuber*, Mannheim 1782: Franz
besieged in the blazing castle in Act v. From the painting by H. A.
Melchior. The style of acting suggests the influence of Garrick and Schröder
(cf. no. 3, and contrast the statuesque manner of no. 8).

Iffland, who as director of the Prussian court theatre in Berlin from 1796 was to be responsible for memorable productions of Schiller's later plays.

In his second play, *Die Verschwörung des Fiesco zu Genua* (*The Conspiracy of Fiesco at Genoa*), Schiller turned for the first time to history, which was to furnish the characteristic themes and subject-matter of the plays of his maturity. *Fiesco* is not, however, a play about history in the sense that *Götz* or *Egmont* is: it is a character drama, the portrait of a great man, and the history of sixteenth-century Italy serves only as a colourful background against which the protagonist can be exhibited. But neither is Fiesco a great man like Götz or Egmont as Goethe saw them, assured and self-confident in their greatness; he is rather a man obsessed, like Karl or Franz Moor, with the ideal of achieving greatness, and hesitating in his choice of means to this end. He poses as the champion of political liberty, plotting with fellow-republicans to overthrow the despot Andreas Doria, but all the time contemplating seizing despotic power for himself. What matters to Schiller is not so much Fiesco's actual choice between republican idealism and despotic ambition as the hesitation which reveals both as no more than alternative forms of self-aggrandisement; the decision itself is not as important as the grand histrionic gesture with which it is made. 'To win a diadem is noble, to throw it away is godlike', reflects Fiesco at the end of Act II; but then, when we next see him, in Act III, ii, 'It is contemptible to empty a purse, it is impudent to embezzle a million, but it is noble beyond telling to steal a crown' (III, ii). Schiller himself was almost as undecided as his hero, for he wrote two endings to the play, though again it was Dalberg who was principally responsible for the change. In the original, published version Fiesco dons the ducal purple, but is assassinated by the fanatical republican Verrina for his betrayal of the ideal; but in the version performed at Mannheim in 1784 Fiesco renounces power, liberty is restored and he lives on as an ordinary citizen. (Neither ending is historically accurate, for the historical Fiesco, at the moment of his triumph over Andreas Doria in 1547, fell into the harbour and drowned by accident.) The outcome of the plot is relatively unimportant: what matters is the portrayal of Fiesco's character, the ambiguity of the hero's aspiration to greatness.

Very like Goethe in his progression from *Götz* to *Egmont*, Schiller in *Fiesco* moves from the dynamic style of *Die Räuber* to a more static manner of presentation – from life-story, as it were, to portrait. But whereas in Goethe's case this meant a change from the rapid movement of many short scenes to a greater breadth and a more leisurely pace, here Schiller takes the opposite course. In *Die Räuber* the individual scenes are long and often somewhat static and slow; in *Fiesco* this is replaced by busy movement and rapid comings and goings – emphasised on the printed page by the adoption of the French convention of scene-division, numbering a new scene ('Auftritt') for each entry or exit, which had been used by Lessing and his predecessors, whereas the original version of *Die Räuber* marks a new scene ('Szene') only at a change of décor. (The 'Trauerspiel' version already adopts the French convention, perhaps like the subtitle itself a sign of compromise with more traditional dramatic and theatrical practice.) As in *Götz*, however, all this surface activity does not necessarily add up to a coherent plot. Rather, the portrait of the hero is rounded out through the depiction of his relations with, and the reactions he produces in, a variety of other characters, often sharply contrasted among themselves. These include the austere Verrina and the other conspirators, many of them pursuing selfish ends of their own; the dignified patriarch Andreas Doria and his vicious, depraved nephew and heir-apparent Gianettino; Fiesco's gentle wife Leonore and the imperious Countess Julia, Gianettino's sister, to whom he pays half-pretended court; and, perhaps most interesting of all, his henchman the Moor Muley Hassan, one of Schiller's few comic characters, who makes one regret that he did not essay the vein more often. The Moor does most of Fiesco's dirty work for him, while Fiesco stands by making the grand gestures; at the end, he is hanged for his pains. 'The Moor has done his work, the Moor can go' (III, iv) is probably the play's most often-quoted line.

*Fiesco* has generally been assigned a minor place in Schiller's dramatic output, but it marks a further stage in his treatment of the theme of individual autonomy, and though it lacks the elemental forcefulness of *Die Räuber* it represents in some ways a stylistic advance. Its prose is generally more restrained and homogeneous, though it rises to heights of considerable rhetorical power, notably in Fiesco's two great monologues in Acts II and III. In recent years it has enjoyed more favour with both critics and producers, its searching portrayal of political intrigue and corruption seeming perhaps more in accord with modern taste than the supposed 'idealism' of the later Schiller. It develops further the themes of political freedom and of charismatic political leadership, which Goethe had broached in *Götz* and *Egmont*, and to which after 1789 the events of history were to give a new and urgent topicality.

The ringing denunciation of political abuses in Schiller's third play, *Kabale und Liebe* (*Intrigue and Love*), has no doubt also played its part in ensuring this work's continuing popularity. Originally entitled *Luise Millerin* after its heroine, it was renamed at Iffland's suggestion, as 'double' titles of this kind were coming into theatrical fashion (Verdi's operatic version reverts to Schiller's original title, but retains little else of his play in recognisable form). It is a 'bürgerliches Trauerspiel' with a highly realistic contemporary German setting which, though no real names are named, transparently represents Schiller's own native Württemberg, just as the Prince who looms so large in the background (very unlike the ultimately benign Frederick the Great of *Minna von Barnhelm*) strongly suggests Schiller's own Duke Karl Eugen. (In a famous Berlin production of the 1960s, the stage was dominated by the legs of a colossal figure representing the Duke, so that the whole action was literally played out by 'petty men' walking 'under his huge legs' and scurrying between his feet.) The play was completed in 1783 and followed its predecessors on the Mannheim stage in April 1784, by which time Schiller had fled from Württemberg and taken up residence in Mannheim as official playwright to the National Theatre. The Palatinate was, of course, foreign territory from which the Duke of Württemberg could not extradite him: for Schiller, as for Gottsched before him, the political divisions of eighteenth-century Germany did have their advantages.

Quite apart from the obvious specific references to Württemberg, the play attacks the abuses of contemporary absolutism much more directly than Lessing or even Lenz had done. Lessing had, or so he claimed, deliberately depoliticised the story of *Emilia Galotti* in order to concentrate on its purely human content. Lenz had attacked peripheral manifestations of class conflict rather than the heart of the political system itself. Schiller shows us the corruption and oppression upon which that system rests: the criminal intrigues by which a minister overthrows his rival and keeps himself in power, and the financing of princely extravagance by the exploitation of the people, as young men are forcibly recruited and sold off to fight in America to pay for jewels for the Prince's mistress. The hero, Baron Ferdinand von Walter, son of the corrupt President (chief minister), falls in love with Luise Miller, daughter of a humble professional musician ('Millerin' is an archaic feminine form of the name). Inspired by his love, he rebels against his father and against the whole vicious system which he represents: 'I will pierce the fabric of his intrigues – tear asunder all these iron fetters of prejudice – free as a man I will make my choice, and these insect souls shall reel before the towering edifice of my love' (II, vi). But Ferdinand's rebellion is broken, and he is destroyed. He succumbs to the intrigues of the 'insect souls', the President and his appropriately named henchman Wurm (the German means not only 'worm' but also 'serpent'), to the 'fetters of prejudice' and not least to the fatal weakness of his own character, the egocentricity of the idealist which his own extravagant rhetoric all too plainly betrays. With breathtaking ease the President and Wurm persuade him of Luise's infidelity, for as Wurm observes, 'Either I have no skill in reading the barometer of the soul, or milord the Baron is as fearsome in his jealousy as in his love' (III, i). Ferdinand denounces her as a whore and poisons her, then drinks the rest of the poison himself and dies, but with his last breath he forgives his father, who is brought to justice for his crimes.

*Kabale und Liebe* is a highly effective piece of stage writing, much better constructed in a traditional sense than either *Die Räuber* or *Fiesco*, with its principals clearly drawn and its minor characters and episodes much more successfully integrated with the plot than are some of their equivalents in the earlier works. Its continuing success is not undeserved. But as our brief summary will have suggested, it does have a strong streak of melodrama about it. This seems, paradoxically enough, to be underscored by Schiller's realism and by the forcefulness of his social criticism. In a well-known study the critic Erich Auerbach speaks of the 'hair-raising rhetorical pathos' of Schiller's portrayal of the contemporary world, and of the failure of

*Kabale und Liebe* (and of the 'bürgerliches Trauerspiel' in general) to achieve a convincingly realistic style.[6] There is certainly a disparity of style in the work, between the traditional elements of tragedy – individual passion and emotion, and the suggestion of an inevitable fate awaiting the 'star-cross'd lovers' – and the more modern elements of critical realism and social satire. Yet essentially it is not the realistic but the tragic side of Schiller's play which is melodramatic, and for 'hair-raising rhetorical pathos' we should look not at the denunciations of princely extravagance such as the famous scene between the Prince's mistress Lady Milford and the lackey in Act II, in which the fate of the conscripts is revealed, but rather at the expressions of Ferdinand's heaven-storming egoism, such as that already quoted, 'Free as a man I will make my choice. . .', or his later declaration of his decision to kill Luise and die with her, 'An eternity bound with her upon a wheel of damnation – eye rooted in eye – hair standing against hair on end in terror – even our hollow moaning melted in one together – And now to repeat my endearments, and now to recite to her again her oaths of fidelity – God! God! the betrothal is fearful – but eternal!' (IV, iv).

Yet this, in the violence and extravagance of its imagery and its disruptions of normal prose syntax, is the authentic voice of the young Schiller, his own personal version of 'Sturm und Drang'. With *Kabale und Liebe* Schiller's dramatic writing reached a crisis. In his own, anonymously published, review of *Die Räuber* he had identified as one of that work's principal deficiencies its failure to achieve a consistent style: 'The language and the dialogue ought to be more harmonious', he had written, 'and on the whole less poetic.' In *Fiesco* and *Kabale und Liebe* he had tried on the whole, and with a good deal of success, to curb the 'poetic' excesses and to achieve a more generally realistic manner. But the rhetoric and the melodrama remain, and it is they – no mere pose as in Klinger – which seem to express the authentic Schillerian sensibility. The three prose plays are also 'poetic' in their use of pervading patterns of imagery which underline their unifying themes. Animal imagery runs through all three: Schiller had concluded his medical studies at the Karlsschule with a dissertation entitled *Über den Zusammenhang der tierischen Natur des Menschen mit seiner geistigen* (*On the Connection between the Animal and the Spiritual Nature of Man*), and the theme continued to preoccupy him.[7] Wild beasts and bestiality are repeatedly invoked in the imagery of *Die Räuber*. In *Fiesco* the hero himself tells the citizens of Genoa a parable of the animal kingdom, in which he appears, naturally, as the lion (II, viii), but the language of the play would furnish a whole menagerie, from the elephant to the worm. In *Kabale und Liebe* we move generally on a lower level, amidst vermin, insects, scorpions and treacherous serpents; much of this, of course, has biblical associations too, and there is much talk of death and judgement, of heaven and hell, of angels and devils. *Kabale und Liebe* is also rich in imagery relating to money, appropriate enough in the realistic setting, and constantly intimating that this is a world in which human beings are accounted mere chattels to be bought and sold. Despite the stylistic uncertainties, language and imagery constitute one of the most important unifying factors in these plays. The real answer to Schiller's perceived stylistic problem lay therefore in making his language not on the whole less poetic but more so: that is, in aiming for the higher degree of uniformity of register which goes with poetic stylisation, rather than for a greater degree of realism, which if it does not bring variety can only lead to flatness. The prose plays constitute a series of stylistic explorations whose true if unconscious goal is the creation not of a realistic but of a poetic form of drama.

Schiller's early development can thus be seen to parallel Goethe's. Each of them, in his next dramatic work, was to take the decisive step from the rebellious exuberance of 'Sturm und Drang' to the discipline of a classical style, most conspicuously in the adoption of verse instead of prose. But this does not mean that they had abandoned the ideals of their youth. On a higher level of dramatic expression, those ideals, the highest ideals of the age, could be given a form appropriate to their seriousness and dignity. Others too had felt the inadequacy of prose for this purpose. Perhaps most surprisingly, Lessing himself, the pioneer of realism, had himself chosen to give final and definitive expression to his own enlightened humanitarianism in the form of a 'dramatic poem'.

CHAPTER V

# *The triumph of humanity:* Nathan der Weise, Iphigenie auf Tauris, Don Carlos

Laocoon, Lessing tells us, was portrayed in the nude, rather than in the vestments appropriate to a priest and a king's son, because the sculptor wished to portray essential humanity, not the trappings of rank and status. The ideals of universal humanity, of the brotherhood of man, of liberty, equality and fraternity, inspired the noblest minds of the eighteenth century – writers, thinkers and men of action. In an age of increasing secularisation, when traditional religious doctrines were being revalued and reinterpreted, the Christian teaching that all men are equal in the sight of God led to the growing feeling, even the demand, that they should enjoy equal rights on earth. Sir William Sampson, in Lessing's first tragedy, rewards his faithful servant Waitwell by raising him to his own status, observing that they will in any case be equals beyond the grave. Luise Miller dreams of being reunited with Ferdinand after death, when the barriers of class which separate them will be removed; Ferdinand seeks to overcome those barriers in life, even to destroy them. Secret societies, such as the Freemasons, enabled men of different social classes to meet as equals; many of the leading writers and artists of the time were Freemasons, and similar societies and orders, devoted to enlightened and humanitarian goals, are depicted in works such as Goethe's *Wilhelm Meister* and Mozart's *Magic Flute*. When in Mozart's opera the Speaker asks Sarastro, the High Priest, whether the hero Tamino will pass the test of initiation – 'will Tamino master the arduous tests which await him? He is a prince' – Sarastro replies: 'More than that. He is a man' ('Mensch'). Religious and racial barriers were also attacked by the idealists of the eighteenth century: 'Am I not a man and a brother?' asks the kneeling, fettered figure on Josiah Wedgwood's anti-slavery medallion.

In stripping his tragic characters of the traditional 'pomp and majesty', in inviting sympathy and even admiration for ordinary, contemporary middle-class people, Lessing was seeking to express this ideal of universal humanity. But the realistic mode of presentation tended not so much to achieve universality as merely to replace one set of particulars by another. And when the 'Stürmer und Dränger' proclaimed the goals of emancipation and the rights of man, the tone of their protest was often too fiercely individualistic, and the freedom which they demanded, and which in the form of their works they practised, came to verge too closely upon anarchy. A truly universal theme called for a more truly universal mode of expression: the highest ideals of civilisation demanded to be expressed in civilised form. This meant a reversion away from realism and individualism towards some kind of classicism, a voluntary submission to some kind of artistic discipline; not, of course, the mechanical obedience to external 'rules' which both Lessing and the 'Stürmer und Dränger' had so forcefully denounced, but an acknowledgement that true freedom, whether social, political or artistic, can only be achieved within a framework of order.[1] And so we find Lessing and Goethe at the end of the 1770s, followed by Schiller a few years later, producing works which exhibit a high degree of stylisation. The universality of their themes is reflected in the removal of the action from the present to historical or legendary times, in accordance with the classical principle of *éloignement* – the reverse of the principle of modernisation which Lessing had followed in his tragedies, but differing also from the realistic evocation of the particulars of a historical epoch which Goethe had introduced in *Götz*. And the elevation of character and sentiment is enhanced through the deliberate unreality of its expression in verse.

Lessing had seemingly abandoned active interest in the drama after *Emilia Galotti*, declaring (though not for the first time in his life) that he was firmly resolved never to have anything more to do with the theatre, and following the activities of the 'Stürmer und Dränger' with a detached and often disapproving eye. In his years at

Wolfenbüttel he became more and more absorbed in theological speculation and controversy. Freedom of religious belief had been one of his most passionate concerns from his early years, and had found dramatic expression in *Die Juden* and *Der Freigeist*. But in 1778 the controversies in which Lessing was involved became so fierce that he was forbidden to publish any more works of theological polemic. Not to be deprived, however, of his freedom of expression, he turned once more to his 'old pulpit, the theatre', as he called it. Taking up a sketch which he had made some years before, he completed within a few months his last and greatest play, *Nathan der Weise (Nathan the Wise)*; it was published in May 1779. In March of the same year, Goethe, by now a minister in the service of the Duke of Weimar, had completed the original version of his *Iphigenie auf Tauris*, and it had been performed at court: a professional actress played the title role, but Goethe took the part of Orest and the Duke himself that of Pylades. This version of the play was in prose, and it was not until 1786, during his Italian journey, that Goethe recast it in verse for publication. But nothing of substance was altered: if we read the original version it seems only waiting to be formally versified, its restrained and elegant prose worlds away from the rough immediacy of *Götz von Berlichingen*, often falling naturally into the rhythm of blank verse. Schiller began his fourth play, *Don Carlos*, in 1783, immediately after *Kabale und Liebe*, but found himself unable to complete it with his customary rapidity. The complexity of the historical subject-matter, and a change or growing uncertainty regarding his dramatic intentions, drew out the process for three years, and though the work had been conceived very much in the spirit of *Fiesco*, as a historical anecdote offering scope for vivid character portrayal, the finished play of 1786 is something very different. However, just as Schiller had from the outset welcomed the opportunity to write about elevated historical characters as offering an escape from the confines of contemporary realism, so he very soon decided that verse rather than prose was after all the proper medium for serious drama.

All three plays are in a sense domestic dramas, their plots turning upon family relationships. Lessing's is basically a comedy of mistaken identity. The setting is Jerusalem during the Crusades. Sultan Saladin is executing Christian prisoners when suddenly, moved by

6 Grecian authenticity: Goethe and Corona Schröter in the original
version of *Iphigenie auf Tauris*, Weimar 1779. Engraving by F. W. Facius
after the contemporary painting by G. M. Kraus. Goethe's appearance as
Orest was commended as 'godlike'.

some half-recognised feature in the man's face, he spares the life of one Knight Templar. The Templar, wandering through Jerusalem, finds a house on fire, rushes in and saves the life of a girl – Recha, daughter of Nathan the Jew. The Templar falls in love with Recha; and Daja, Nathan's Christian housekeeper, reveals to him that she is really only Nathan's foster-daughter, and the baptised child of Christian parents – a Christian like himself, it seems. But in the end it turns out not only that the Templar and Recha are in fact brother and sister, but that their father was the brother of the Muslim Saladin: religious divisions are transcended in family reunion. Goethe's play, based upon Euripides, tells of the reunion of the children of Agamemnon, Iphigeneia and Orestes, in the land of Thoas, king of the Taurians. At the end they leave Tauris to return home to Greece, hopeful that the fearful curse of internecine destruction which the gods had laid upon their family, the house of Tantalus, may at last be expiated. Schiller's play, unlike Lessing's or Goethe's, has a tragic outcome. It deals with the fatal love of Don Carlos, son of Philip II of Spain, for his stepmother Elizabeth of Valois. Here the family (Schiller said that his play would not be a political one, but 'a domestic scene set in a royal household') is not a happy union, but a hotbed of jealousy and suspicion. But this is no natural family: Carlos had been betrothed to Elizabeth, but his father had then taken a fancy to his son's bride and married her himself. The situation is brought to a head by the intervention of Carlos's friend, the idealistic Marquis Posa. After many complications (the details of the plot are, it must be admitted, not always easy to follow), Posa attempts to save his friend by sacrificing himself to the King's vengeance. But his death is in vain: the play ends with Elizabeth fainting as Philip hands his son over to the tender mercies of the Inquisition.

Lessing's plot is flagrantly artificial, Goethe's legendary, Schiller's a romantic travesty of historical fact. We are far away from contemporary domestic realism. The truth which these plays convey is not literal but symbolic: the family with which all three are really concerned is the universal family, the brotherhood of mankind. Lessing is concerned with the essential unity of all true religions and the falsity of religious bigotry. The Templar, a man whose life has been devoted literally to fighting for Christianity, is thrown into confusion and doubt, almost into despair, at the seemingly incomprehensible twist of fate by which his life is spared by one enemy (the Muslim) only for him to save in turn the life of another (the Jew). But, as Nathan asks, 'Are Jew and Christian rather Jew and Christian / Than men?' (II, v). And the message symbolised in the working-out of the plot is also expounded in the parable of the three rings, the centrepiece of the play, which Nathan tells Saladin in Act III. Saladin, originally intending only to trap Nathan so that he can coerce him into lending him money, challenges Nathan to prove to him which of the three great religions, Christianity, Judaism and Islam, is the true one. But Nathan's answer is that 'truth' is not such a simple matter, that no one religion can claim its exclusive ownership. The three sons in the parable, left three indistinguishable rings by their father, quarrel about which is the true one, the magic ring which

> had the secret power
> To make the man who wore it in good faith
> Beloved by God and man. (III, vii)

But the judge whom they ask to settle their dispute observes that it appears from their behaviour that the true ring has been lost and that all three are forgeries: rather than each of them jealously seeking to establish the authentic origin of his own ring, he tells them:

> Let each one show his zeal in love, beyond
> Venality and prejudice exalted!
> Let each one seek in rivalry to prove
> And manifest the power that dwells within
> The stone of his own ring! And strive to aid
> That power with sweet amicability,
> Good deeds, and glad submission to the will
> Of God! (III, vii)

Goethe's play proclaims a similar message. In Euripides' *Iphigeneia in Tauris*, which provided its basic model, we are presented with a conflict between Greeks and barbarians, in which the gods ultimately intervene on the side of the Greeks and King Thoas is left to curse the folly of opposing the divine will. Goethe's play is also about a victory of civilisation over barbarism, but the Greeks by no means enjoy a monopoly of civilised values. Iphigenie, and subsequently Orest, reject the course of deceit, treachery and if need be violence which Orest's friend Pylades urges in pursuit of their goal of escape from Tauris. They seek to win over Thoas by persuasion, to bring out the potential for civilised behaviour which he shares with them and with all men:

THOAS       And do you think the raw
 And barbarous Scythian will hear the voice
 Of truth and sweet humanity, to which
 The Grecian Atreus was deaf?
IPHIGENIE                       It can be heard
 By any man, born beneath any sky,
 If in his breast the source of life flows pure
 And unimpeded.                                    (v, iii)

And just as Lessing's play rejects literal obedience to the dictates of any religion, be it Christianity, Judaism or Islam, so Goethe, departing from his Greek source, rejects a literal interpretation of the oracle of Apollo, according to which Orestes and Pylades had been instructed to steal the image of Diana from the temple in Tauris and return it to Greece, in favour of a figurative and purely human reading: it is not Apollo's sister Diana who is to be returned to Greece, but Orest's sister Iphigenie, and so there is no need for them to quarrel with Thoas over the image.

 Schiller's play takes place, of course, in a modern and a more realistically political world. Lessing's advocacy of religious toleration is here intensified into an impassioned plea for freedom of conscience in general. The unnatural domestic situation, with the father married to his son's intended bride, is symbolic of a general perversion of the natural order in the autocratic political system of Philip's Spain, and the play's idealists, Carlos and Posa, and their ally the Queen, dream of replacing this 'sad perversion of the laws of nature' (Posa in III, x) with a natural society in which the relations of human beings to each other – of friends, of lovers, of parents and children – can be normal and free. Posa, the self-proclaimed 'ambassador of all humanity' (to Carlos in I, ii), urges King Philip (III, x) to grant his subjects freedom of thought ('Geben Sie / Gedankenfreiheit' – the famous cry whose enthusiastic reception by audiences in Nazi Germany led to a ban on further performances of the play). In doing so, Posa urges, the King will become a king of kings, like God himself, who does not rule His subjects with the iron rod of despotism, but through allowing them their liberty:

> Will you not look about you
> Within His glorious realm of nature! Liberty
> Is its foundation, and what riches flow
> From liberty! The great Creator casts
> The humble worm within a dewdrop, grants
> Free play of forces even in the realms
> Of death and of decay – but *your* creation,
> How poor and withered! Let a leaf but stir,
> It frights the lord of Christendom –                    (III, x)

The language and imagery closely resemble those of Schiller's great hymn to liberty and the brotherhood of man, the Ode to Joy ('An die Freude'), which appeared at the same time as *Don Carlos*, in 1786. In the play Schiller also attacks the Church and the Inquisition in an almost Voltairean spirit, showing them to be the powers behind the throne and the ultimate authors of political as well as of overtly religious repression. In one of its most striking scenes (memorably and in this case faithfully reproduced in Verdi's opera) King Philip, ostensible 'lord of Christendom', seeks advice from the blind, aged Grand Inquisitor, only to learn that the Inquisitor has the whole situation in his command already. The King is humbled before this terrifying figure (whereas the Patriarch of Jerusalem, who takes a somewhat similar role in *Nathan der Weise*, threatening though he may appear, is ultimately comic in his impotence). Philip's excuse that he longed for the confidence of a fellow human being is cut down with the savage rebuke 'Men / For you are numbers, nothing more', and his plea that to hand his own son over to the Inquisition would be unnatural is silenced with the brutal 'The faith / Allows no voice of nature' (v, x).

Though Schiller's play fully shares the humanitarian idealism of Lessing's and Goethe's, it appears at first sight that it does not share their optimism. The worlds of *Nathan der Weise* and of *Iphigenie auf Tauris* are governed by a benevolent power (be it divine Providence or the gods of classical antiquity) which ensures that all will eventually turn out for the best: the families are reunited and humanity is triumphant. In *Don Carlos* the family is destroyed, the cause of liberty is defeated, and tyranny, bigotry and repression apparently reign supreme. Yet the whole movement of the play, and in particular the imagery of nature and of natural growth which pervades it, surely endorse the view so passionately put before the King by Posa, that the victory of repression can only be temporary and that the cause of liberty must ultimately triumph:

> More gentle times
> Will take the place of Philip's century;
> They will bring milder wisdom, reconcile
> The subject's happiness and the ruler's glory,
> And give necessity a human likeness.                    (III, x)

Even Philip himself seems to admit as much when in his final paroxysm of vengeful rage he lets slip the phrase 'The world / Is mine yet for an evening' (v, ix, my emphasis): he is fighting against the tide of history. The Providence which, despite appearances, governs the world of Schiller's play is a historical teleology, a sense of immanent historical progress. Only in the course of writing *Don Carlos* did Schiller discover this sense of meaning in history. After the completion of the play he turned to writing works of historiography, notably his *Geschichte des Abfalls der vereinigten Niederlande* (*History of the Revolt of the United Netherlands*, 1788). He was then appointed to a chair of history at the University of Jena, and there in May 1789, a few weeks before the outbreak of the French Revolution, delivered his inaugural lecture under the title *Was heißt und zu welchem Ende studiert man Universalgeschichte?* (*What is, and to what end do we study, Universal History?*). Schiller's answer to the question is that the historian's task is to make plain the meaning of history, the story of the gradual advance of humanity to freedom. That this advance is not achieved without setback and sacrifice Schiller knew well, and this is the meaning of the tragedy of *Don Carlos*.

But this Lessing and Goethe knew too. Nathan, the hero of Lessing's play, is a man who has known and overcome tragedy, whose faith in Providence and humanity have been subjected to the severest possible test. He reveals that his adoption of Recha followed hard upon the bitterest of losses, the murder of his wife and seven sons by Christians in a pogrom. After three days and nights of the deepest despair, he realised that this affliction was nothing but a test of his faith in the ultimate wisdom and benevolence of God:

> But reason gradually was heard again,
> Speaking with gentle voice: and yet, God is!
> And yet, this too was God's command! Why then,
> Come, practise what you long have understood,
> And what to practise is no harder than
> To understand, if you but have the will.
> Rise up! – I rose! and cried to God, I will,
> If Thou wilt only that I will! (IV, vii)

The ideals of tolerance and humanity will not triumph of their own accord, even in a world ruled by a benevolent Providence: they have to be fought for, gambled on, as in *Minna von Barnhelm*, even against the apparent odds. Providence demands the active cooperation of man in the fulfilment of its designs. Lessing did not believe in miracles, if by that word is meant the miraculous intervention of divine agency in human affairs. For the Patriarch, Nathan's adoption of the orphaned Recha is an interference in the divine plan, a human usurpation of the divine prerogative:

> What business has
> The Jew to do God's work? God can deliver
> Whomever He may please, without the Jew. (IV, ii)

But Lessing's view is rather that also expressed by Arkas, the King's confidant in *Iphigenie auf Tauris*, that the gods carry out their designs through the use of human agents: 'Through men it is their wont men to deliver' ('Sie pflegen Menschen menschlich zu erretten', *Iphigenie* IV, ii). In Goethe's play too the heroine faces a crisis, a test of her faith in the benevolence of the gods. The appearance of Orest in Tauris offers no straightforward prospect of a happy family reunion, for Taurian custom demands that he, as a stranger, be sacrificed in the temple of Diana – and that Iphigenie, as Diana's priestess, herself perform the sacrifice – a fratricide which would bring the story of their family, the house of Tantalus, to a fittingly gruesome end. Both Iphigenie and Orest have to struggle, to win through to a recognition of their true roles in the divine plan, and to gamble on their own faith in that plan before it can be realised. When this happens, there is no need for the miraculous intervention of the gods by which the Greeks are saved from the angry Thoas in Euripides' play: Thoas himself magnanimously consents to their returning home.

Neither Lessing's play nor Goethe's, then, is facile in its optimism. Goethe has been accused of the 'avoidance of tragedy' in *Iphigenie*;[2] but it is rather the case that he has deepened the elements of potential tragedy in the story as he took it over from Euripides, and introduced further elements of inner conflict which are not present in Euripides at all. There is no hint in Euripides of the struggle undergone by Goethe's Iphigenie, of the conflict between her ties of blood, and her natural desire to return to her homeland, and the loyalty and gratitude which she feels towards King Thoas, who has become her 'second father', as she says in IV, iv; of her reluctance to betray Thoas as Pylades urges her to do, or of her deep conviction that she can only expiate the curse on her family by preserving the purity of her own conscience. In telling the truth to Thoas she resembles not so much Euripides' Iphigeneia as Antigone, the heroine of Sophocles' tragedy, who does what she believes to be right regardless of what the consequences may be.

In all three plays, a central character is called upon to stand up for his or her beliefs, to proclaim those ideals which the author himself is seeking to express in his work, to a potentially hostile listener: Iphigenie to King Thoas, Nathan to Sultan Saladin, Marquis Posa to King Philip of Spain. In each, the listener is the supreme earthly authority within the play, who holds all the other characters' lives in his power. In each case, therefore, the encounter, the conviction with which the character who is the playwright's mouthpiece proclaims his or her ideals, and the impression which he or she makes upon the potential adversary, are crucial to the outcome of the plot. This is obvious in Goethe's play, where the confrontation takes place in the final act and the heroine herself points out to Thoas that

> The two of us, the last of Tantalus'
> Descendants, I have placed thus in your hands:
> Destroy us – if you must![3]                    (v, iii)

In *Nathan der Weise* and *Don Carlos* the fateful encounter takes place earlier, in the third act, and its crucial function in the plot is less obvious. But it would be wrong to suppose (though some critics, and some performances, tend to give this impression) that the playwright is simply using his favourite character to proclaim his own ideals, and that the action of the play has been suspended. By rising successfully to the challenge of Saladin's question, Nathan wins Saladin's friendship and support, a vital factor in ensuring the eventual happy outcome and the revelation of the Providential design: in Lessing's play as in Goethe's, the family reunion, literal and symbolic, is achieved under the patronage of an enlightened secular authority, but that authority has first to be converted to the enlightened cause. The outcome of the confrontation between Philip and Posa is more complex. Up to a point, Posa too succeeds in persuading his adversary; but his success is not of the kind he had hoped for. By his passionate advocacy of his ideals Posa convinces the King not of the truth of those ideals, but of his own sincerity and trustworthiness; upon which the King decides to make Posa his confidant and to use him in the furtherance of his own designs. Posa is caught in a trap of his own making, from which all the complications and the eventual tragic outcome of the plot may be seen to spring.

Both Lessing and Goethe present a vision of a world capable of overcoming tragedy, of leaving tragedy behind it. But the awareness of tragedy is fully contained within their optimism, in the story of Nathan's bereavement and in the past history of the house of Tantalus. And just as the protagonists have to fight for their convictions within the play, so they, or their successors in the march of humanity, will have to fight again. In the last act of *Nathan* we learn that Saladin's enlightened rule is coming to an end, that 'the Templars are astir again' and that the bloodshed of the Crusades is likely to recommence (v, i-ii). And though it is with high hopes that Orest and Iphigenie leave Tauris, we do not know what will happen to them when they return to Greece (Goethe planned a sequel, *Iphigenie in Delphi*, but did not execute it) – nor indeed to King Thoas, threatened by his rebellious subjects, after he has let them go; for his response to Iphigenie's challenge, 'Destroy us – if you must', was as much of a gamble on 'virtue and Providence' as was the challenge itself. The ending of Goethe's play is curiously muted, with Thoas' final 'Farewell!' ('Lebt wohl!') leaving the verse hanging in mid-line.[4]

Iphigenie herself is fully aware of the risk that she is taking in standing up to Thoas and telling him the truth. She is even challenging the gods themselves, disobeying what appears to be their literal command – to assist Orest in stealing the image of Diana – and insisting on doing what she herself feels to be right, defying the gods as she defies Thoas to gainsay her if they dare:

> If
> True Gods you are, and such is your repute,
> Then show it by your aid, and glorify
> The truth in me! (v, iii)

This is heroic behaviour, very different, at least in appearance, from Lessing's 'glad submission to the will of God'. There is even a hint of the old Promethean rebellion about it. Iphigenie has indeed become 'godlike' ('göttergleich', one of the play's key words), and it is her behaviour before Thoas in the final confrontation which inspires Orest with the realisation that it is she, rather than the mere idol which stands in the temple, who must be returned to Greece. In Goethe's play, humanity seems to be outgrowing the need for gods. Similarly in *Don Carlos* the priest Domingo tells the Duke of Alba of his fear that Carlos, if he becomes King, will replace the old religion with a new one, the religion of humanity:

> His heart is all aglow with a new virtue,
> Proud and secure, sufficient to itself,
> Which bows the knee before no faith. – He *thinks*!
> His brain is all aflame with prodigies
> Most strange – what he reveres, is man . . . (ii, x)

But Lessing's play too, though no miracles of divine intervention occur in it, bears on its title-page the motto 'Introite, nam et heic dii sunt' – 'Enter, for here too are gods'.

Religion needs ritual. In all three plays, the realism and immediacy which all three writers, in their different ways, had sought to achieve in their earlier works give way to deliberate and overt stylisation. This is most obvious in externals such as the *éloignement* of the setting and the use of verse, and in the case of *Iphigenie* a

77

complete reversion to the 'prison' of the unities from which the young Goethe had been so eager to escape. But all three also manifest or at least aspire to a more profound discipline of form. This is perhaps least obvious in the case of *Nathan der Weise*. Lessing's earlier plays, in accordance with his dramatic theory, had been fundamentally Aristotelian in character. *Nathan der Weise*, with its complicated plot, its network of family relationships deliberately elaborated with obvious artifice, appears in many ways less, rather then more, 'classical' than his previous work. It also treats the unities with much greater freedom, employing a number of settings, and one of the implications of its subtitle 'dramatic poem' ('dramatisches Gedicht') appears to be that Lessing is no longer bothered by the traditional distinctions of genre, which he had previously always observed in practice and rigorously insisted on in theory. Although Lessing himself had praised Shakespeare and so prepared the way for the exaltation of Shakespeare by the 'Stürmer und Dränger', little if any Shakespearian influence can be detected in the form or style of his earlier plays; but the plot of *Nathan* is not unlike that of a Shakespearian comedy, and in its colourful style and range of effects – serious and touching, didactic and witty – it seems to turn its back on all neo-classic precedent. The range, of course, is still narrow compared with that of Shakespeare (or even of *Götz* or *Die Räuber*), and Lessing's design is still very carefully controlled and, for all the complications, economical, requiring a cast no larger than that of *Minna von Barnhelm* or *Emilia Galotti*.

If in *Nathan der Weise* Lessing has moved away from Aristotelian and towards Shakespearian form, Goethe and Schiller have moved in the opposite direction and come to meet him. Both had begun their careers as playwrights with character tragedies in full accord with the non-Aristotelian or indeed anti-Aristotelian theory of the 'Sturm und Drang'. They had, however, both also written plays to the domestic formula pioneered by Lessing – *Clavigo*, *Stella*, *Kabale und Liebe* – in which situation and relationship are at least as important as character portrayal, and it is these elements which come to the fore in *Iphigenie* and *Don Carlos*. In *Iphigenie* Goethe has, it seems, turned his back completely on Shakespeare and reverted to the Racinian formula of a very small cast (five, one of whom, Arkas, is a mere confidant and go-between) and a crisis long prepared but brought to a head by the appearance on the scene of a new character or characters (Orest and Pylades). Almost the whole play is conducted in monologue and duologue, and only once, in the penultimate scene, are all the characters present on the stage together: Arkas and Pylades then make their exits, leaving only Iphigenie, Orest and Thoas on stage for the final scene. (Goethe also reverts here, like Schiller in *Fiesco*, to the French convention of scene-division.) The shifting relationships between the five characters are brought visually, one might say choreographically, before us by the careful patterning of their entrances and exits. Iphigenie is undoubtedly the central figure, but in a more essentially dramatic way than is the case with Götz or Egmont: she is the focal point about which the whole situation turns and upon which its tensions and perspectives resolve. But Goethe retains the modern, unclassical designation 'Schauspiel', which he had used for *Götz* and for the original version of *Stella*, indicating that the Greek legend is really being treated in an essentially modern way and that his play, like Lessing's, consciously transcends the neo-classic separation of the genres.

*Don Carlos* bears the same generic subtitle as *Nathan der Weise*, 'dramatic poem', although it is quite plainly a tragedy. It completes the evolution, begun in *Kabale und Liebe*, from the character-based structure of *Die Räuber* and *Fiesco* to a much more Aristotelian structure grounded in action and situation. The complexity of the situation, the large cast (twenty named characters and numerous extras) and the frequent changes of scene are, it is true, still unclassical features, and Schiller's Aristotelian evolution seems to have happened to some extent by accident. Carlos was originally conceived, when Dalberg suggested the subject to Schiller, as a hero very much in the 'Sturm und Drang' mould, taking, as Schiller wrote to one of his friends, 'his soul from Shakespeare's Hamlet, his blood and sinews from Leisewitz's Julius [J. A. Leisewitz's *Julius von Tarent* was another 'Sturm und Drang' tragedy of fraternal hatred], and his pulse from me'. But as the work developed, Schiller's interests and sympathies shifted, so that the finished work no longer revolves about a single, subjective point of view. The situation and plot are indeed so complex that not only the characters but Schiller himself, on occasion, seem none too sure of exactly what is going on or of why people act as they do; the dramatist gets himself into complexities from which he has to extricate himself by *coups de théâtre* which themselves create further problems. But although Schiller is not always in perfect control of his material, the complexity is not inappropriate to the play's subject-matter and theme – the shifting pattern of alliances, the deceptions and the self-deceptions which make up the world of politics, and which present a constant challenge and a constant frustration to the reforming zeal of the idealist. (Verdi's opera, however, offers an interesting comparison: his librettists have successfully simplified Schiller's intrigue and thereby rendered the course of the action a good deal more easily comprehensible, while retaining most of the great climactic scenes in which the themes of the work – love, friendship, the desire for liberty – are most forcefully articulated.) Character and action are here much more fully integrated than in *Die Räuber* or *Fiesco*, and this marks an important step towards Schiller's eventual mastery of a classical style.

All three plays employ elevated characters and remote settings, which raise their significance from a particular to a more universal level. In realistic terms one might see the characters of *Nathan der Weise* as socially not unlike those of *Emilia Galotti*, with Sultan Saladin, the rich merchant Nathan and the Templar corresponding to the Prince, Odoardo Galotti and Count Appiani. But social hierarchy plays little part in the action, and the 'pomp and majesty' for which Lessing has so little regard are attributed not to the Sultan, but to the villainous Patriarch, who is indeed directed to appear 'with full ecclesiastical pomp' (IV, ii). Jerusalem at the time of the Crusades provides a plausible setting for the encounter between representatives of the three great religions, but superficial plausibility is not Lessing's concern:

DAJA                           O! this is the land
  Of wonders!
TEMPLAR             (Well! – a wondrous land, indeed.
  It must be so, for all the world is found
  Foregathered here.)                                          (III, x)

Oriental settings, with their air of exotic mystery, were often used in the eighteenth century: familiar examples are again furnished by

Mozart's *Seraglio* and *Magic Flute*. Lessing studied historical source material and adopted one or two little touches of local colour which happened to take his fancy, but he makes no attempt to create a genuine historical atmosphere. Like the geographical setting, the historical one – which can be identified as the year 1192, when there was a truce between Sultan Saladin and the Crusaders – is symbolic rather than literal in its significance.

The Greece of *Iphigenie* is similarly symbolic rather than real. Drama in the classical style had, of course, regularly been set in classical antiquity, but Dryden and others had observed that characters such as we meet in Racine are not really ancient Greeks but seventeenth-century Frenchmen. Goethe seems to have gone to some trouble to create what he believed to be a genuinely Greek atmosphere, insisting, for example, upon something approaching authentic Greek costume when the play was performed, instead of the traditional anachronistic mixture of wigs and armour. But it was still, of course, a Greece seen through eighteenth-century German eyes. In his early farce *Götter, Helden und Wieland* the Goethe of the 'Sturm und Drang' had portrayed ancient Greece as a land fit for 'Kerls' to live in, and had indeed introduced just such a 'Kerl' in the person of Hercules, whose large size, loud voice and earthy rumbustiousness provoke the fastidious Wieland of the play to the rebuke: 'I will have nothing to do with you, you colossus.' The Greece to which Iphigenie longs to return, the Greece whose spirit she and her brother Orest embody, is very different. It is the Greece of *kalokagathia*, 'the good and the beautiful', the Greece of the 'edle Einfalt und stille Größe' (noble simplicity and calm grandeur) praised by the art-historian Winckelmann as the hallmark of Greek art and Greek humanity. This was, of course, an idealised view, and had been attacked for its one-sidedness by Lessing in *Laocoon*. And in relation to *Iphigenie* it should not be overstressed, for the play itself contains enough intimations of a very different and probably more authentic ancient Greece – the Greece of the bloodthirsty family of Tantalus, or of the wily, deceitful Ulysses whom Pylades acknowledges as his hero.[5]

Both *Nathan der Weise* and *Iphigenie auf Tauris* depict the coming-into-being of a new, more humane and civilised set of attitudes and sensibilities, in each case one more characteristic of eighteenth-century Western Europe than of the time and place in which the action is set. Schiller wrote in 1802, when he was working on *Iphigenie* for a new production at Weimar, that the play was 'extraordinarily modern and un-Greek'. But a similar kind of anachronism can be found in his own *Don Carlos*, especially in the figure of Marquis Posa (incidentally a wholly fictitious character, unlike the other major figures of the drama), whose ideals of liberty and fraternity are very much those of Schiller and his contemporaries. In realistic terms, *Egmont*, which treats closely-related historical subject-matter from a different viewpoint (the same Duke of Alba appears in both plays), is probably more authentic; but Schiller's choice of setting and period is again of symbolic rather than realistic significance.[6] Goethe in *Götz* and *Egmont* portrays the sixteenth century as a time when traditional, established liberties were being extinguished; Schiller in *Don Carlos* sees it rather as a time when new ones were being born, or at least conceived in men's minds. (There is, of course, a strong hint of this at the end of *Egmont*, in that visionary transformation when the whole perspective of the work seems to change so radically.) Similarly, in the preface to his *Revolt of the Netherlands*, Schiller the historian describes that rebellion as the first chapter in a story of progressive liberation continuing into his own day and, by implication, into the future which he and his contemporaries so eagerly and confidently awaited.

The last common feature which unites the three plays and sets them apart from their authors' earlier works and from the movement towards realism in earlier eighteenth-century drama is, of course, their adoption of blank verse instead of prose. From the seventeenth century to the first attempts of Lessing, the alexandrine had reigned supreme in serious German drama. (Some writers, such as Schlegel, had also used it in comedy, though Gottsched and his followers generally favoured prose for this 'lower' form.) It was dignified and elevated, but inflexible and relentlessly formal. The desire for increased realism and immediacy which began with *Miss Sara Sampson* and continued through the 'Sturm und Drang' had naturally led to the adoption of prose. A number of dramatists had felt the need for something in between the two extremes; and the generally developing interest in English drama had led to experiments in blank verse, the unrhymed iambic pentameter which the

Elizabethan playwrights had established as the standard form of dramatic verse in English. The first such experiment to be completed was Wieland's *Lady Johanna Gray* (1758), an adaptation of a play by Nicholas Rowe. But no dramatist of the first rank had successfully essayed the metre (two or three attempts by Lessing at about the same time had remained fragments). Goethe's first attempts at drama, the comedies written while he was a student at Leipzig in the late 1760s, still employ alexandrines. Goethe had also tried free verse in *Prometheus* and the old German 'Knittelvers', the metre of Hans Sachs, in the as yet unfinished *Faust* and in such pieces as *Das Jahrmarktsfest zu Plundersweilen*. But between 1755, the year of *Miss Sara Sampson*, and 1779, that of *Nathan der Weise*, no dramatic work of major importance in German had appeared in any form of verse. Schröder in advertising his competition of 1776, while not ruling out verse, had expressed a decided preference for prose.

Then, however, first Lessing, then Goethe and Schiller, felt the need for a stylistic heightening, a degree of linguistic *éloignement*, and turned to what was to become the standard verse form of German classical drama. The advantages of blank verse over the alexandrine were obvious. Its iambic rhythm and the built-in asymmetry of its five stresses as easily fit the natural cadences of German as they do of English. It is inherently a varied and flexible metre: if rhythm is handled freely and the sense run on from line to line, it can flow almost as unemphatically or informally as prose, while if a regular rhythm is maintained and the lines are emphatically end-stopped it can be almost as formal as the alexandrine. Further emphasis can be added by the occasional use of rhyme. All these resources were to be fully exploited by the German dramatists. Very rarely, though, do they employ a mixture of verse and prose, as we so often find in Shakespeare: in this respect their use of the medium can be called more classical, for here discipline and uniformity are preferred to freedom and variety. The overall tone or mean stylistic register of German blank verse is also usually rather closer to the classical 'grand style' than to the unrestricted Shakespearian manner: though it may range from the sublime down to the near-colloquial, the lowest and most familiar register is generally absent.

Lessing's blank verse, as might be expected, tends strongly to the informal, even the colloquial, avoiding 'pomp and majesty': even the play's greatest set-piece, Nathan's parable of the three rings, is conversational in tone, and elevated rhetoric occurs only to be parodied, in the 'sermon' which the unctuous Patriarch preaches to the Templar in IV, ii. The Romantic critic Friedrich Schlegel, describing the verse of *Nathan* as some of the best prose Lessing ever wrote, objected to its colloquialisms and homely proverbial phrases, and took particular exception to the use by Sultan Saladin's sister of an expression like 'Noch bin ich auf / Dem Trocknen völlig nicht' ('I'm not yet / Quite stony broke', II, ii), as unbecoming to a princess. Lessing himself made a number of self-deprecatory remarks about his verse, claiming, for example, that he had chosen verse in order to be able to complete the play more quickly, since verse was easier to write than good prose. But he plainly knew exactly what he was aiming at: the colloquial tone is quite deliberate – he told his brother that 'the verse would not be nearly as good if it were better' – but the adoption of verse gives distance, a touch of unfamiliarity, even of deliberate artificiality, appropriate to the exotic setting. Goethe and Schiller both adopt a more elevated manner, but their blank verse is still warm and human. As in parts of *Egmont*, so in the original version of *Iphigenie* we can sense the verse, as it were, emerging from the prose, the speech falling again and again into an iambic cadence, needing only that slight further degree of regularity, harmony and grace which the formal division into lines will supply. Often a comparison of prose and verse forms of the same passage – Iphigenie's opening monologue, for example – will show how slight the necessary alterations were. The prose version even contains instances of such classical rhetorical devices as stichomythia, the allocation of single lines to two speakers in strict alternation. The exchange between Iphigenie and Arkas in the second scene, for example, is virtually identical in the two versions. I quote the original 'prose' form:

IPHIGENIE Soll ich beschleunigen, was mich bedroht?
ARKAS Willst du sein Werben eine Drohung nennen?
IPHIGENIE Es ist's, und mir die schrecklichste von allen.
ARKAS Gib ihm für seine Neigung nur Vertraun.
IPHIGENIE Wenn er von Furcht erst meine Seele löst.
ARKAS Warum verschweigst du deine Herkunft ihm?
IPHIGENIE Weil einer Priesterin Geheimnis ziemt.
ARKAS Dem Könige sollt' nichts Geheimnis sein.

IPHIGENIE Am I to hasten that which threatens me?
ARKAS The King pays suit: is that for you a threat?
IPHIGENIE It is, most terrible of all to me.
ARKAS Why can you not reward his love with trust?
IPHIGENIE Let him first lift from me the weight of fear.
ARKAS Why will you not reveal your name to him?
IPHIGENIE The veil of secrecy becomes a priestess.
ARKAS Before the King no secrets should remain.             (I, ii)

If an example such as this shows that Goethe's dramatic blank verse, in its balance and polish, is already classical rather than Shakespearian in character, it also indicates how natural was the transition from prose to verse and how unforcedly the rhythms fit the German language. We can see this again if we compare the blank verse of *Iphigenie* with the alexandrines of Schlegel's *Orest und Pylades*, where a number of closely parallel passages can be found: the alexandrines strike rhetorical attitudes, the blank verse seems to express the movement of genuine feeling.[7]

With Schiller too we have seen how the language of his earlier plays, with its passionate expressiveness and profusion of imagery, seemed to be demanding the additional heightening which the formal adoption of a poetic style would give. It was, as Schiller acknowledged in his preface to the first, incomplete published version of *Don Carlos*, the example and precept of Wieland which led him to blank verse. From the first he handles the medium with masterly assurance. Schiller's plays, like Shakespeare's, are 'full of quotations', and *Don Carlos* already has its fair share of them, from the almost, but not quite, colloquial ease of the opening words, spoken to Carlos by Domingo, the King's confessor –

> Die schönen Tage in Aranjuez
> Sind nun zu Ende. . .

> The happy days here in Aranjuez
> Are at an end. . .                                      (I, i)

– through the various emotional high points, the scenes of confrontation and passionate appeal, to King Philip's bitter and laconic words which end the play, as he hands his son over to the Grand Inquisitor:

> Ich habe
> Das Meinige getan. Tun Sie das Ihre.
>
> I have
> Done my part. Now you do yours. (v, xi)

Both *Nathan der Weise* and *Don Carlos* bear the subtitle 'dramatic poem'. It is sometimes suggested that one of the implications of this term is that they were intended in the first instance as 'closet dramas', plays to be read rather than performed. Schiller indeed says as much in his preface, and though such disclaimers should not be taken too seriously, the length of *Don Carlos* is certainly a practical drawback, necessitating severe cutting. But of *Nathan* Lessing wrote: 'I know of no place in Germany where this piece could be performed today. But all honour to the stage where it is first performed.' His concern for eventual stage performance, and his awareness that the adoption of blank verse created problems for actors and actresses used increasingly only to prose, is also indicated by the careful attention he paid to the punctuation of the printed text, which he claimed to be intended specifically to aid correct delivery of the lines. He proposed to explain his 'new system of dramatic punctuation' in a prefatory essay, but unfortunately this was never written. The problems he anticipated were indeed encountered by Goethe and Schiller. Goethe's play was of course originally written for performance rather than printed publication, but it is noteworthy that the acting version is in prose, the published version in verse. Schiller, conversely, was forced to recast *Don Carlos* in prose for stage performance in Mannheim, Berlin and elsewhere, though the original verse text was used in Hamburg. Though *Don Carlos* owes its inception to Schiller's association with the Mannheim theatre, in that it was Dalberg who first drew his attention to the story, the finished work represents a degree of estrangement between Schiller and the stage – and indeed after its completion he abandoned playwriting altogether for a number of years. For Goethe too the period of composition of *Iphigenie* was one of reappraisal, in which many other activities began to oust the theatre and the drama from the forefront of his concerns. But from the union forged between classical drama and the German-speaking stage at the court of Weimar in the late 1770s the great age of German literary drama was nevertheless to spring.

# CHAPTER VI

# Crisis and response: the beginnings of Weimar classicism

Goethe was invited to the Duchy of Saxe-Weimar in 1775, when he was in his twenty-sixth year. The Dowager Duchess Anna Amalia, who had ruled the small principality since her husband's early death in 1758, had identified the author of *Götz von Berlichingen* and of *Werther* – the novel whose appearance in 1775 had made him almost overnight into a European celebrity – as the brightest of the rising stars in the literary firmament of Germany, and she wished to add him to the ornaments of her court. In particular, he was to act as companion to her son, the young Duke Karl August, who had just attained his legal majority, and with it the responsibility of governing the small duchy and its 90,000-odd subjects – the capital, Weimar, had at that time only 6,000 inhabitants, a tenth of its present population. Despite the modest size of her domain, Anna Amalia had kept up a tradition of patronising the arts. A well-equipped opera house had been built in 1696; this was also used for spoken drama, and in the mid-eighteenth century some of the best actors in Germany could be seen there. After the collapse of the National Theatre enterprise in Hamburg, the Hamburg troupe under its then director Abel Seyler, and including Ekhof, had established itself in Weimar. In May 1774, however, professional theatre in the town had been brought to a sudden end by a disastrous fire which devastated the buildings of the ducal palace. The actors were dispersed, many following Ekhof to the neighbouring duchy of Gotha, where he set up an official court troupe: in the palace at Gotha his theatre, with its eighteenth-century machinery still largely intact, can still be seen. It was here that

Iffland served his apprenticeship, moving to Mannheim after Ekhof's death in 1778.

Theatre in Weimar had to go on in some form. A portable stage was erected in a private ballroom, owned by a citizen named Karl Hauptmann: it could be dismantled when the room was needed for its original purpose. This stage was used for amateur performances for the next five years, and in this world of amateur court theatricals Goethe now became involved.[1] For it he wrote a number of pieces, though of these only *Iphigenie auf Tauris* is of major importance. For the production of *Iphigenie* in 1779 he engaged a professional actress and singer, Corona Schröter, whom he had admired in his student days in Leipzig ten or twelve years before. This was the first step towards the re-establishment of professional theatre in Weimar.

The theatre was only one of many claims upon Goethe's time and attention at this time, however. His duties as the Duke's companion were not precisely defined, but he soon found himself taken into the young man's confidence to a degree which displeased the more conservative members of the Weimar establishment: engaged, as they had thought, merely to furnish intellectual conversation and to produce literary works, he was made a member of the Duke's Privy Council and in consequence granted a patent of personal nobility. By 1782 young Dr Goethe, academic jurist and avant-garde author, had become Geheimrat von Goethe, and had taken on various duties in the government of the duchy. Some of these were profoundly to influence his own personal intellectual development. His responsibility for the duchy's mineral resources, for example, led to a passionate interest first in geology, then in the natural sciences in general, which remained with him all his life. There were other, very different, matters too, notably an intense, but almost certainly platonic, relationship with the unhappy, introverted Charlotte von Stein, wife of one of the Weimar court dignitaries.

Goethe's first years in Weimar were for him as man and as artist a period of stock-taking. In particular he took stock of his own dramatic and theatrical aspirations, and of the aspirations which the cultivated classes of the German nation had come to attach to the idea of a National Theatre, in the novel *Wilhelm Meisters theatralische Sendung* (*Wilhelm Meister's Theatrical Mission*), which he began soon after his arrival there. Wilhelm undoubtedly bears, in fictional transformation, many features of the young Goethe himself: a young man of comfortable middle-class origins who develops an infatuation with the stage, traced back ultimately (as in Goethe's own autobiography) to the delights of a puppet-theatre enjoyed as a child. But like Goethe's previous fictional *alter ego*, Werther, Wilhelm lives out to the full what his creator had only dreamt of. Further inspired by a love-affair with a beautiful young actress, Wilhelm rejects what he sees as the philistine bourgeois world of his upbringing and joins a company of strolling players. The novel then presents us with a panorama of German theatrical history from the time of Gottsched and Frau Neuber (represented in the novel by Madame de Retti) to the introduction of Shakespeare to the German stage in the 1770s by Schröder (represented by Serlo). Madame de Retti's discussions with Wilhelm on the course of her professional career embody Goethe's own view of the Gottschedian reform of the theatre: it had been to a considerable extent necessary and justified and yet, as Lessing had observed, was bound to fail because it did violence to the natural tastes and character of the German nation. The novel also paints a lively and by no means flattering picture of the theatrical profession and of the social, economic and emotional problems of its members and its motley crew of hangers-on.

Goethe made slow but steady progress on the *Theatralische Sendung* during his first ten years in Weimar, but then abandoned it for the time being. To some extent he was writing the theatre out of his system. In the new environment of Weimar, and with the first flush of youth behind him, he was undergoing, as we have said, a period of profound self-reappraisal, involving all the different aspects of his personality: his artistic creativity, his public, social life and responsibilities, his private emotions, and their relation to each other and to the world in which he found himself living. Eventually the tension became unbearable, and could be resolved only in flight. In 1786 Goethe suddenly and without warning left Weimar for Italy, where he spent the next two years, a period which he thereafter regarded as one of spiritual rebirth and as one of the high points of his life. In Italy he developed a completely new attitude to life and art, to nature and science, to poetry and the world. It was also in Italy that he did most of the work on his play *Torquato Tasso*, conceived in Weimar in 1780 and completed in 1790 after his return, in which he gives powerful dramatic expression to the crisis he had undergone. It is one of his finest dramatic works. It is also one of the first literary works whose hero is himself an artist, and whose principal theme is the perils of the artist's calling. Goethe's Tasso is the ancestor of that familiar Romantic stereotype, the lonely artist at odds or in actual conflict with the rest of the society in which he lives.

The play is of course no more directly autobiographical than *Werther* or the *Theatralische Sendung*. Indeed, the tension between the artist and society, or the 'disproportion between talent and life' (as Goethe is said to have defined the play's theme) manifests itself in Tasso's case in a form quite different from that in which it affected Goethe. Tasso, court poet to Duke Alfonso of Ferrara, complains that he is valued – or perhaps only tolerated – as a producer of goods (in his case, poetry), but is not allowed to live his life as a complete human being; he complains that the Duke will not take him into his confidence as a man, or discuss affairs of state with him. Goethe in Weimar, on the other hand, was coming to feel that the personal confidence of Karl August and the responsibilities of public admin- istration left him too little time for his own artistic and intellectual pursuits. The relationship between Goethe and Charlotte von Stein is no doubt to some extent reflected in that between Tasso and the Duke's sister, the Princess Leonora, who perhaps appreciates the poet's worth more truly than do the other characters, but is horrified when Tasso interprets her signals of affection in a directly erotic sense; this should not, however, be over-emphasised. And Weimar offers no obvious real-life models for the play's other two char- acters, the Countess Leonora Sanvitale, the Princess's friend but also her rival for possession of Tasso, and the statesman Antonio, jealous of what he sees as the undeserved acclaim and favour enjoyed by the idle poet. But for all this, and despite the classicism of its outward form, *Tasso* is still perhaps the most complete and successful realisation of the 'Sturm und Drang' ideal of drama as the self- expression of a creative personality. It has indeed been called 'the tragedy of a creative artist'.[2]

But the problem which the play treats has more than merely personal or poetic significance. The figure of Tasso – once again

Goethe turns to the sixteenth century for the embodiment of a theme characteristic of the self-awareness of his own age – can be seen as exemplifying the relationship between any creative or productive individual and the society which consumes the product of his labours. Tasso sees himself as the victim of a conspiracy of exploitation, and though the other characters, notably Antonio, regard this view as exaggerated or even paranoid, it has been shared by some Marxist interpreters of the play. And Tasso's vision of a Golden Age in which human beings can be complete in their humanity, not confined within particular functional roles (the poet or the man of action) seems indeed to anticipate the Utopia of Marx and Engels' *German Ideology*, in which the individual would be free to 'do one thing today and another tomorrow, to hunt in the morning, fish in the afternoon, rear cattle in the evening, criticise after dinner, just as I have a mind, without ever becoming hunter, fisherman, shepherd or critic'.[3] Goethe seems though to be expressing the realisation that the ideal of pure or complete human-ity so dear to his age may be difficult or even impossible to realise in any actual human society. He offers us a vindication of art and the artist, a sympathetic portrait of the perils of the artistic tempera-ment, but also a justification of the accommodations which are necessary for civilisation to survive.

It is no accident that *Tasso*, like *Iphigenie*, is classical in form. As in that work, the unities are carefully observed (there are three changes of scene in *Tasso*, but the whole action takes place at the Duke's country retreat of Belriguardo, moving only from outdoors to in, from park to palace) and Goethe is as much at pains to observe the rules of propriety and decorum as he had been in *Götz* to defy them. In *Iphigenie* Goethe had adopted that most civilised of dramatic forms in order to depict the power of civilisation; in *Tasso* he observes the rules of artistic decorum in order to expose the rules of social decorum to critical, but not ultimately disapproving scrutiny. In the vision of the Golden Age which Tasso evokes for the Princess in II, i, 'All that gives pleasure is permitted' ('Erlaubt ist, was gefällt'); the phrase is taken from historical Tasso's *Aminta*. But the Princess counters with the more restrictive, but also more realistic maxim 'All that is seemly is permitted' ('Erlaubt ist, was sich ziemt'), based on words from his rival Guarini's *Pastor fido*. The abuse of such a code of conduct is seen in the famous quarrel scene in Act II, when Antonio, the practised diplomat and master of decorum, gives carefully controlled vent to his jealousy of Tasso in such a way as to provoke the younger and less wordly-wise man to forget himself and where he is, to the extent of drawing his sword on Antonio in the precincts of the Duke's palace, a grave breach of the social code. The Duke, arriving on the scene, sees plainly that the real responsibility lies with Antonio, for 'When two men quarrel, we may prudently / Regard the wiser as the guilty' (II, v). But he, as ultimate guarantor of the code, has to punish Tasso for breaking the letter of the law. This Tasso cannot understand; but Antonio, who after all really is an experienced and sensible man, accepts the Duke's reproof, comes to understand his own and Tasso's position more clearly, and at the end of the play is able to offer Tasso some measure of support when the poet's impetuous behaviour has lost him the favour of the Duke and the Princess.

The ending of the play is ambiguous, however, and has given rise to a good deal of interpretative controversy. The Duke and the two ladies leave Belriguardo in their carriage and Tasso launches into a passionate speech of eloquent despair, punctuated by Antonio with sober adjurations to calm and finally with a silent gesture of sympathy, as he takes Tasso by the hand. Tasso responds by acknowledging the nobility of the man he had previously regarded as a deadly and malicious enemy. But then he warns Antonio not to look too patronisingly, in his calm and stability, upon the storm-tossed poet who clings to him for support as the shipwrecked mariner clings to 'the very rock on which he thought to perish' ('an dem er scheitern sollte'). With these words the play ends. Once again, despite many classical features of form and spirit, Goethe has created a work which is ultimately, like *Iphigenie*, 'extraordinarily modern and un-Greek'. Though some critics have called it a tragedy, Goethe did not: he gave it, as he had latterly given *Iphigenie*, the unclassical designation 'Schauspiel', for it is another work which transcends the traditional generic subdivisions and arouses responses other than those traditionally associated with the different dramatic genres. *Tasso* is not simply, to quote Lessing's summary definition of tragedy, 'a poem which excites compassion': it evokes a more complex response, intellectual as much as emotional. It is in essence a problem play: with his most wholly successful attempt at dramatic classicism, Goethe simultaneously crowns his achievement in this characteristically modern type of drama.

For all its uniquely personal and essentially modern qualities, *Torquato Tasso* is undoubtedly more reminiscent of the Racinian manner than any other classical German play. It has only five characters, a minimum of external action – the two climaxes formed by Tasso's two offences against both courtly and dramatic propriety, his drawing of his sword against Antonio in Act II and his attempt to embrace the Princess in Act V – and a highly polished linguistic form: the blank verse is more regular than that of *Iphigenie*, and there are no deliberate variations of metre such as we do find in the earlier play. It has been called 'the most purely eloquent play in the whole of dramatic literature'.[4] But this eloquence is strictly subordinated to dramatic purpose. In the quarrel scene, for example, Tasso's actual drawing of his sword is preceded by a sharp verbal battle in which key words and phrases serve as weapons of thrust and parry – not only words of obvious thematic significance like 'permit' and 'beseem' ('erlauben', 'ziemen'), but even the simple spatial adverb 'here', which is linked to a pattern of spatial metaphors running throughout the play:

ANTONIO This lofty tone, this hot impetuousness
    Beseem you not, before me in this place.
TASSO What you here grant yourself beseems me too.         (II, iii)

Not a word is idle. Like Racine, Goethe creates drama from the exploitation of a limited vocabulary; though this is not, as in Racine, a conventional and indeed often highly artificial vocabulary relating to the themes of high tragedy (*feux*, *fers*, *flamme* and the like), but a vocabulary of ordinary social relationships, given its intensity by Goethe's particular thematic focus. Racinian too is the sense of potential violence underlying the smooth surface: beneath the polite exchanges, the characters are constantly manoeuvring against each other for position and influence, and every scene is laden with personal, social or sexual rivalry. Goethe completed *Tasso* at a time when he was perhaps least interested in, or most disillusioned with, the possibilities of the German theatre. It is a highly literary work; Goethe himself described it as 'stage-shy' ('theaterscheu'), and it was not until 1807 that it was actually performed. But it is nevertheless a work not only of great poetic beauty and deep thematic interest, but also of high dramatic and theatrical potential.

In Italy, Goethe formed a clearer idea of the shape he wished his life and the development of his personality to take. He wished his energies to be devoted to the discovery and celebration of the eternal truths and eternal laws of art, science and nature, and not to be dissipated in the chores of administering a petty German principality. When he returned to Weimar in 1788 it was on condition that he should be relieved of these chores – though he retained the title of Privy Councillor and the emoluments that went with it. If henceforth he undertook any public duties, they were to be exclusively of a cultural, artistic or scientific kind. One such duty very soon presented itself. A new, permanent theatre had been built in Weimar in 1780 to replace the one in Hauptmann's ballroom. But by this time the best professional actors and actresses had all found themselves employment elsewhere. In the mid–1780s the Weimar court was served by a distinctly second-rate company under the leadership of one Joseph Bellomo. Karl August made some attempts to find a better troupe elsewhere in Germany and to attract it to Weimar, but nothing was actually done until 1790, when Bellomo suddenly left Weimar on receiving the offer of a more favourable engagement at Graz. It was then decided not simply to engage another actor-manager and his troupe bag and baggage, but to set up a court theatre under full official supervision. Lessing, after the failure of private enterprise in Hamburg, had reflected that the best hope for the German theatre lay in some form of enlightened court patronage, and this course had already been followed in the 'National Theatres' of Mannheim and Vienna. In Weimar, with commendable modesty (or perhaps prudence), this grandiose title was not used. (It was conferred upon the Weimar theatre only in 1919, when – by another of the ironies of German history – it was the scene of the adoption by the new German republic of the ill-fated Weimar constitution.) In January 1791 Goethe accepted appointment as artistic director. There was a financial director as well (Franz Kirms, another member of the Privy Council), and various subordinates who were responsible for day-to-day tasks both administrative and artistic. Supreme authority rested, however, with Goethe, and so it was to remain for the next quarter of a century.

With his appointment as director of the Weimar theatre Goethe found himself in real life plunged into the thick of battles such as he had described in his novel, where the idealistic Wilhelm Meister struggles to maintain artistic standards against the various forces which threaten them – commercial pressures, the demands of patrons, and various forms of personal and professional jealousy. Money was the first problem. Theatre tickets were no longer to be free, as in Anna Amalia's early days as Duchess, and so concessions to public taste had to be made to ensure some degree of commercial viability. There was, of course, a subsidy from ducal revenues, but this was not large; Kirms exercised strict financial control, and indeed Goethe himself took some pride in keeping his requests for subsidies as low as possible. But Weimar was such a small place that even at the best of times no very large audiences could be expected nor many repeat performances given. Audiences and receipts were usefully supplemented by students from the University of Jena, about twelve miles from Weimar, and by the visitors who came to take the waters at Bad Lauchstädt, a spa near Halle, some forty miles north-east of Weimar, where the company regularly played a summer season. But what the general public undoubtedly liked best was sentimental domestic drama such as that of Iffland and Kotzebue. During Goethe's directorship over a hundred performances were given of plays by these two writers, far more than any other dramatist could match. However, there were of course also plays by Lessing, by Goethe himself and subsequently by Schiller, and by other German writers. Gradually the repertory was extended to include works representative of all the major European dramatic literatures: plays by Shakespeare and Racine, by Gozzi and by Calderón. (From this time on, Calderón has probably been more popular in Germany than in his native Spain.)[5] Opera was performed too – many of the leading actors were also singers – and Mozart's operas in particular enjoyed great success. *The Magic Flute* was performed in January 1794 and soon became one of the most popular works in the repertory; for many years Goethe toyed with the project of writing a libretto for a sequel to it. A representative cross-section of the Weimar repertory is presented in the 'prelude'

*Was wir bringen* (*What We Offer*), which Goethe wrote for the reopening of the theatre in Lauchstädt after its rebuilding in 1802. Allegorical figures represent Nature and Art, Comedy, Tragedy and Opera; Mercury fulfils the office of master of ceremonies. Actors and actresses are given the opportunity to interpolate excerpts from their favourite roles. On the occasion for which it was written the 'prelude' was followed by a performance of Mozart's *La clemenza di Tito*, making a lengthy and weighty evening's entertainment, before a packed house of 672 spectators.

It was only very gradually and little by little that Goethe could introduce into the repertory works designed to educate public taste in the direction of a classical form of drama. Indeed, it is by no means clear that he had at the outset any such intention. Some indication of his attitude to the theatre in the early 1790s can be inferred from the new direction which he gave to his novel *Wilhelm Meister* when he resumed work on it at this period. The published version which appeared in 1796, *Wilhelm Meisters Lehrjahre* (*Wilhelm Meister's Apprenticeship*), was naturally based to a considerable extent on the *Theatralische Sendung*, but the earlier version had of course never been published, and indeed a copy of the manuscript survived only by accident, to be discovered in 1910. The *Lehrjahre* is no longer a novel about the ideal of a National Theatre. It is the story of a young man's growth to self-cultivation and to the emancipation of his personality, in which the theatre appears not so much as the repository of the hero's and the author's highest ideals, but rather as an aberration, even if a necessary and in some ways fruitful one, which the hero must suffer on his way to his eventual and now very different goal. Much of the original description and discussion of theatrical matters is excised. In one respect the novel does carry through what can be presumed to have been its original intention: Wilhelm's performance of *Hamlet*, only anticipated in the final completed chapter of the *Theatralische Sendung*, forms a new climax in Book v of the *Lehrjahre*. But instead of going on from triumph to triumph in the theatre – from Shakespeare, perhaps, to a new form of classical drama? – Wilhelm is now abruptly advised to give up his theatrical career, for which, as he and we are rather surprisingly told by his new mentor Jarno, he has no real talent anyway.

But even if Goethe did hope from the beginning to use the

Weimar court theatre as a base on which to build a living classical drama, the taste of the theatre-going public was a formidable obstacle in his way. So too was the generally established realistic or, as Goethe called it, naturalistic style of acting which had developed in accordance with it, even if the work of an actor such as Iffland raised that style to its highest potential. There were also, though chiefly in later years, intrigues against Goethe, instigated from various quarters, notably by Kotzebue (not satisfied, apparently, with the very considerable success his own plays were enjoying) and by the actress Karoline Jagemann. Jagemann was an actress and singer of some distinction; she was also the Duke's mistress, and in this capacity made a good deal of trouble for Goethe over the years. It was probably Jagemann who was chiefly responsible for his eventual resignation from the directorship in 1817.

Goethe's commitment to the theatre in the early 1790s was thus by no means whole-hearted, and for long periods he took little interest in its day-to-day running. Various causes may have contributed to his increasing interest in it towards the end of the decade, and to the reawakening of some at least of the idealistic aspirations which had been expressed in the *Theatralische Sendung*. The decisive one was undoubtedly his friendship with Schiller.

Schiller too had undergone a period of profound self-appraisal after the final, protracted and painful completion of *Don Carlos*. The flood of spontaneous creativity which had engendered the three prose plays had apparently ebbed; and it was evident, or so it seemed to Schiller himself, that the inspirational method of writing which had produced his earlier work – essentially, of starting at the beginning and continuing by improvisation, which in the case of *Don Carlos* had resulted in awkward changes of direction – would no longer do. After 1786 – at the same time as Goethe was undergoing his 'rebirth' in Italy – Schiller accordingly embarked upon a period of intense reflection upon the nature, the subject-matter and the intended effect of his particular chosen art-form, tragedy. To set this reflection in a wider intellectual context, he flung himself enthusiastically into the study of history and philosophy, of ethics and aesthetics, of the history of poetry and of the evolution of human society towards its presumed eventual goal. Though in *Über naive und sentimentalische Dichtung* he offers a profound analysis of different types of creative personality (very much with Goethe's and his own in mind), Schiller was not so much concerned with the character of the artist or with his relation to society in the sense in which these problems find expression in *Torquato Tasso*. And with regard to the drama, he was no longer occupied, if he ever had been, with the notion of art as essentially serving the expression of the artist's own creative personality. Like Lessing, or indeed Aristotle, he had always been interested in the effect of tragedy on its audience and in its consequent potential as an instrument of moral education: even during his own 'Sturm und Drang' phase he had expressed himself enthusiastically on this subject in his essay *Die Schaubühne als eine moralische Anstalt betrachtet (The Stage considered as a Moral Institution*, 1784). He was also fascinated by another familiar concern of eighteenth-century aesthetics, but one upon which Lessing, with his strong preference for domestic subjects, had largely turned his back: the problem of the beautiful and the sublime, the distinction between those experiences which give us sensuous or aesthetic pleasure and those which through the invocation of grandeur or terror give us also (or so we like to think) a sense of moral elevation. These phenomena, particularly as they are portrayed in tragic art, are the subject of a number of his essays of the 1790s. In his discussion of these matters Schiller was much influenced by the philosophy of Kant, whose three *Critiques* appeared in 1781, 1783 and 1790. Kant's views on ethical and aesthetic questions were particularly important for Schiller, although he adopts on many issues a standpoint significantly different from Kant's.[6]

He was also, as was Goethe, profoundly affected by the outbreak of the French Revolution, and in particular by the turn taken by events in 1791–3, with the execution of Louis XVI and the establishment of the Jacobin Terror. The events of 1789 had seemed to many intellectuals of the day to promise the immediate realisation of their ideals, the fulfilment of that grand design of history which Kant had intimated in his essay *Idee zu einer allgemeinen Geschichte in weltbürgerlicher Absicht (Idea for a General History in Cosmopolitan Intent)* and which Schiller had developed in his own lecture on Universal History. His early plays had voiced many of the same hopes and ideals; the revolutionary spirit of *Die Räuber* was recognised by the French themselves, who on the strength of that work proclaimed Schiller, on 26 August 1792, an honorary citizen of the French republic. But by this time Schiller, like so many others, had been disillusioned and disgusted by the chaos and bloodshed which the intervening years had brought. What had seemed in 1789 to presage the veritable triumph of humanity – the dawn in which, as Wordsworth put it, it was bliss to be alive – now looked more like a reversion to barbarism. In such times as these, was not art perhaps an unnecessary or unjustifiable luxury? Goethe was from the beginning an enemy of the Revolution, which he saw as an aberration from those universal laws of harmonious evolution – physical, biological, social – of whose timeless validity his Italian experience had convinced him; the Revolution made powerful demands upon his art, but it did not lead him to question further the legitimacy of the artist's calling as such. Schiller's more rigorous moral conscience would not allow him to evade the question. He faces squarely up to it in the opening paragraphs of his *Briefe über die ästhetische Erziehung des Menschen* (*Letters on the Aesthetic Education of Man*, 1795) – and answers that in times of social and political upheaval, art is more of a necessity than ever. The reason why the promise of the early days of the revolution was not fulfilled was, Schiller argues, that man was still, essentially, a savage: the process of civilisation was not far enough advanced for him to be able to rise adequately to the challenge of the historical occasion. The process must be resumed where it had been interrupted; and it was art, above all, which was to carry out the task of civilisation. The mission of 'aesthetic education' was the most important of all; the vocation of the artist – in particular, as we are no doubt to understand, the vocation of the tragic dramatist, such as Schiller himself – was triumphantly vindicated.

Having thus undergone and resolved his own artistic crisis, Schiller was ready to return to playwriting. Since Goethe had returned from Italy to find Schiller established in Jena as his near neighbour, the two men had regarded each other with a certain mutual suspicion or even hostility, rather like Tasso and Antonio. Goethe saw in Schiller, *Don Carlos* notwithstanding, the embodiment of the 'Sturm und Drang' which he had now so determinedly put behind him; Schiller saw Goethe as barring his way to the summit of artistic success. But in 1794 the ice was broken, and a

decade of friendship and collaboration began. Schiller very soon put
the relationship to a severe test with his adaptation of *Egmont* for the
Weimar stage in 1796, his first work for the theatre since *Don Carlos*.
Many years later, in the course of his conversations with Eckermann, Goethe observed that the adaptation revealed a streak of
cruelty or violence in Schiller's nature. It certainly does violence to
Goethe's play, sacrificing its characteristic, if elusive poetic and
thematic unity in favour of a more obvious, indeed sometimes
melodramatic theatricality. Schiller had described Goethe's ending
as a '*salto mortale* into the world of opera', but some of his changes
have themselves a distinctly operatic character: thus Alba, who in
Goethe's original, it will be remembered, encounters the hero on
stage only once, in Schiller's version reappears in disguise in
Egmont's prison to hear the death-sentence read out and to enjoy his
moment of triumph, like Pizarro in Beethoven's *Fidelio*. The
adaptation is interesting as an illustration of the radical difference of
Schiller's dramatic mentality from Goethe's. But their friendship
withstood the test, and until Schiller's death in 1805 they worked in
partnership to try to make the Weimar court theatre into the
instrument of that 'aesthetic education' which Schiller had so passionately advocated. Goethe himself wrote few new dramatic
works, and none of them (with the possible exception of *Die
natürliche Tochter*) is of major artistic importance. His work was in
the theatre itself, directing, training the actors, and developing a
suitably elevated, classical style of performance. In all this Schiller
assisted him. Schiller was also responsible for translating Racine's
*Phèdre*, Shakespeare's *Macbeth* and Gozzi's *Turandot*. (*Macbeth* was
subjected to a good deal of classicising bowdlerisation, and in
*Turandot* the more extravagant elements of the *commedia dell'arte*
style were similarly toned down.) But Schiller's principal contribution was the writing of new plays of his own, one a year until he
died. The series of plays and the theatrical style go hand in hand, for
each was conceived with the other in mind. The series begins with
the *Wallenstein* trilogy, the first part of which, *Wallensteins Lager*
(*Wallenstein's Camp*) received its first performance on 17 October
1798. It was a momentous occasion in the history of the German
drama: the date on which Weimar classicism came of age. It was also
an occasion in the history of the Weimar theatre in a more literal

sense, for it marked the reopening of the building after a fairly extensive reconstruction.

The theatre built in 1790 had been of course a great improvement on the previous temporary one as far as stage facilities were concerned, but its auditorium was of an awkward shape, and it was this which was principally affected by the rebuilding of 1798. The new theatre was designed to accommodate about 500 people, with rows of benches on the ground floor and a horseshoe-shaped balcony, divided into boxes, with a gallery above. Seats in the balcony cost twelve groschen (about one-and-sixpence in contemporary English money, or 7½p in its modern equivalent; Goethe's annual salary was about £200). In the pit they cost eight groschen and in the gallery four. The stage was slightly reduced in size by the alterations, but remained basically unchanged in its arrangements. These can still be seen, somewhat restored, at the theatre in Lauchstädt, where the stage, for obvious reasons, was constructed to the same dimensions as in the parent theatre in Weimar. The proscenium opening was about seven metres wide and the stage area behind it about nine metres deep. There were five sets of tracks with chariots and pulleys for movable wings, which would all be changed simultaneously; and at the back of the stage there would always be a painted curtain or backdrop. The stage floor sloped upwards, increasing the illusion of perspective depth, and had in it no less then seven mechanically operated trapdoors. Stage lighting was by oil-lamps, of the newly invented Argand model (allegedly smokeless), replacing the earlier candles. The footlights could be retracted into the floor, and the upstage lighting was mounted in revolving pillars between the wings, so that it could be 'dimmed' if these pillars were turned away from the stage area. The theatre was thus equipped – unlike either Shakespeare's or Racine's – to provide a high degree of spectacle and, by the standards of those pre-cinematic days, of illusion. That favourite of the repertory, Mozart's *Magic Flute*, demands a number of spectacular effects, such as the sudden appearances and disappearances of the Queen of the Night, or Tamino and Pamina's ordeals by fire and water (the latter were a particular favourite with audiences of the time, and are repeated in Goethe's projected continuation), and several transformation scenes. Schiller's later plays also make full use of these

7   Goethe's theatre at Bad Lauchstädt, as it still appears today. The stage is
set with three sets of wings and a perspectively painted middle drop: the
scene is an Egyptian temple, for Mozart's *Zauberflöte*, a favourite of the
repertory. Each of the footlights consists of a pair of Argand oil-lamps with
a circular metal reflector. The ceiling of the auditorium is of stretched
canvas, but the curvature of the panels is painted in a *trompe-l'œil* effect.

visual resources. Indeed, some of the more spectacular scenes in
*Wilhelm Tell* make demands which the Weimar stage had difficulty
in fulfilling, but which could easily be met by a more technically
sophisticated theatre such as Iffland's in Berlin: a lake with rocking
waves for a storm, a moon with a halo and an Alpine sunrise calling
for transparent scenery with back lighting. The scenic descriptions
in these plays are thus to be taken quite seriously as stage directions,
not merely as 'epic' interpolations intended only for the reader.

In addition to the flat wings and backdrop, there was a middle
drop or curtain, which would also be painted with an appropriate
scene, and which was lowered behind the second or third set of
wings to create a smaller stage area. This was known as a short stage
('kurze Bühne' or 'kurzes Theater') as opposed to the long or deep
stage ('tiefes Theater') extending all the way to the backdrop. This
device was used for scenic variation rather than actually to increase

or decrease the acting area, for the actors were in any case not encouraged to move too far upstage, where they began to look out of proportion with the perspective scenery. (For the Zwing-Uri scene in *Wilhelm Tell*, Schiller recommended that the workmen on the castle in the background should be played by children.) The raising or lowering of the middle drop would of course effect a change of scene: this was a well-established practice in the German theatre, against which Gottsched's pedantic insistence on the unity of place had made little headway. The directions 'kurzes Theater' and 'tiefes Theater' are often found in plays of the period, and dramatists will generally be found to alternate short and deep settings – a characteristic, if nowadays little appreciated, feature of the scenic rhythm of their plays.

Most of the scenery was painted on the wings and drops, and not many movable properties were used: for the banquet scene in Schiller's *Piccolomini*, for example, the production notes specify sideboards painted on the wings, rather than real or 'practicable' ones. Stage settings could therefore be changed quickly, without breaking the flow of dramatic action: scene-changes within the course of an act were carried out on the open stage, without lowering the curtain. The curtain was raised at the beginning of an act (hence the usual German term for act, 'Aufzug') and lowered at the end. Thus the curtain was used not simply to facilitate scene-changes but also to articulate the dramatic structure of the play – a classical feature which modern stage practice has largely abandoned, so that it is nowadays more readily appreciated by readers than by theatre audiences. The division of a play into a set number of acts, usually five, may of course be regarded as essentially a literary rather than a theatrical convention; it dates effectively from Horace's *Art of Poetry*, Greek drama having no act divisions. It was in any case not pedantically insisted upon in the eighteenth-century German theatre. If the necessary scene-changes were not practicable within the limits of this convention, then the curtain had to be lowered and the scenery changed behind it, even if this technically meant creating another 'act'. The Mannheim prompt-copy of *Die Räuber* divides the text into seven acts rather than five; Goethe's satirical drama *Der Triumph der Empfindsamkeit* (*The Triumph of Sensibility*) of 1777 has six, because, as one of the characters observes at the end of Act v, when it becomes clear that more time will be needed to unravel the complications of the plot, 'in the German theatre anything goes'. On the classical Weimar stage such irregularities were generally avoided. When, however, the First Part of Goethe's *Faust*, which in the printed text has no act divisions, finally reached the stage in 1829, in a number of productions designed to celebrate the poet's eightieth birthday, it was variously divided into five, six and at Weimar itself into eight acts.

Scenery was sometimes specially painted for a new production, but a good many standard settings were kept in stock and used whenever appropriate: rooms painted in different colours, a street, a wood. This was also standard practice. Thus, as we have mentioned, *Die Räuber* was backdated from the eighteenth to the sixteenth century for the first production, but the famous picture-gallery set, allegedly used for that first production, which was preserved at Mannheim until it was destroyed in the bombing raids of the Second World War, was, as surviving photographs show, unmistakably eighteenth-century in style – no doubt a set that was already in stock. It was in any case only during the late 1770s and 1780s, largely because of the vogue for historical drama created by *Götz von Berlichingen*, that theatres were beginning to pay serious attention to period authenticity in costume and setting. (Wilhelm Meister as Hamlet wears a 'schöner Federbusch', presumably the traditional feathered turban of the hero of the 'Haupt- und Staatsaktion'. But the Hamlets of Shakespeare's day would of course have worn the costume of their own time.) Costumes were generally the responsibility of the actors and actresses themselves, though at Weimar they received a modest allowance for this. In general the budget for scenery and costumes was tight, but with ingenuity and improvisation a little was made to go a long way, and Goethe took care to avoid gross inconsistency, inappropriateness or anachronism.

Most of these features were fairly typical of the late-eighteenth-century German stage. But the distinctive style of acting which was developed in Weimar between the first performance of *Wallensteins Lager* in 1798 and the death of Schiller six years later was a different matter. The scenic resources of the theatre pointed in the directions of illusion – that is, of realism – and spectacle. Most actors of the day

8 'Sturm und Drang' classicised. *Die Räuber* in Goethe's statuesquely stylised production at Weimar in 1812: Karl Moor discovers his father imprisoned in the tower in Act IV. Aquatint by J. C. E. Müller.

cultivated the former, using a natural, even prosaic delivery, treating the auditorium as a 'fourth wall' of the stage and playing, as Diderot and others in the 1750s and 1760s had advocated, to each other rather than to the audience. The reaction against the alexandrine had gone so far that by now any kind of competent verse speaking was almost unknown. Some actors and actresses suffered from such 'rhythmophobia', as Goethe called it, that they claimed to be unable to learn verse parts and had to have them copied out as prose, while some, including Iffland himself, would deliberately repeat words or insert interjections to break the rhythm of the verse – practices revived by anti-classical schools of acting in our own day. Goethe and Schiller would have none of this. Despite the fair degree of illusion which their stage was capable of creating, in the Weimar acting style they sought not so much an illusion of reality as a picturesque stylisation of it. The players were encouraged to address the audience, to deliver their lines downstage rather than to each other. Gestures were carefully studied, indeed prescribed with a degree of choreographic precision which seems at times absurd –

as do the exaggeratedly statuesque poses which are depicted in contemporary illustrations. Sometimes, even allowing for obvious artistic licence, one finds oneself wondering how the actors ever got into these strange attitudes, or out of them again. Goethe himself seems to have realised the difficulty, for in 1800 we find him advising one of his actors to pay particular attention to the transitions between different poses and gestures, to prepare them carefully and to execute them slowly, preferably not in mid-speech. He encouraged the players to study the poses of Greek statues and to seek to emulate their 'unaffected grace in sitting, standing and moving'; indeed, the characteristic gestures and attitudes of the Weimar style seem to owe a great deal to the essentially static ideal of physical beauty which Goethe had derived from his study of antique art, chiefly during his years in Italy. And despite his insistence that gesture and attitude should be meaningful and expressive rather than just gratuitously beautiful, affectation and self-conscious statuesqueness were the impressions the style made on many contemporary observers, both outside and inside Weimar. Left to himself, Schiller (like Partridge in *Tom Jones*) would probably have preferred something more like the old baroque bravura. Thus when Friederike Unzelmann played Maria Stuart in 1801, while others praised her dignity and restraint, Schiller found her too 'natural' and lacking in 'Schwung' or panache. The Weimar style as it manifested itself in the presentation of Schiller's later plays was probably something of a compromise between this Schillerian panache and Goethean ideas of statuesque classical beauty. But both men were agreed that they did not want humdrum, everyday realism. Their art had to be seen to be art, not a pretence of nature.

It had likewise to be heard to be art – verse delivered as verse, not like Lessing's verse in *Nathan der Weise*, already turned halfway back into prose. Blank-verse delivery was carefully taught, and here again unfriendly observers were apt to criticise the 'sawmill' style of declamation practised in Weimar. Goethe took great pains to eradicate provincialisms and to make all his actors and actresses speak a pure, dialect-free German – an artificial language spoken then, as now, by relatively few people, not consistently even by Goethe himself and certainly not by Schiller, who retained his Swabian accent to the end of his days (he would have called Faust

'Fowsht'). But the National Theatre – and that, if not in name, was what was being created here – had of course to stand above regional differences. There were other reforms too. Goethe aimed to break the typecasting system, which was the mainstay of the older troupes (the *Theatralische Sendung* gives a vivid impression), and to create a team of actors any of whom had in principle to be willing and able to take any part, large or small; this met with considerable opposition, notably from Jagemann. Goethe was trying to create an ensemble, in which no individual performer would be allowed excessive prominence, but all would be subordinated to the service of the dramatist and his work. He was of course not an actor himself, though there are anecdotes of impressive performances by him at rehearsals, when he would demonstrate to the actors how he wished their roles to be played. Indeed, one of the most significant features of Weimar in theatrical history is that it is one of the first major examples of a 'director's theatre': most directors had hitherto been actor-managers, leading their companies from within rather than with the detached, over-all view of a director sitting in the audi-torium.

All this was necessary if the Weimar court theatre was to carry out its civilising mission, its work of 'aesthetic education'. And if the actors and actresses were to be worthy of their roles as public educators, then their private lives and conduct should also be, as far as possible, beyond reproach. Earlier in the century the social standing of the acting profession had been very low. When young men and women of breeding and education left home to go on the stage, it was often because of debt or family scandal. Actors and actresses were refused communion or even burial in consecrated ground: even the great Frau Neuber died in poverty, neglect and misery. Again the *Theatralische Sendung* gives a good idea of this state of affairs. Ekhof in Schwerin, Dalberg in Mannheim and the Emperor Joseph II and his Burgtheater committee in Vienna had all sought to regulate the private lives of their actors and actresses in order to enhance the social respectability of the theatre in general. Similarly Goethe in Weimar, to the best of his ability, and with the full weight of his authority as a Privy Councillor, attempted to impose discipline on his often unruly charges. They were governed by a special set of regulations, with a graduated scale of penal sanctions running from fines to actual imprisonment. Of one recalcitrant, Goethe commented in 1809: 'Something must be done with this fellow, who will go on acting the strolling player ('der noch immer den Komödianten fortspielt') and will not understand what it is to be an actor by appointment to the court of Weimar.'

The essence of Goethe's views on speech and delivery, on gesture and movement, on the conduct of the actor in general, is enshrined in the *Regeln für Schauspieler* (*Rules for Actors*) which he dictated in 1803, in the first instance for the use of his favourite young protégé of the time, Pius Alexander Wolff.[7] They contain much which seems excessively prescriptive or pedantic, naively idealistic or even suspiciously authoritarian. But Goethe and Schiller were making a supreme effort, which at that crucial period of European history they conceived to be supremely necessary, to raise the German theatre once and for all out of the rut of popular entertainment and everyday realism. Schiller expressed their programme in the Prologue which he wrote to precede *Wallensteins Lager* on that first night in October 1798:

> The fresh, new dawn Thalia's art begins
> Upon this stage today has also made
> The poet bold to leave well-trodden paths,
> And carry you beyond the confines of
> Domestic life, on to a wider stage,
> That will not be unworthy of the high,
> Momentous times in which we live and strive.
> Only an object of sublimity
> Can stir the deepest depths within man's soul;
> In narrow confines men grow narrow too,
> But greater when their goals are higher set.

Few others were to rise to the challenge. But in the series of his great historical plays, from *Wallenstein* to the unfinished *Demetrius*, Schiller, exploiting the possibilities of the Weimar style to its limits, created a drama which was indeed not unworthy of those 'high, momentous times'.

# CHAPTER VII

## The high tide of Weimar classicism: Schiller and Goethe, 1798–1805

For the Hamburg National Theatre in 1767, Lessing had been able to write a play on a subject embodying the theme of national reconciliation, of peace and harmony between the peoples of the various German states. For Weimar in 1798 Schiller produced something of more ominous import: a drama illustrating the fragility and the dubious unity of the Holy Roman Empire of the German Nation. *Wallenstein* is the only one of Schiller's plays to be written, like Shakespeare's histories, on a truly 'national' subject; the later ones turn to England, France, Sicily, Switzerland and Russia. In general Schiller disclaimed and even disapproved of patriotic or similar 'material interest', as he called it. He was aiming at the wider, more 'philosophical' significance which according to Aristotle distinguishes the poet from the mere historical chronicler. Though Karl Moor had wished 'that the spirit of Hermann still glowed in the ashes', one can hardly imagine Schiller himself following in the footsteps of Klopstock and Schlegel with a Hermann drama. But the subject of *Wallenstein* was not only a national one: it was one of particular relevance to the times in which it was written.

Schiller points out the contemporary relevance of his subject in the Prologue:

> Crumbling before us in these days we see
> The old, assured, familiar form, that once
> A welcome peace, one hundred and fifty years
> Ago, gave Europe's kingdoms, precious fruit
> Of thirty years of war and suffering.

General Bonaparte's redrawing of the political map of Europe under the Treaty of Campo Formio in 1797 effectively brought to an end the dispositions of the Peace of Westphalia which had concluded the Thirty Years' War in 1648. It also heralded the final dissolution of the Holy Roman Empire, which was formally abolished in 1806. For all its many and obvious imperfections, the Empire had represented a principle of order and stability, a foundation upon which, given unceasing human effort, an edifice of civilisation could gradually rise. Schiller in 1789 had viewed the course of history as one of slow but inevitable progress; now, nine or ten years later, Europe seemed to be reverting to chaos and barbarism. More specifically, the social and political order was being torn apart, very much as it had been in the seventeenth century, by a conflict in which ideological slogans – then Reformation and counter-Reformation, now revolution and counter-revolution – served often merely as the mask for personal, dynastic and territorial ambition. As Brecht's Mother Courage observes of the official causes of the Thirty Years' War: 'When you hear the big nobs talk, they say they're making war out of the fear of God and for everything what's good and beautiful, but when you look closer, they're not really so stupid, they're making war for profit.' For all Brecht's scorn for Schiller and his 'idealism', *Mother Courage and her Children* owes a good deal to *Wallenstein*, and Schiller too does much to expose the ideological rhetoric with which the various parties disguise their true motives – to a large extent even from themselves. This is true of the Catholic and Imperial party; it is true of the Swedes, ostensible champions of the Protestant faith; and not least it is true of Schiller's tragic protagonist, Wallenstein himself. He, the Imperial and Catholic generalissimo who is conducting secret negotiations with the Swedes, dreams of a new order of peace and religious toleration in Europe; but it is one with himself as King of Bohemia, firmly established at Europe's strategic centre. Wallenstein too had his equivalents in Schiller's own day. Goethe noted a resemblance to the turncoat French general Dumouriez, who had gone over to the Austrian side in the anti-revolutionary campaign of 1793; but even more suggestive is the parallel with Napoleon himself, the charismatic war-lord, whose star was rising rapidly at the time Schiller was writing, and whom some of Schiller's contemporaries, such as

Hölderlin in his poem 'Buonaparte' of 1798, were already beginning to hail as the potential saviour of a Europe torn by a decade of revolutionary strife. But it does not really matter whether Schiller intended any such particular parallel. As history repeated itself, it added new layers of meaning to his historical play; similarly, the riots against the Emperor Joseph II in Brussels in 1787 had, as Goethe noted, added a new layer of meaning to *Egmont*, which he was working on at the time but had of course conceived many years before, and so too the dropping of the atomic bomb in 1945 was to add a new layer of meaning to Brecht's dramatic portrait of Galileo.[1] Like Napoleon, Wallenstein is a 'man of destiny', a man elevated by the fortunes of war and the collapse of old systems of power and authority and thus given the power to change the course of history. Ever since Wallenstein's death, into Schiller's time and even down into our own, historians have debated whether, if he had had the courage and resolution to seize his opportunity, he could indeed have brought the disastrous war to an end and ushered in a new age.[2] All that is certain is that he failed. In 1634 his enemies at the Imperial court themselves seized the opportunity that his hesitation offered them and had him outlawed and assassinated; and the war dragged on for another fourteen years, just as the wars resulting from the French Revolution were to drag on for another sixteen years after Schiller's *Wallenstein* was completed.

Despite Schiller's determination to exercise strict formal control over the work and not to let it grow in its own unpredictable way as *Don Carlos* had done, it did in fact come to assume quite unforeseen proportions: a trilogy (the whole work bears again the designation 'a dramatic poem') consisting, after the Prologue, of a dramatic prelude, *Wallensteins Lager* (*Wallenstein's Camp*), and two full-length five-act plays, *Die Piccolomini* (*The Piccolomini*) and *Wallensteins Tod* (*Wallenstein's Death*). Schiller aimed to show in analytic or, as he called it, 'Euripidean' fashion the connection between Wallenstein's treason against the Emperor and his downfall and death. This was a closer and more complex connection than that of simple cause and effect, for, as Schiller the historian had written in his own account of the Thirty Years' War, 'Thus Wallenstein fell, not because he was a rebel, but he rebelled because he fell.' To show this demanded an extensive examination of Wallenstein's complex motives. These include his political visions and his personal ambition, his desire for revenge on the Emperor for his earlier dismissal from his command at the Diet of Regensburg in 1630, and above all the desire of the 'man of destiny' ('der Mann des Schicksals', *Tod* III, xv) for absolute freedom, for the assurance (powerfully symbolised in his addiction to astrology) that while all other men are subject to necessity, caught up inextricably in the mechanisms of cause and effect, he and he alone stands free above those forces, sharing the counsels of fate, able to know the consequences of all possible courses of action and therefore able to choose correctly between them. This in turn led Schiller to consider in general the processes of human decision-making, and to illustrate further the complexity of his central character by flanking him with two contrasting, simpler figures who exemplify more straightforward patterns of decision and action. From history Schiller took the figure of Octavio Piccolomini, Wallenstein's chief adversary and rival, and made him the embodiment of what he called 'realism', the cast of mind which refers all decisions to practical necessity and expediency; and, contrary to the historical record, he gave him a son, Max Piccolomini, who is made the complementary embodiment of 'idealism', which refers all decisions to fundamental moral principles. (In their fierce debates we hear many an echo, sharpened by anger, of the arguments of Goethe's Pylades and Iphigenie.) Schiller's philosophical and psychological analysis is thus given the dramatic shape of a conflict between father and son – a familiar Schillerian motif – which is expanded to provide the major subplot of the work. It is indeed this subplot which furnishes most of the actual dramatic movement in what would otherwise be a rather static play, characterised by expectancy and hesitation, both in Wallenstein himself and in the allies and enemies who are all waiting upon his decision. The naive young idealist Max hero-worships Wallenstein and will believe no ill of him. When his father Octavio tells him that his idol is plotting treason, he is at first utterly incredulous: 'Your judgement may speak false, but not my heart' (*Picc.* v, i). Then, when he hears the truth from Wallenstein's own lips, he is plunged into a crisis of despair from which there is no escape but death. Octavio, the politician, who despite his constant appeals to duty (a word of solemn weight in Kantian and Schillerian moral philosophy) seems rather the all too willing, unquestioning executant of his superiors' orders – 'I split no hairs, I only do my duty, / I carry out my Emperor's commands' (*Picc.* v, i) – is shattered by the loss of his son. So too is Wallenstein, for Max was perhaps the one human being for whom he had felt a genuine affection and regard, as if he had been his own son. The tensions and conflicts between the three male protagonists – Wallenstein, Octavio and Max – are echoed and varied by a similar if more muted contrast between the play's three principal female characters – Wallenstein's wife, the Duchess of Friedland, a hesitant creature, with all her husband's weakness and none of his compensating strength; her sister, Countess Terzky, a Lady-Macbeth-like figure, bloody, bold and resolute in her political ambition; and Thekla, Wallenstein's daughter, a figure of selfless, noble purity in whom Max finds a worthy ally. This complex action is further played out against a background which brings to life the historical and political context of the Thirty Years' War. Ranged against Octavio, at first almost alone in his defence of the Imperial cause, is the group of high-ranking officers surrounding Wallenstein. Illo and Terzky are brutal political realists who yet remain loyal, in their fashion, to their master Wallenstein when all the rest have gone. Isolani, the fickle gambler, soldier of fortune in every sense of the word, is the first to desert him. Buttler, the rough Irish mercenary who has worked his way up from the ranks, remains fiercely loyal until he learns that Wallenstein has repaid his loyalty with double-dealing, when he in turn vows and exacts revenge. Nor do we meet only the generals, the 'big nobs' in Mother Courage's phrase. In the *Lager* Schiller paints a lively picture of the common soldiery, the base upon which Wallenstein's power rests, which offers noisy vocal support in times of success, but melts away in adversity; he even offers us a glimpse of the common people over whose fields and homes and bodies the war was raging.

The work thus grew, as it were, backwards and outwards in Schiller's hands from the final catastrophe – Wallenstein's downfall and death; and what had been originally intended as a single play turned into a complex and spacious piece of dramatic architecture. It is not simply a long play in which a lot of incidents and complications succeed one another, as might with some degree of justice be maintained of *Don Carlos*. Nor is the relation of the three parts of the trilogy merely sequential, as in Aeschylus' *Oresteia* (which provided Schiller with a reassuring classical precedent when the scale of his work was causing him concern) or in later German examples of the form such as Grillparzer's *Golden Fleece* trilogy or Hebbel's *Nibelungen* (or Wagner's *Ring* tetralogy). The whole is more like a pyramid on whose steps we gradually mount to the summit: from the common soldiery in the *Lager*, through the officers and the world of power politics in *Die Piccolomini*, to the hero himself, his fatal decision and its nemesis in *Wallensteins Tod*. It is like a portrait in an elaborate compound frame; or a dramatic tableau enacted on a perspective stage, which becomes deeper and deeper as successive curtains are raised. Rather as in *Egmont* – perhaps Schiller had after all imbibed something of the poetic spirit of Goethe's play – we are introduced to the hero only gradually, and at first indirectly. We do not meet him at all in the *Lager*, though we hear a great deal about him, and he appears only in one act, the second, of *Die Piccolomini*. Only in *Wallensteins Tod* do we begin to know his complex character at first hand and to understand the springs of his actions. And at the end Wallenstein withdraws again from our sight, disappearing into the inner recesses of the stage – for this scene, Schiller prescribes 'a hall opening on to a gallery which recedes far into the distance' – to meet his murderers, lurking behind the scene like Agamemnon's in the *Oresteia*.

*Wallenstein* has many features which can be called 'Shakespearian': its large cast, its almost epic breadth, and its striking crowd scenes – the *Lager*, the council and banquet scenes in *Die Piccolomini*, in which all the generals are assembled, and the climax of the whole trilogy, the scene in the town hall of Pilsen in Act III of *Wallensteins Tod*, where on a stage filled with armed men, to the accompaniment of offstage cannon and martial music, Wallenstein and Max are both forced to declare themselves publicly for one side or the other, for or against the Emperor. Variety is furnished by the idyllic scenes depicting the love of Max and Thekla, a welcome (if to some tastes too 'idealistic') contrast to the harsh world of war and power politics, and by touches of comedy, chiefly in the *Lager*, but also notably in the banquet scene and in Buttler's briefing of the murderers (reminiscent of Shakespeare) in Act V of *Wallensteins Tod*. The language of the play is memorable – again full of quotations –

and of a near-Shakespearian range, encompassing powerful rhetoric, vision and mystery, and the cut and thrust of argument.
Schiller avoids extreme earthiness or vulgarity: even his most brutal
characters at their most brutal moments – Illo, for example, drunk at
the banquet, and again in Act IV of *Wallensteins Tod*, or Buttler and
the murderers – continue to speak blank verse rather than lapsing
into prose. The whole *Lager* is written in rhymed Sachsian 'Knittelvers', as befits its generally lower tone and its character as a piece of
expository genre-painting.[3] But the work also has eminently
classical qualities, which may be summed up in the architectural or
perspectival nature of its dramatic structure. In his letters Schiller
names Shakespeare and Sophocles as his two principal dramatic
models. *Wallenstein* typifies German classical drama at its best: it
combines Shakespearian with Greek or neo-classical formal
features, and it combines realism of content – in its unsparing
analysis of the realities of politics and history, and of the ambiguities
and moral shortcomings of human motivation – with a high degree
of artistic stylisation.

The same qualities are again held in skilful balance in Schiller's
next play, *Maria Stuart*. The subject of the rivalry between Queen
Elizabeth of England and her 'sister' Mary Queen of Scots has much
in common with the favourite 'Sturm und Drang' theme of fraternal
strife, and it had indeed attracted Schiller's attention as early as 1782;
but it was only after the completion of *Wallenstein* in 1799 that he
took it up in earnest, making extensive studies of the historical
source material – including Robertson and Hume in German
translations. Progress was smooth and the play was completed the
following year. It is to some extent a double character study like *Die
Räuber*, just as *Wallenstein* can be seen to resemble *Fiesco* as a study in
ambition and hesitation. But whereas in *Die Räuber* the two protagonists' actions are shown unfolding *from* their contrasting characters, the mature Schiller of *Maria Stuart* is more concerned with his
two characters' contrasting reactions *to* the common situation in
which history has placed them. Like the *Titanic* and the iceberg in
Hardy's poem 'The Convergence of the Twain', they are

> bent
> By paths coincident
> On being anon twin halves of one august event.

They cannot therefore be presented simply as parallel figures like Karl and Franz Moor, but must be brought into actual dramatic confrontation, and Schiller finds it necessary to bring them together on stage, although in historical fact, like the brothers in the original version of *Die Räuber*, they never met face to face.[4] The contrast in their reactions gains in paradoxical intensity from the contrast in their physical and political circumstances. Elizabeth, enjoying freedom and power, is able physically to destroy Mary, but refuses to accept responsibility for the execution, blaming her ministers and in particular the luckless Secretary Davison (as in historical fact); by pleading necessity or even mere accident as the author of the deed, Elizabeth effectively denies her own moral freedom. Mary, on the other hand, physically imprisoned, has no choice (as she discovers after various fruitless attempts at escape or evasion) but to submit to her fate; but by her final acceptance of responsibility for her own life and death she demonstrates her moral autonomy, and makes the execution *her* execution in virtually an active rather than a merely passive sense. As Schiller wrote in his essay *Über das Erhabene (On the Sublime)*, published the year after *Maria Stuart*, 'The man ('Mensch') of moral culture, and he alone, is perfectly free . . . Nothing which happens to him is mere force, for before it touches him, it has become his own action.' Elizabeth is sometimes seen as merely the villain of Schiller's play, but she is rather, like Franz Moor, a tragic or at least near-tragic figure in her own right, of a significance approaching that of the titular heroine. The play is a study in how and how not to rise to the challenge of a historical occasion. Elizabeth fails, though she appears victorious; Mary succeeds, but only at the cost of her own life and the total defeat of her political ambitions.

The clash of the two protagonists also embodies an ideological conflict which, as in *Wallenstein*, has its parallels in Schiller's own day; once again historical developments had given the subject a new topicality. The conflict between the Catholic Mary and the Protestant Elizabeth is also a clash between traditional, 'legitimate' authority, resting ultimately upon the individual will of the ruler, and a new form of social and political order in which these traditional sanctions of authority are no longer acknowledged and the ruler must appeal to the consent of her subjects, to the general good, the 'general will' (as Rousseau had called it) – or, if all else fails, to expediency and superior physical force. Schiller does not take sides in this ideological battle. Though he, born and brought up a Protestant, underlines his emotional and moral sympathy with Mary by lavish use of Catholic symbolism – including the presentation on stage of her confession, absolution and taking of the last sacraments, which gave considerable offence in religious circles – both Catholic and Protestant ideologies are, as in *Wallenstein*, shown as serving at least in part as masks for political or personal ambition. In Act II and again in Act IV, the balanced recapitulation emphasising the point with classical symmetry, we witness scenes of political debate at Elizabeth's court. Burleigh counsels Mary's execution, in the name of England, the Protestant cause and the will of the people ('Obey / The people's voice, it is the voice of God', IV, ix). Leicester in Act II advises mercy, then in Act IV severity, but on both occasions in the name of the royal prerogative; by flattering Elizabeth as an absolute ruler, however, he seeks of course to preserve his own position as her favourite. In between them stands Talbot, Earl of Shrewsbury, in whom we can perhaps most clearly see both Schiller's own viewpoint and the relevance of the historical case to his own times. Against the claims both of the Bourbon absolutism of 'l'État, c'est moi' and of the revolutionary populism of the *volonté générale*, Talbot pleads for a new relationship between the ruler and her people, founded not, like both those other forms of government, upon force and fear, but upon mutual trust, respect and love. And, as the essential foundation of this, he urges that Elizabeth should follow neither her own personal desires nor the alleged dictates of any external necessity, but only the voice of her own moral conscience, leaving the consequences to take care of themselves. It was the course which Kant had prescribed in his moral philosophy – and which Goethe's Iphigenie had followed, to be rewarded not only with moral triumph but also with the granting of her dearest wish: to return to Greece with her brother. But Elizabeth lacks the strength to follow Talbot's advice, and he resigns his office, lamenting his failure to save her 'nobler part' (v, xv). Burleigh is banished as a scapegoat, and Leicester goes into exile, shamed (not unlike Octavio Piccolomini at the end of *Wallenstein*) as he recognises where his policy of selfish expediency has led. Mary has been executed, after her final moment of moral victory; and, as the play ends, Elizabeth is left alone on the throne, to continue as best she may with the task of ruling England, of coping with the chaotic world of history and politics. But there is a faint suggestion that had she followed Talbot's advice, the course of history might have been changed. We are reminded of Schiller's diagnosis of the failure of the Revolution: a great historical opportunity was there for the taking, but human nature was not equal to the challenge.

In *Maria Stuart*, as in *Wallenstein*, Schiller employs an unclassically large cast (eighteen named characters) and is elastic in his treatment of the unities, especially that of place. Once again, as in *Die Räuber*, Schiller divides his play between his two protagonists, each in her own setting: Mary in prison at Fotheringhay, Elizabeth at her court in Westminster. Here, however, there is a much more conscious balance and symmetry in the alternation between the two than in the earlier play, and the central climax, the meeting between the two queens in Act III, takes place in a third, semi-neutral setting, the park at Fotheringhay, where Mary has been granted a moment of limited feedom from her prison. The psychological and dramatic significance of this scene is thus emphasised by its setting, and of course by its visual impact: it is the only scene in the play which takes place out of doors, with open space, trees, and a view into the distance, and Mary responds to this taste of liberty with ecstatic, lyrical joy, the blank verse breaking into rhymed stanzas. (Schiller's German audience would no doubt have been less disturbed than a British one by Mary's claim to be able to see the mountains of Scotland from Northamptonshire.) The unities of time and action are, however, obeyed, as in *Wallenstein*, in spirit if not to the letter, giving the play the essential concentration of the classical form: in his letters Schiller speaks again of the 'Euripidean method' of presenting a dramatic action, and cites the Greek dramatists as his principal formal models. The action of the play begins at the first climactic moment, when Burleigh comes to tell Mary that she has been condemned, and the lengthy and complicated history which has led up to this moment is all skilfully conveyed by recapitulatory narration. Mary's actual death takes place, like Wallenstein's, behind the scenes, though Mortimer, hero of the play's most important subplot and a character recalling Schiller's earlier idealist figures, is allowed to kill himself on stage in defiance of classical propriety. Again as in *Wallenstein*, the blank verse is varied with rhyming passages and lyrical interpolations as well as with more obviously classical forms of ornamentation such as stichomythia; and though the tone is serious throughout, the decorum of the grand style is stretched to allow some passages of remarkable force and directness, culminating in Mary's defiant assertion of her own legitimacy and divine right, which crowns the confrontation scene in Act III:

> A bastard sits on England's throne, and dupes
> This noble race with cunning and deceit.
> If right was might, then you would crawl before
> My feet this moment, for I am your Queen.          (III, iv)

In *Wallenstein* and *Maria Stuart* a combination of realism of content and classical stylisation of form marks the summit of Schiller's dramatic achievement. There are romantic elements in these plays too, indeed George Steiner has described *Maria Stuart* as 'with *Boris Godunov*, the one instance in which romanticism rose fully to the occasion of tragedy'.[5] Schiller was at his best as a dramatist when what was probably a naturally romantic imagination was subjected to the twin disciplines of historical realism in subject-matter and the classicism of form which, as we have seen, was undoubtedly his intention.

In Schiller's next two plays, *Die Jungfrau von Orleans* (*The Maid of Orleans*) of 1801 and *Die Braut von Messina* (*The Bride of Messina*) of 1803, the element of realism is largely discarded in favour of a much more thoroughly stylised and artificial manner. This stylisation appears at first sight to take quite different forms in the two works. *Die Jungfrau von Orleans* is actually subtitled 'a romantic tragedy', and treats the story of Joan of Arc in a free, episodic style, beginning with her visions and ending with her death. It has a large cast and employs thirteen different stage settings, one of them, 'A wild forest with charcoal-burners' huts' (v, i), stongly reminiscent of the gypsy scene in *Götz von Berlichingen*, or of their common ancestor, the heath scene in *King Lear*. It also calls for a number of elaborate and spectacular scenic effects, including thunder and lightning and a trapdoor for the disappearance of the mysterious Black Knight whom Joan encounters on the battlefield in III, ix. The visual climax of the work is the coronation scene at Reims in Act IV, for which Iffland's production in Berlin reportedly employed 200 extras. (The Weimar production was a more modest affair, and it was only with great difficulty that Kirms, the financial director of the Weimar theatre, was persuaded to authorise the purchase of a new coronation robe for the Dauphin: could they not, he asked, make something up out of an old curtain?) In contrast with this, as it might seem, pseudo-Shakespearian, or perhaps proto-Hollywood historical extravaganza, *Die Braut von Messina* appears of all Schiller's plays the one most closely imitative of the Greek manner. Its plot and setting are not Greek, however, but of Schiller's invention – a historical transplantation of classical motifs, in this respect perhaps recalling Lessing's tragedies. Don Manuel and Don Cesar, rival heirs to the throne of Sicily, are in love with the same girl, Beatrice – who turns out to be their long-lost sister, banished by their mother Isabella in the hope of frustrating a prophecy that the birth of a daughter to her would bring ruin and destruction upon their house. Isabella attempts to reunite her children in amity, but Don Cesar kills Manuel in a blaze of jealousy and then commits suicide in atonement for his deed – leaving the spectators wondering:

> I stand appalled, and know not whether I
> Should grieve for him, or should approve his fate.
>
> (IV, final scene)

If the confrontation of hostile brothers again recalls *Die Räuber*, the incest-motif and the oracular prophecy are plainly deliberate echoes of *Oedipus Rex*. The play has only four principal characters – the three siblings and their mother – and alternates regularly, like *Maria Stuart*, between a small number of stage settings. The most important classical feature of all is indicated by the play's subtitle, 'A Tragedy with choruses'. No other modern European dramatist in the classical tradition has imitated this feature of Greek drama so closely, if at all, as does Schiller here. The chorus is an almost constant presence, commenting on the action throughout, and lengthy choric passages, in contrasting metres, alternate with the dialogue of the protagonists. (The play also in its original form dispenses with act-divisions, though Schiller later divided it into

9   The fully-fledged Weimar style. *Die Braut von Messina* in Goethe's Weimar production of 1808–9: Isabella, Don Cesar and Beatrice with the body of the murdered Don Manuel in Act ɪv. Chorus as well as principals all adopt carefully studied poses. Aquatint by J. C. E. Müller after J. F. Matthaei.

four acts.) Sometimes the chorus is divided into rival factions which take sides with the rival brothers, sometimes it speaks with a single voice. In an important prefatory essay, *Über den Gebrauch des Chors in der Tragödie (On the Use of the Chorus in Tragedy)*, Schiller argues for the reintroduction of the chorus into modern drama on two principal grounds. It is to restore the 'public' dimension which modern tragedy, in its concentration upon 'domestic' subjects, has largely foregone; and it is to 'declare open war upon naturalism', justifying and indeed making essential the use of an elevated style, and making clear beyond all doubt the artificial and deliberately *poetic* character which all serious drama must in Schiller's view have.

But though *Die Jungfrau von Orleans* is 'romantic' and *Die Braut von Messina* ostensibly Greek in manner, the difference between the forms of stylisation employed in these two plays is perhaps less important than their common tendency to stylisation in general, and their seeming abandonment of any form of realism. Both plays move away from the solid ground of history which had furnished such convincing tragic subject-matter in *Wallenstein* and *Maria Stuart*, even if in both those works Schiller had naturally exercised the dramatist's traditional privilege of altering the details of the historical record. The subject of *Die Jungfrau* is legend rather than history, and Schiller emphasises this by the spectacular style of his play, by his use of apparently supernatural elements such as the Black Knight, and not least by his rejection of the historical death of Joan of Arc at the stake in favour of a legendary ending of his own invention. Schiller's Johanna, captured and imprisoned by the English, learns of the imminent defeat of the French on the battlefield: by a supreme effort, Samson-like, she breaks her chains and leaps from her prison window to rally the French and lead them to victory, but is fatally wounded and dies transfigured, her banner in her hand, beneath a sky tinged with a rosy glow. History is here, as Shaw put it in the preface to his own *Saint Joan*, 'drowned in a witch's caldron of raging romance'. And the Sicily of *Die Braut von Messina* is not historically authentic, but Schiller's own invention – again a kind of proto-Hollywood version of the Norman-ruled Sicily of the twelfth century. However, the historical setting of these plays is by no means mere escapist romance. It is rather to be understood in a symbolic or even mythical sense. It embodies a vision of history, a transfigured version of the pre-Revolutionary historical optimism which Schiller had derived from Kant and the Enlightenment. This vision is expressed not only in Schiller's own essays on aesthetics and philosophy, notably *Über naive und sentimentalische Dichtung*, but in the works of many other writers and thinkers of this period of crisis and revolution, known in the history of European thought and sensibility in general as the age of Romanticism. Man once lived in a 'state of nature', a Golden Age of 'wholeness' and unconscious, idyllic harmony. He then entered the realm of consciousness and with it the world of history, characterised by division, alienation and strife. But one day – perhaps very soon, as some believed in those apocalyptic days – he would somehow progress, by a revolutionary transformation, beyond this alienated state and achieve a reintegration with himself and with nature, a new Golden Age which would restore the original, paradisal harmony on a higher plane. As Shelley wrote in his ode 'Hellas':

> The world's great age begins anew,
> The golden years return. . .

This Romantic myth of history has been identified as a secularised version of the Christian story of the Fall of man and his eventual redemption;[6] Marx's materialist dialectic of history was to take the process of secularisation one stage further. The world which *Die Jungfrau von Orleans* and *Die Braut von Messina* portray is the world of history as it is characterised in this myth. The protagonists are alienated from themselves, suffering inner conflict and a loss of the sense of their own identity. They are alienated from their families: Johanna is estranged from her sisters and her father, and family strife is of course the very essence of *Die Braut von Messina*. They are alienated from the communities in which they live: Johanna from the French, who first acclaim her as a saviour, but then reject her as a witch, and the protagonists of *Die Braut*, as members of a foreign ruling house, from the native inhabitants of Sicily. Dissension in the human sphere is even reflected by dissonance and tumult within nature – by the storms and lightning of *Die Jungfrau* and by the volcanic menace of Etna in *Die Braut*. But both Johanna and Don Cesar, the younger of the two brothers in *Die Braut*, die exemplary and (more clearly in the case of Johanna) triumphant sacrificial deaths which appear to have some kind of redemptive function, intimating the possibility of a transcendence or transformation of the historical world.

In both plays, however, this symbolic or mythical pattern is combined, not wholly convincingly, with a more realistic psychological conflict. The protagonists labour under a burden of personal guilt which is partly self-incurred, partly laid upon them by some mysterious external agency whose objective reality, however, appears to be in doubt. In Johanna's case, this is constituted by the 'mission' enjoined upon her by her 'voices' and by the concomitant vow of chastity, which she then breaks, in her own eyes, by falling in love with the English captain Lionel; in the case of the Sicilian brothers, it is the 'fate' which makes them ignorant of the identity of the sister with whom they both fall in love. In both plays, sexual guilt appears as the immediate dramatic cause of the alienation and inner struggle which the characters suffer, and which they can only overcome in death. But the real or ultimate nature of this guilt is obscure, so that their inner struggles seem to lack, as T. S. Eliot said of *Hamlet*, a genuine 'objective correlative'.[7] This is particularly true in the case of *Die Jungfrau von Orleans*. Johanna's falling-in-love with Lionel reflects, or results from, a sudden loss of nerve, a loss of her previously instinctive and unquestioning faith in her mission. But Schiller is evidently unwilling to motivate the action purely, if at all, on the level of realistic psychology. He therefore externalises Joan's loss of faith in the form of her encounter with the Black Knight, which has prompted a good deal of unfruitful speculation as to the 'real' identity or significance of the Knight himself. In fact the Knight is best regarded as simply a theatrical device, or indeed an operatic one – another *'salto mortale* into the world of opera' of the kind of which Schiller had been so critical in the case of *Egmont*.[8] In *Die Braut von Messina* it is similarly unclear whether the prophecy that the birth of Beatrice will bring disaster upon Isabella's family is to be regarded as the voice of a genuine objective necessity or fate, as a symbol for the characters' subjection to an inner, psychological compulsion, or as, at worst, a rather arbitrary device to make the play look 'classical' – in contrast to Goethe's confidently 'modern and un-Greek' treatment of the oracle in *Iphigenie auf Tauris*, or Schiller's own complex, but psychologically and dramatically convincing treatment of astrology in *Wallenstein*.

The tendency to a stylised, poetic or even operatic, rather than a realistic, manner of presentation was, however, becoming more and more characteristic of Weimar classicism, as it confronted the new and ever more threateningly unpoetic world of the nineteenth century. It was, as we have noted, a distinctive feature of the Weimar stage style; it was also a prominent feature of the later dramatic and theatrical works of Goethe.

*Tasso* had closed a major chapter in Goethe's career as a playwright. Conceived in his early years in Weimar, before the journey to Italy, it had arisen, as had all his works before that watershed in his creative life, out of personal, subjective, expressive needs. The Italian journey had led to a joyous affirmation of external, objective reality on Goethe's part: in the *Roman Elegies*, the sequence of poems which sum up the essence of the Italian experience, he celebrates it as a liberation from the prison of subjectivity. More grimly, the Revolution and the continuing upheavals which followed it had in their very different way confirmed the message: in future the poet must heed and respond specifically to the objective demands of the outside world. Virtually all the dramatic works which Goethe conceived after 1789 are deliberate attempts to come to terms with the Revolution and its consequences, to face up to the profound challenge which these events offered to his own conservative, evolutionary and anti-theoretical view of politics, history and the social life of man. These attempts take a variety of forms. At first, the technique is satirical. In a number of political comedies, *Der Groß-Kophta* (*The Grand Copt*) of 1791, *Der Bürgergeneral* (*The Citizen General*) of 1793 and the unfinished *Die Aufgeregten* (*People in a Stir*), begun in the same year, advocates of revolutionary political views are exposed as fools or charlatans. The style is the exaggerated or distorted realism typical of satirical comedy, and the medium is prose. But these attempts did not prove successful, and Goethe pondered for some years on the problem of devising a dramatic vehicle for what was after all not a comic subject. The result was *Die natürliche Tochter* (*The Natural Daughter*), Goethe's last full-length conventional drama, which appeared in 1803.

It is in fact a fragment, for it is but the first part of a projected but never completed trilogy. Eugenie, illegitimate daughter of the Duke, is brought to court by her father and publicly acknowledged as his child. But an intrigue instigated by her jealous legitimate brother (whom we never meet) leads to her disgrace and banishment. At the end of the play she is faced with the choice between exile and almost certain death in 'the islands' (evidently some kind of pestilential penal colony like the French Devil's Island) and the renunciation of her noble identity and status in marriage to the middle-class Magistrate. With their betrothal the 'tragedy', very oddly, ends, and we can only speculate as to the further course of the action, for there remain only the briefest of notes and sketches for the projected continuation. An optimistic interpretation would see Eugenie's *mésalliance* in the light of the similar betrothals across class barriers which take place at the end of *Wilhelm Meisters Lehrjahre*, and which seem to promise both individual happiness and some kind of regeneration of society at large, combining the best and most truly forward-looking elements of both aristocracy and bourgeoisie. But it might rather be the case that, although the Magistrate seems on his first appearance to be a selfless and admirable character, Goethe intended him later to be unmasked as a political agitator; Eugenie's marriage to him would then be seen to represent her contamination by revolutionary politics, from which she could only save herself by some kind of counter-revolutionary self-sacrifice. On either view, however, Goethe is plainly addressing himself in *Die natürliche Tochter* to the same kind of issues as is Schiller in the plays of his maturity: to themes of directly contemporary relevance and urgency – the legitimacy of power and the crisis of the traditional political and social order, as in *Wallenstein* and *Maria Stuart* – and to the relation of the individual to the historical process in a more abstract sense, as in *Die Jungfrau von Orleans* and *Die Braut von Messina*. Goethe, however, moves much further than Schiller in the direction of a purely symbolic or even allegorical manner of treatment. At a realistic level, the motivation and the sequence of events in *Die natürliche Tochter* are obscure almost to the point of incomprehensibility; possibly even deliberately so, for Goethe may have wished to depict the world of political intrigue, against which the heroine stands out in her fatal purity, as not merely corrupt but fundamentally senseless. As in *Die Jungfrau von Orleans*, we are in an 'alienated' world from which only the sacrifice of the heroine offers any hope of redemption. Goethe's characters, however, lack the human depth and complexity which Schiller's, even in *Die Jungfrau*, still possess. It is noteworthy that they are all designated only by titles – King, Duke, Magistrate and so on; only the heroine Eugenie has a name, and even that is a symbolic or allegorical one, for it is the Greek for 'well-born'. The characters also speak a language of extreme refinement and artificiality which contrasts sharply with the theme of political upheaval and disintegration. One wonders whether, when Goethe makes the King speak lines such as these –

> Entfernten Weltgetöses Wiederhall
> Verklinge nach und nach aus meinem Ohr.
> Ja, lieber Oheim, wende dein Gespräch
> Auf Gegenstände, diesem Ort gemäßer.

> May far-off cosmic trouble's echoing roar
> Cede fainter yet and fainter from our ear.
> Yes, dearest uncle, let your speech be turned
> To subjects more becoming to this place. (I, i)

– he is actually satirising the obfuscation of present reality by linguistic artificiality, using this highly studied language to show us the King refusing to face that reality and thereby effectively bringing nearer the cosmic upheaval which he finds so distasteful. But this seems not to be the case. For one thing, there is little or no stylistic differentiation between the various speakers, and the language therefore seems to lack the psychological dimension which was still very strongly felt, for all the polish and formality, in *Torquato Tasso*. Also, the self-conscious refinement of such lines as these is very much in accord with the aesthetic ideals cherished by Goethe at this time, when the hostile challenge of the new century was to be met by the uncompromising pursuit of beauty. The language of *Die natürliche Tochter* is the verbal equivalent of the self-consciously statuesque attitudes of the actors in the Weimar theatre.

In this play Goethe is moving away from drama, in the familiar sense of the word, in the direction of more purely allegorical forms of theatrical representation, such as the masques which had been so popular at the courts of the Renaissance, and which were indeed now being revived at the ducal court of Weimar. Goethe had already essayed the form in the brief *Paläophron und Neoterpe* (the Greek names indicate allegories of the Old and the New), written in celebration of the Dowager Duchess Anna Amalia's birthday in 1800. He turns to it again in *Pandora* (begun in 1807, but unfinished), based upon another episode in the myth of Prometheus, and in *Des Epimenides Erwachen* (*Epimenides' Awakening*, 1814–15). These three works all have the same theme: the movement of history, the reconciliation of old and new, and the eventual overcoming of the conflict and alienation of the present age. All employ a frankly symbolic rather than an in any sense realistic mode of presentation, and all are written in highly stylised language, often of intensely wrought poetic beauty, and incorporating a variety of metrical forms, including some imitated directly from those of Greek drama. They are also designed to exploit the resources of the stage in spectacular fashion: *Pandora* begins with the specification of an elaborate stage setting, and Goethe's surviving notes for the Weimar production of *Des Epimenides Erwachen* in 1816 contain detailed observations on the effects to be achieved in the transformation scenes and on the costuming of the allegorical 'Army of Hope', which was to allude to (rather than directly imitate) the uniforms of 'the modern northern and north-eastern nations'. A similar quasi-dramatic treatment of history as poetic myth can be seen in Shelley's *Prometheus Unbound* of 1819. Shelley's revolutionary optimism, however, is very different from the conservatism of the older Goethe. Indeed, the dour Prometheus of *Pandora* is a very different figure from the rebellious Titan evoked by Goethe in his 'Sturm und Drang' days: he seems to represent a merely material form of 'progress', lacking the idealism or imaginative vision embodied in his brother Epimetheus. Well might a Karl Moor now think that 'The bright spark of Promethean fire is burnt out.'

In these works of the early 1800s Weimar classicism seems to be moving away from that synthesis of realism and poetic stylisation which had produced its greatest achievements, in the direction of a more consistently poetic, but also more abstract and less humanly moving style. However, Schiller's last completed play, *Wilhelm Tell* (1804), makes a satisfying return to that synthesis. Perhaps this was not what Schiller intended. *Tell* was originally conceived as an 'idyll', and in *Über naive und sentimentalische Dichtung* Schiller had defined the 'sentimental' or 'reflective idyll', which he further declared to be the highest possible goal of modern poetry, as a depiction of the reintegration of the real and the ideal in the restored Golden Age. In other words, *Wilhelm Tell* was once again conceived as a mythical representation of history, and indeed the hero, even more than Joan of Arc (whose trial and death are historically attested, whatever the legends that have been built up about her), is a figure of legend rather than of sober historiography. But he is not, at all events in Schiller's play, a figure of allegorical abstraction like Goethe's Eugenie or Epimenides. It may be the case that, as some critics have argued, he is intended as the embodiment of some Schillerian philosophical abstraction such as the ideal of Aesthetic Man. But if this is so, then at any rate this airy nothing is given a local habitation and a name. He is indeed portrayed as a typical Swiss (and Schiller emphasises this by making powerful use of the spectacular Swiss landscape in the stage settings of his play): dour and taciturn, a man of action rather than words; a devoted husband and father, but an essentially solitary, asocial figure, always ready to help a fellow human being in need, or to rescue a lost lamb, but preferring to avoid the society of men, and above all wanting nothing to do with their political deliberations. The patriot Stauffacher tries to persuade him to join the league which the Swiss have formed to resist Austrian oppression. Tell refuses, but promises that he will not fail his country if it really needs him. The call duly comes, in the climactic scene of Act III. Tell refuses to salute the hat which the Austrians have raised on the green at Altdorf as a symbol of Imperial authority; or rather, he ignores it in his belief that the world of politics does not concern him. In punishment, Gessler, the sadistic Austrian governor, orders Tell to prove his prowess as a marksman by shooting an apple off his little boy's head, mockingly exhorting him to save himself as he has saved so many others – the words deliberately recall the priests' taunting of the crucified Christ (Matthew 27.42). Tell wrestles with his conscience in silence (but Schiller's stage directions indicate the anguished gestures with which he undergoes this struggle) and resolves to obey the tyrant's command, but then to kill him. He has discovered how tyranny can affect even the most innocent and unpolitical of men. Gessler is duly killed, and Tell is acclaimed as the saviour of his people: he has successfully risen to the challenge of history. Many of the features of the Romantic myth of history to which we have previously referred can in fact be discovered in *Wilhelm Tell*; but stronger and more convincing, even if the story is itself a legend, is the sense of real human beings acting in a concrete historical and political situation. In Schiller's last completed play, humanity is once again triumphant, and for the first and only time in his dramatic output both 'physical' and 'ideal' freedom are successfully achieved.

The play is also a fine example of Schiller's stagecraft. As has been mentioned, it makes lavish and effective use of the resources of the contemporary stage and of the grandeur of the Swiss setting. The two climaxes, the apple-shooting scene in Act III and the killing of Gessler at the end of Act IV, are both masterly. The former takes place on an open meadow with a background of towering mountains. Two soldiers guard the Imperial hat. Tell enters, crossbow in hand, with his little son. Gessler appears on horseback, with a large retinue. He plucks the fateful apple from a branch which hangs above his head – a superb, casually imperious gesture. Others press around him, imploring him to be merciful – and distracting our attention from Tell on the other side of the stage, until suddenly all are startled, Gessler himself as much as any, to hear the cry 'The apple's fallen!' (III, iii). The scene in Act IV, in contrast, is set in a narrow pass through the mountains. Tell now waits brooding for his quarry. The stage again fills with people; again they press about Gessler, vainly imploring his mercy; again, suddenly, Tell's arrow finds its target, and Tell appears triumphant from his hiding-place: 'You know the marksman, look to find no other!' (IV, iii).

*Wilhelm Tell* is not Schiller's greatest play, but it forms a worthy conclusion to his career as a dramatist. His next project, *Demetrius*, based on a subject from seventeenth-century Russian history, might well have proved a greater work even than *Wallenstein*, similarly combining a soberly realistic, even pessimistic vision of history with the basic discipline of classical form and the fuller range of Shakespearian drama, and exploiting still further the resources of the contemporary stage. But work on it was cut short by Schiller's tragically early death, on 9 May 1805, in his forty-fifth year.

'Schiller's talent', as Goethe observed to Eckermann, over twenty years later, 'was simply made for the theatre.' He was a natural dramatist, with a powerful sense of conflict and the gift of creating memorable, if often larger-than-life, characters and striking theatrical situations. He undoubtedly had a liking for the grand gesture, for rhetoric and melodrama, and the scale of his works (by which is meant not simply their length) is not always to modern tastes. But he also had, as the later plays in particular bear witness, a keen sense of history, and the true tragedian's blend of compassion and admiration for men (and women) seeking to maintain their human dignity against the adversities of life, the threat of force, or the blind play of impersonal chance or causality. Critics in their discussion of Schiller's work often give the impression that he wrote his plays to exemplify preconceived theories of tragedy or of human character and behaviour – of realism and idealism, of sublimity, of the 'beautiful soul' or of the 'aesthetic state'.[9] It is surely rather the case that the theorising is the work of a natural dramatist who had reached a stage of uncertainty in his own playwriting, and of an artist of great integrity who wished to make sure that he really was fulfilling the highest demands that could be placed upon an artist at that crucial period of European history. In his mature plays he shows us men and women similarly facing up, often through similar processes of uncertainty and critical reflection, to the responsibilities, albeit very different ones, which history has thrust upon them. His theoretical writings are fascinating in their own account, and the writing of them undoubtedly helped to clear his mind for further dramatic composition, but the plays can stand on their own feet without reference to them.

When Schiller died, Goethe felt that he had lost, as he put it, a part of himself. He remained as director of the Weimar theatre for another twelve years, but the task seemed less and less congenial; the hopes which he and Schiller had invested in a classical German literary and dramatic revival seemed more and more impossible to realise. He continued to encourage (or sometimes, as we shall see, to discourage) new talent, but despite the popular success of Schiller's plays the general level of public taste remained low. Intrigues were mounted against Goethe with increasing frequency and hostility: it was probably Karoline Jagemann who finally engineered his resignation in 1817. The occasion was provided by the proposed visit to Weimar of the Viennese actor Karsten with the play *Der Wald bei Bondy* (*The Wood at Bondy*), in which he was accompanied on the stage by a trained poodle. This seemed like a reversion to the worst crudities of days gone by, and Goethe declared that he would not hear of it. But Jagemann exerted her influence upon the Duke, Karsten and his poodle came to Weimar, and Goethe resigned the directorship. A chapter of theatrical history had come to an end. The epilogue, strangely enough, was a repetition of the event of 1774 which had formed the prelude to Goethe's theatrical career in Weimar. In the small hours of Tuesday 22 March 1825, the theatre caught fire and was burned to the ground.

Goethe had, however, one more contribution to make to the classical German drama, the work which forms the summit of its poetic achievement and is Weimar's most memorable contribution not merely to German but to world literature. It was, however, as we have already observed, in the generally accepted sense of the words neither classical, nor a drama. It was his life's work, *Faust*.

# CHAPTER VIII

# Nordic phantoms: Goethe's Faust

Dr Johann Faust is a shadowy figure on the borders of history and legend. Though the small town of Knittlingen in Württemberg claims to be his birthplace, no one knows for certain whether he really existed. Even his name, authentically German though it looks, could well be a Latin pseudonym (*faustus*, fortunate or lucky), one which was traditionally adopted by wizards and necromancers from the days of late classical antiquity. But the traditional name and many traditional tales of magical accomplishments (miraculous transformations, prodigious feats of eating and of speed, a familiar spirit in the form of a black dog) gather about a particular personality at the turn of the sixteenth century. We are back, once again, at that crucial period of the birth of modern Europe, of the emergence of the European nations – in the case of Germany, imperfect and problematic – from the ruins of the medieval world. The tradition places his death around 1540. If this is true, then he would have been making his pact with the devil, the term of which was twenty-four years, about the time that Luther was nailing his ninety-five theses to the church door in Wittenberg – one of Faust's legendary haunts. Another tradition, dating his life and death somewhat earlier, identifies him with Johann Fust, who was one of the pioneers of the new and, to the conservative mind, diabolical art of printing. Whoever he was, Dr Faust is a figure admirably suited to symbolise the birth of modern Europe and of the modern European mind.[1]

To the traditional Christian believer, Faust's wicked life and terrible end were simply a warning example of the dangers of forbidden speculation, of a second tasting of the forbidden fruit of knowledge. It was in a Lutheran spirit of pious exhortation that the Frankfurt printer Johann Spies published in 1587 his *Historia von D. Johann Fausten*, the ancestor of all subsequent literary, dramatic and musical treatments of the story. Translated into English, it immediately seized the imagination of Christopher Marlowe, whose *Tragical History of Doctor Faustus* was probably composed in 1593, the last year of his life. Faust chapbooks and, as we have seen, Faust plays and puppet-plays continued to appear in Germany until well into the eighteenth century, to be execrated by Gottsched in his *Dichtkunst* – and praised by Lessing in the seventeenth *Literaturbrief* – as examples of the popular native dramatic tradition. Like Marlowe's play, the German Faust plays will have contained elements of spectacle, dance and comedy, as well as the debates and confrontations between Faust and his evil familiar-cum-adversary Mephostophilis or Mephistopheles.[2]

Despite Lessing's professed enthusiasm for the Faust theme, his essentially enlightened spirit seems in fact to have been unable or unwilling to grasp its tragic aspect – the elements of 'the mighty, the terrible, the melancholic' to which the *Literaturbrief* itself refers. The 'Stürmer und Dränger' had no such inhibitions. For the young Goethe and his contemporaries, Faust was another Promethean 'Kerl', straining furiously at the bonds laid upon his high-flying spirit by society, convention, religion, morality and the limitations of the human condition in general. They were also fired with enthusiasm for popular culture: for folk-song and ballad, for national tradition, for forms of utterance unrestrained by the rules and proprieties of neo-classicism. Several of them seized upon the theme, including Lenz and Klinger: the latter wrote a Faust novel, though it did not appear until 1791. Goethe tells us that he saw a Faust puppet-play in Frankfurt as a child; as a student in Leipzig he visited Auerbach's Cellar, a favourite haunt of students and the scene of one of Faust's legendary exploits, the turning of water into wine (in blasphemous emulation of Christ at the marriage-feast in Cana). In Strasbourg, Herder opened his eyes to Shakespearian drama and to folk-ballad and other elements of popular tradition. Back at home in Frankfurt he steeped himself in occult lore. He followed the trial, and may even have witnessed the execution, of a girl who had killed her illegitimate child, and had pleaded in her defence that she had been seduced with the aid of black magic. In his poetic explorations and experiments he had discovered the earthy vigour of Sachsian 'Knittelvers'. And so, some time in the early 1770s, he created a miraculous amalgam of all these elements. It begins, as does Marlowe's *Doctor Faustus*, with a monologue of 'the man that in his study sits', in this case at night in a narrow, high-vaulted Gothic chamber, symbolising the constrictions of the medieval world from which modern man yearns to break free:

> Hab nun, ach, die Philosophei,
> Medizin und Juristerei,
> Und leider auch die Theologie
> Durchaus studiert mit heißer Müh.
> Da steh ich nun, ich armer Tor,
> Und bin so klug als wie zuvor.
> Heiße Doktor und Professor gar,
> Und ziehe schon an die zehen Jahr'
> Herauf, herab und quer und krumm
> Meine Schüler an der Nas' herum
> Und seh, daß wir nichts wissen können,
> Das will mir schier das Herz verbrennen. . .

> Why then, Philosophy is mine,
> In Medicine and in Law I shine,
> Divinity too, to my regret,
> I've mastered them all by toil and sweat.
> So here I stand, poor foolish man,
> No wiser than when I began.
> They call me Doctor and Professor too,
> It must be all of ten years, it's true,
> That I've led my students by the snout,
> Dragged them hither and thither and round and about,
> And I see that all knowledge is out of our grasp:
> It brings me to my heart's last gasp.[3]

But this is quite un-Marlovian. The 'Knittelvers' is anything but a 'mighty line'. It is short-winded and often bumpy in rhythm, and these characteristics are reinforced by the insistent rhyming couplets. The diction, like that of the contemporary *Götz von Berlichingen*, has a flavour both old-fashioned and homely. The opening lines are indeed more appropriate to a puppet Faust than to a 'tragic

134

hero' in any sort of hitherto accepted literary mode. But from this beginning Goethe gradually intensifies the atmosphere and heightens the tone, until the scene culminates in the overwhelming apparition of the Erdgeist or Earth Spirit, before whom Faust the 'superman' ('Übermensch', as the Spirit with contemptuous irony calls him – one of the first recorded occurrences of that ominous word) reels in terror. The whole scene occupies 160 lines, nearly three times the length of Faustus's opening monologue in Marlowe and virtually a self-contained Faust monodrama on its own. What follows is an inconclusive series of fragmentary episodes. Faust's visionary conjurations are interrupted by the nightcapped appearance of his 'famulus' or assistant Wagner, the caricature of a dusty pedant, for whom those conjurations are nothing but an exercise in 'declamation'. We meet Mephistopheles, his entry unheralded and unexplained, in professorial disguise, haranguing a naive and earnest freshman in yet another satire on the traditional academic faculties. Faust and Mephisto join the students drinking in Auerbach's Cellar and play tricks on them. And then, in a sequence of fifteen short scenes which make up two-thirds of the original text, Faust encounters Margarete (Gretchen), an ordinary small-town girl, falls in love with her, seduces her with the aid of Mephistopheles' magic arts, and abandons her to bear their child alone. She kills the child and is condemned to death for infanticide. Faust returns to find her delirious in prison, awaiting execution, and offers to rescue her. But this would again involve the assistance of Mephistopheles, and Gretchen refuses. Mephistopheles bears Faust away, leaving her to her fate.

This concludes the so-called *Urfaust* or 'original *Faust*', as scholars have named the manuscript, not discovered until 1887, which appears to contain most if not all of what Goethe had written on the Faust theme up to about 1775. We know that the readings from his works which he gave to the Duke and his circle in Weimar included selections from the Faust material, and it was the Weimar lady-in-waiting Luise von Göchhausen who made the copy which we now possess. The *Urfaust* is only a fragment, or a series of fragments. It has a certain elusive poetic unity – of theme, of imagery and of style, but no over-all design or dramatic shape. It contains neither of the two scenes essential to define the scope of any Faust drama: neither the signing of the contract between Faust and the devil, nor his eventual death and damnation. It has economy, force and immediacy, and has repeatedly been successfully performed on stage; but it is not, strictly speaking, comprehensible as it stands, and such performances must presume that their audiences know the work in its final form or at least know the legend on which it is based – as was, of course, the case with Goethe's courtly audience at Weimar in 1775. The immense potential but also the drawbacks of the material, the poetic and dramatic strengths but also some of the problematic features of the finished work, can already be detected in it.

Some of the strengths are immediately apparent in the opening scene. We find there a unique blend of the familiar, the archaic and the mysterious; the intensity of Faust's vision of a world of nature and the spirit, from which the cultivation of dry book-learning has cut him off; the terror and the courage of the man struggling to break free from the prison (as he characteristically calls it) of his narrow Gothic cell. As we proceed, we find lively satire of the academic world: of its students, from the naive, eager yet apprehensive freshman to the bored and disillusioned drinking party in Auerbach's Cellar, and of its professors, whether myopic pedants like Wagner or cynics in whom the devil appears but thinly disguised. The tragedy of Gretchen and her love for Faust combines a depth and intensity of emotion with a breathtaking simplicity of form and utterance: a symmetrical arch-form, rising from initial encounter to consummation and falling again to the final catastrophe, but presented with the elliptical brevity, the 'leaps and bounds', which Herder had taught Goethe to see as characteristic of folk-song and ballad. Here the popular, even primitive element in the 'Sturm und Drang' programme, the deliberate rejection of sophistication, urbanity and polish, comes into its own. And running through the whole there is the relationship, undefined though it may be in formal terms, between Faust and Mephistopheles: the one the embodiment of an intense desire, spiritually idealistic and greedily sensuous by turns, to savour and to affirm life and all it has to offer, and the other of a sarcastic nihilism, often expressed in mordant wit, which looks upon the world and upon all forms of human aspiration and activity with contempt.

Problems are apparent too, however. One of the major innovations in the dramatic revolution of the 'Sturm und Drang' was, we remember, the abandonment of the Aristotelian principle of unity of action and of the Aristotelian conception of plot as the essence of tragedy in favour of a unity of character only, of the adoption of an episodic structure in which a series of incidents and encounters forms a composite or cumulative portrait of a great 'Kerl'. Goethe's procedure in the early years of his work on *Faust* was entirely in conformity with this programme. He put off writing the scenes which would give dramatic articulation to the whole, and wrote instead a series of scenes or episodes illustrating various aspects of Faust's character and aspirations. There is little or no continuity or connection between these episodes, and we do not see in any but the most general way, if at all, how they contribute to the final outcome. That outcome itself remains in doubt: though according to the traditional story Faust had of course finally been carried off to hell, a number of eighteenth-century writers had already proposed his redemption or salvation – in Paul Weidmann's *Faust* of 1775, for example, he is saved through love and repentance, and in one of Lessing's Faust sketches he is saved through his very yearning for knowledge and wisdom – and it has been suggested that even at this early date Goethe had already decided that his Faust too was to be saved rather than damned. And the Gretchen episode – an invention of Goethe's quite unrelated to the traditional Faust material – had taken on such independent life and, in particular, attained such a dramatic wholeness of its own that it threatened to divert attention from the larger issues implicit in the Faust theme, just as Gretchen herself tends to divert our interest and sympathy away from Faust whenever she appears. These problems dominated Goethe's intermittent work on the project for the next half-century or so. He had to devise a suitable framework for the whole action, formulate a pact defining more precisely the terms of the relationship between Faust and Mephistopheles, decide Faust's eventual fate and provide an appropriate conclusion, and accommodate the Gretchen episode within the greater whole without sacrificing its own poetic unity and strength. Style was also a problem, for the scenes which make up the *Urfaust* are composed in a variety of linguistic forms: 'Knittelvers' and other forms of rhymed verse, free verse and prose, with interpolated songs. Eventually, Goethe found solutions to all these difficulties; on their success, critical opinions have often differed.

Goethe soon came to regard the work's deliberately popular and traditional character as itself a serious problem. The popular, national character of the Faust legend and of the plays based upon it had, of course, constituted a major attraction to writers aiming to create a German drama with a genuine national identity. But soon after his arrival in Weimar, when he had begun to establish himself in a courtly environment and to turn back towards a more cosmopolitan and classical form of drama, Goethe began to fall out of imaginative sympathy with his puppet-hero Faust, his ballad-heroine Gretchen, his semi-comic medieval morality-play devil. He appears to have stopped work on *Faust* soon after his arrival in Weimar – at about the same time, in fact, that he began his imaginative stock-taking in *Wilhelm Meisters theatralische Sendung*. In the otherwise comprehensive panorama of the eighteenth-century German theatre which that work offers us, it is surprising, but perhaps significant, that there is no mention of a Faust play.

However, Goethe took his Faust manuscript to Italy with him in 1786, and while in Rome he made some attempt to complete the work for publication. He wrote to Duke Karl August that he thought he had 'found the thread' again, and that he had written a new scene which, if he 'smoked the paper', no one would be able to distinguish from the original material. But it seems rather that the thread, the shadowy unity of inspiration and conception that had underlain the fragmentary and heterogeneous *Urfaust* scenes, had been lost, and that Goethe was now approaching his own work as it were from the outside, as if it had been another's, and trying to extend it by a kind of self-pastiche. Much of this is remarkably successful, some of it less so; and far from helping to unify the work, it often creates more formal and stylistic disparities and thus new problems to be solved in their turn. The new scene referred to in his letter to the Duke is a case in point: the scene 'Witch's Kitchen', in which Faust, his disillusionment with the academic world complete, is prepared for entry into the world outside and, specifically, for the erotic encounter with Gretchen, by drinking a magic potion with rejuvenating and, evidently, aphrodisiac powers. This is another invention of Goethe's which forms no part of the traditional Faust material. It is plainly designed to link the two principal components of the *Urfaust* – the 'Gelehrtentragödie' or 'scholar's tragedy', as the opening scenes have been called, and the Gretchen tragedy; in fact it calls attention to the gap between them. The Faust of the original conception had evidently needed no such rejuvenation. But for Goethe, himself reborn, basking in the clarity of the Italian sunlight and revelling in what he now believed to be the objectivity of classical art-forms, the romantic passion of the Gretchen tragedy now belonged to a different world, the dark northern world of intense subjectivity which he believed he had left behind him for ever. In the Witch's Kitchen even the devil appears transmogrified – so much so that the witch fails to recognise her lord and master. As he tells her:

> Civilisation, moving on apace,
> Has even on the devil left its trace;
> That Nordic phantom's no more to be seen;
> Horns, tail and cloven hoof might never have been.    (ll. 2495ff)

The traditional, popular, 'Nordic' and legendary elements which originally had constituted a major attraction of the Faust material Goethe now found something of an embarrassment, like Mephisto-pheles' cloven foot, which he tries to disguise by wearing false calves when appearing in polite society. Subject-matter which Goethe had in earlier years grasped eagerly and directly has now to be held at arm's length and treated with condescending irony.

Not surprisingly, Goethe was unable to finish *Faust* in Italy. Part of the *Urfaust* material, filled out with the 'Witch's Kitchen' scene and other new interpolations, but shorn of the final scenes of the Gretchen tragedy (which in their original form were in stark, harrowing prose), he published in 1790 under the title *Faust, A Fragment*. By doing so he probably intended to signify that he wished to have no more to do with the subject.

In 1794 Schiller, in the course of his overtures of friendship to Goethe, expressed the desire to see the remaining unpublished Faust material: the *Fragment* he describes, in an inappropriately classical comparison, as like the torso of Hercules. But Goethe was unwilling even, as he put it, to untie the string that held the papers together. In the summer of 1797, however, he told Schiller that he was taking the work up again, reconsidering the existing material and trying to proceed further with 'the plan, which is really only an idea'. Over the next few years the project was much discussed between the two friends. It was probably the influence of Schiller's more analytic, schematic cast of mind that led Goethe himself now to try to schematise and abstract from what he had written, rather than simply to write new scenes and 'smoke the paper'; to try to rediscover and define that lost thread, or perhaps to spin a new one to take its place; and thus to turn what was 'really only an idea' into an actual plan which would enable him to finish the whole, even if only after many more years and after further amplifications and modifications. *Faust* is a most un-Schillerian work, but without the support and influence of Schiller it would probably never have been completed.

The main problems confronting Goethe were the extent and heterogeneity of the material, the virtual autonomy of the Gretchen episode, and the popular or traditional atmosphere in which the classical Goethe no longer felt himself at home. To each of these problems he found a solution which might be described, from a negative point of view, as making the best of a bad job. The problem of size was solved, or rather shelved, by allowing the work to grow even bigger, and dividing it into two parts – which meant that the execution of the second part and the conclusion of the whole were indefinitely postponed. The problem of heterogeneity was solved by allowing it to become even more heterogeneous, and that of episodic autonomy by creating further autonomous episodes. The first part was to be allowed to focus around the Gretchen tragedy, while the second was to reintroduce the original Faust's legendary paramour, the shade of Helen of Troy; this meant that the first part could be allowed to remain a simple, romantic tragedy of youthful passion, while the second would move on to a more elevated, symbolic and classical plane. The first part could keep its homely, short-winded, popular German metres, but the Helen scenes would be in the majestic long, rolling iambic trimeter, the actual metre of ancient Greek tragedy. If Gretchen represented passion, Helen would represent Beauty, and Faust's encounter with her would constitute a kind of 'aesthetic education' like that propounded by Schiller, through which Faust would be emancipated from subjection to physical necessity and rendered truly free, all his potential released to achieve its full realisation. This is not inconsistent with the original conception of Faust as a typical 'Kerl' of the 'Sturm und Drang' seeking to exercise his 'Kraft', but it gives it a more idealistic and also more optimistic cast. That original fiercely raging, pent-up energy is given some, however vaguely defined, channel and direction; convulsive 'Kraft' becomes that purposeful striving ('Streben') by which, according to the philosophy of Fichte (which Goethe and Schiller discussed together in 1798) the self achieves its final apotheosis. The closed circle of Faust's pact with the devil is broken: the action must lead forward and upward, to Faust's eventual salvation.

Mephistopheles still offers Faust the traditional pact:

> Your service here on earth I will embrace,
> Promptly obey your every beck and call;
> But when we meet there in the other place,
> It will be your turn to be bound in thrall. (ll. 1656ff)

But Faust does not care what happens 'in the other place' ('drüben'), if indeed there is one. Not only is he still, as he had declared in the opening monologue, 'not afraid of the devil or Hell'; he does not believe that the devil can give him anything he really wants. Though he had quailed before the Earth Spirit, he treats Mephistopheles with sovereign contempt, and spurns his services:

> Poor devil, what have you to give?
> The lofty striving spirit of a man
> You do not understand, nor ever can. (ll. 1675ff)

He offers Mephisto a challenge and a wager: if ever he ceases to strive, if ever he expresses satisfaction, if ever he experiences a moment of fulfilment such that he would bid that moment stay, then the devil may claim him. The twenty-four years' time-limit of the traditional pact has disappeared (Goethe had already implicitly abandoned it in writing the 'Witch's Kitchen' scene, where Faust is rejuvenated by thirty years). The devil is given the whole span of Faust's earthly life in which to satisfy him: we shall indeed see him trying to meet the challenge first in Faust's (restored) youth, then in his manhood, finally in his old age. And Goethe sets the wager in a wider context by furnishing the drama with a 'Prologue in Heaven' in which, before the Lord and the assembled heavenly hosts, Mephistopheles wagers that he will be able to win the soul of the Lord's 'servant' Faust and thus refute the archangels' optimistic asseveration that

> all the works Thy hand hath wrought
> Are glorious as on Earth's first day. (ll. 269f)

The Prologue is obviously designed to recall the opening chapter of the biblical Book of Job, and the allusion plainly implies that Faust, like Job, will in the end, despite all intervening trials and tribulations, emerge triumphant, and that the Lord's faith in him and his satisfaction with his creation will thus be vindicated.

The Prologue itself, however, is only part of an elaborate framework which Goethe designed not only to contain the drama of Faust and the devil and its various episodes, both those already written and those still waiting to be composed, but also to make explicit and to justify his work's unique artistic character. It is prefaced further by a 'Prelude on the Stage' – not the stage of a newly refurbished permanent theatre such as Schiller had celebrated in his Prologue to *Wallenstein*, but the temporarily erected boards of a troupe of strolling players, where the Director is addressing his two principal collaborators, the Dramatic Poet ('Theaterdichter') and the Comedian ('Lustige Person' – the 'Hanswurst' who had been the mainstay of so many companies):

> You two, who have so often stood
> Beside me here, through thick and thin,
> Say, do you think this will be good
> To draw the German public in?
> I like to see a smile on people's face,
> For that's the way our profits are increased;
> The posts and boards are hammered into place,
> And all are promising themselves a feast.
> Already, with their eyebrows raised in waiting,
> They're sitting there – it's got to be exciting! (ll. 33ff)

And whereas Schiller in the *Wallenstein* Prologue further celebrates the harmonious collaboration of the various participants in the theatrical experience – actor, poet and public, but with the poet firmly in charge – Goethe's Prelude shows the Director struggling hard to keep the peace between the Poet, who feels his art to be prostituted by concessions to public taste, and the Comedian, who has no such qualms about giving the people what they want. We are given to understand that the work which follows will be a heterogeneous and not altogether harmonious mixture of stylistic elements. It is also intimated that it will exploit to the full the theatre's resources of spectacle ('prospects and machines', l.234) – though plainly, on a stage such as this, much will have to be left to the imagination – and range freely through the whole of creation, 'from Heaven through the world to Hell' (l.242, the last line of the Prelude). There are also hints that the actors in the subsequent play may be to some extent identified with the spokesmen of the Prelude: the Lord, who appears only in the Prologue, with the Director, Faust with the Poet, and Mephistopheles with the Comedian. These hints have been followed in many modern productions, notably the famous Gustaf Gründgens production of the 1950s, later preserved on film.

But even this does not complete Goethe's framework. Even before the Prelude comes a Dedication in the form of a substantial poem – four stanzas of rich and solemn *ottava rima* – in which the author addresses his own creation, the 'shadowy forms' (l. 1) which had appeared to him in his youth, and which he is now seeking to recapture and to endow with firmer substance by a deliberate effort of the imaginative will. Dedication and Prelude together elaborately dramatise Goethe's complex relationship to his own work – the imaginative distance separating the fifty-year-old poet from the inspiration of his earlier years, and the tension between the classical aspirations of the director of the Weimar theatre and the inherent artistic character of a work which had originally been conceived in a deliberately anti-classical, popular, traditional German style.

*Faust*, Part I, comprising the 'scholar's tragedy', the wager with the devil, and the Gretchen tragedy, together with Dedication, Prelude and Prologue (which of course preface the whole work, including the as yet unwritten Part II) was completed in 1806 and appeared in print two years later, after delays caused by the disturbances of the Napoleonic wars. (Life in quiet, provincial Weimar had been severely disrupted in the autumn of 1806 after

10 Faust conjuring the spirits, in Gothic and in classicised forms: (a) Frontispiece to the *Fragment* in Goethe's *Schriften*, VII, 1790, engraved after Rembrandt; (b) drawing by Goethe, *c.* 1810–12, with the Earth

Napoleon's defeat of the Prussians at Jena, only a few miles away.) Even after the formulation of a plan for the whole, it had been a hard struggle, and the work had proved almost unconquerably resistant to classical discipline. As Goethe wrote to Schiller on various occasions in the course of those years, it was still a 'barbaric production', a 'family of fungoid growths' or of 'Nordic phantoms' which insisted on following its own mysterious organic processes. Like the poodle in whose shape Mephistopheles first appears to Faust,

> Banished behind the chimney-flue
> Like an elephant it grew. (ll. 1310f)

The same was to happen again with Part II, even though this had been conceived from the start as moving on a higher plane both thematically and stylistically.

Round about 1800 Goethe had already embarked upon the classical Greek trimeters of the Helen of Troy episode, which was to form the climax of Part II and indeed of the whole vast drama, just as the emotional, if not strictly speaking the dramatic, climax of Marlowe's *Doctor Faustus* is formed by Faustus's encounter with the 'face that launched a thousand ships':

> By men so much admired, so much reproved, I, Helen,
> Have come here from the seashore where our ships have beached,
> Yet still unsteady from the rocking waves and their lively
> Motion that carried us from Phrygia's open plains
> On surging mighty crests, by great Poseidon's grace
> And Eurus' power, to inlets of our fatherland.
> Below King Menelaus at his coming home
> Rejoices too and with him all his boldest men. (ll. 8488ff)

We are indeed worlds away from 'Why then, Philosophy is mine'. And some years later Goethe told his young admirer Sulpiz Boisserée that in his 'best period' – that is, presumably, during those same years of his classical maturity – he had also succeeded in composing the final scenes of Faust's salvation 'in a very fine and grandiose manner'. But even if this is true – like many of Goethe's assertions, at various times between 1808 and 1832, that he had known all along exactly how the work was going to turn out, it should probably be taken with a large pinch of salt – inspiration flagged, and often for years at a time he seems again to have given up all hope of completion. Again the decisive stimulus to put the work finally into shape came from another, in this case from Eckermann. And again, despite Goethe's confidence, during that 'best period', in the absolute and timeless validity of classical art-forms, he himself, naturally enough, had changed as he grew older. The Goethe of the 1820s was as far from the Helen of 1800, in years, experience and artistic temper, as was the Goethe of 1790 from the Gretchen of 1770. Helen too becomes a 'phantom'; and when Goethe put the last touches to Part II in January 1832, two months before his death, not only had it too grown 'like an elephant', but it had also in some ways reverted to its 'Nordic' origins – while in others taking on quite unforeseeably modern, even 'modernist' characteristics, pointing forward into a new, post-Revolutionary world, a world perhaps of new hopes and expectations, but also of new threats and dangers.

In the *Urfaust* Faust's encounter with Gretchen had evidently needed no explanation; by 1788 Goethe had come to feel that it had to be prepared in some way, that the gap between the scholar and the ordinary girl needed in some way to be bridged. Similarly in Part II Faust's encounter with Helen of Troy has to be prepared: some kind of bridge has to be thrown across the gap which separates modern, post-Renaissance man from the ideal of classical antiquity for which he so passionately longs, but which cannot simply and unproblematically, as Goethe in his classical phase had believed, be re-created or recovered in the modern world. At the beginning of Part II Faust undergoes another rejuvenation or restoration, this time at the hands of beneficent spirits of nature, and vows to continue his striving. We then find him at the Emperor's court – Goethe, in a draft of 1816, actually refers to the Emperor Maximilian, but in the final text he is not named (Marlowe's Faustus visits the court of Maximilian's successor, Charles V). Here he seems to have taken over, rather like his creator in Weimar, the combined roles of confidant, finance minister and director of court entertainments – with Mephistopheles, of course, aiding him in all these capacities. A large part of Act I is taken up by an extensive court masque or carnival. After this the Emperor, seeking new entertainment, orders Faust to summon up the shades of Paris and of Helen, 'the perfect shapes of woman as of man' (l.6185). Faust obliges, but when the shadow-Helen appears his passion is so violently aroused that he attempts to embrace her. The result of this contact between flesh and spirit – matter and anti-matter – is an explosion, from which Faust is carried off, paralysed, by Mephistopheles, to return to his old Gothic study, which we find in Act II looking just as he, and Goethe, had left it all those years ago in Part I. (The action of course observes no realistic chronology.) Wagner, still undisillusioned with traditional learning, has taken Faust's place and continued his speculations, to the point at which he is about to realise one of the great ambitions of the medieval alchemists, the creation of a Homunculus or miniature artificial human being. This Homunculus turns out to be ideally qualified to act as guide to Faust and Mephisto on a journey to ancient Greece. For before Faust can be restored to consciousness and encounter Helen once more, he has to be sent on a vast exploration of the world of classical and pre-classical Greek mythology and legend. This takes the form of a 'Classical Walpurgis Night', a huge mythological carnival recalling both the Nordic Walpurgis Night or Witches' Sabbath of Part I and the Renaissance carnival of Act I. At last in Act III Faust meets Helen again. But their encounter now no longer simply represents man's timeless adoration of the absolute of Beauty, as Goethe had intended about 1800. It has come to symbolise something more complex and historically specific: the love of modern Western European man for the ideal of ancient Greece, the union of the Romantic and the classical. Faust, the lover of Helen, appears no longer as a youthful gallant as in the Gretchen tragedy, but as a man in the prime of life (like his creator, the classical Goethe), dressed in the rich costume of a medieval crusader. He has gone back in time to meet her – but she has come forward to meet him. She surrenders herself to him in a striking linguistic gesture. The classical Greek heroine abandons her appropriate linguistic garb, the stately iambic trimeter, and is taught by Faust to speak in the northern manner – that is, to rhyme:

HELEN So tell me then, how can I learn this art?
FAUST Quite simply: you must listen to your heart.
    And when your breast with longing overflows,
    Look round to see –
HELEN                  Who the like feeling shows.

                              (ll.9367ff)

In Arcadia, Faust and Helen enjoy a charmed, idyllic existence. But the idyll is shattered when their son Euphorion attempts to fly beyond the charmed circle. Once, Arcadia was a real place (in the Peloponnese); now it is only a poetic dream, and to mistake the dream for reality, or to imagine that it can be re-created in reality, is to fall into the kind of potentially tragic error to which Faust had already succumbed in trying to embrace the phantom Helen in Act I. Faust has now learnt this lesson, but Euphorion has not. The figure of Euphorion was also associated by Goethe with Byron, who died at Missolunghi in 1824 in the course of a campaign to restore the political independence of Greece, then still part of the Turkish Empire. Goethe said that the action of Act III spanned three thousand years, from the fall of Troy to the surrender of Missolunghi; he also described this part of the work as a 'classical–romantic phantasmagoria'.

After the Arcadian idyll and the birth and death of Euphorion, the shape of Helen once more dissolves into thin air, though peacefully this time, and returns to the underworld of Greek mythology. Faust is left holding her empty garments, which in their turn dissolve into a cloud upon which he is transported back to the real world, the troubled political scene of the German Empire which he had left behind him in Act II. From aesthetic experience he returns to the world of action.

Schiller had argued that the goal of 'aesthetic education' was to emancipate the powers of man to accomplish the tasks of real life – of moral action and, as the context of the *Briefe über die ästhetische Erziehung des Menschen* makes clear, of social and political regeneration. Faust and Mephisto had already dabbled in public affairs in Act I, with predictably questionable results, when they had produced an instant, but bogus, cure for the Empire's economic difficulties in the shape of a diabolical new invention – the printing of paper currency. (Like other conservatives before and since, Goethe was a believer in 'sound money'.) Now these inflationary chickens have come home to roost, and economic anarchy has led to political anarchy, civil war, and the appearance of a rival emperor. We are still (or again) nominally in the sixteenth century, but the scene very soon takes on an obvious, if again somewhat 'phantasmagoric' or symbolical, resemblance to Goethe's own times, when the social and political order of Europe was undergoing such radical upheavals – and, in the view of some pessimists and reactionaries, reaping the fruits of the three centuries or so of emancipation and 'progress' which had followed upon Renaissance and Reformation. Once again Faust and Mephisto spring to the Emperor's aid and the old order is, apparently, restored. In Auerbach's Cellar the students had sung

> The dear old Holy Roman Empire.
> Whatever keeps it going? (ll. 2090f)

– a question even more appropriate, and even harder to answer, in the 1770s, when the scene was written, than in the sixteenth century, when the action nominally takes place. In 1806 the Holy Roman Empire had been formally dissolved. But at the Congress of Vienna in 1815, after the defeat of Napoleon, something very like it had been re-created under the name of the German Confederation ('Deutscher Bund'); and most of the other features of the pre-Revolutionary status quo had also been restored, as if by some kind of political black magic. And Duke Karl August of Weimar, who had managed to trim his sails to a succession of different political winds, was rewarded with the title of Grand Duke. For his services to the Emperor, Faust is rewarded with a grant of land on which to carry out the latest of his schemes. But like the wealth promised by the paper currency in Act I, Faust's new land exists as yet only in the future, and has still to be created. For his plan is to conquer and drain the sea, to fight back the elemental forces of nature with dykes and dams, with all the technological resources at his disposal – that is, in the language of the poem, with the aid of Mephistopheles again – and to create a virgin land which can then be colonised with a new humanity cast in the Faustian mould. The 'superman' who cowered before the Earth Spirit has at last, it seems, in his high old age (Goethe said that the Faust of Act v was a hundred years old) himself inherited the earth. He will be monarch of all he surveys, and the humble old couple Philemon and Baucis, living peacefully minding their own business amid the sand-dunes by the sea, have to be forcibly evicted to make way for the realisation of his visions. Mephistopheles sets fire to their homestead, and they perish in the blaze. Faust feels something like remorse, curses Mephisto and vows to renounce the use of magic, which means that he is no longer physically immortal. Mortality appears to him in the shape of the spirit of Care; though he defies her, she strikes him blind. And so, when he savours in anticipation the fulfilment of his great imperial vision, in which altruism and egoism are as inextricably blended as in that of any Schillerian idealist, he is hopelessly deluded; for the sound which he takes to be that of the workmen digging his great new canal is in fact made by Mephistopheles and his grisly gang of spirits digging Faust's grave:

> And so, where danger from each side appears,
> Youth, manhood, age live out their hardy years.
> O that I might behold them throng around,
> Stand amidst free men on the free-won ground!
> Then I might cry out to the moment's haste,
> Fair one, you shall not leave me, stay!
> The mark my years on earth have traced
> In aeons cannot pass away.
> In knowing foretaste of such rare delight,
> I savour now the moment at its height.          (ll. 11577ff)

It is still an affirmation of human striving and of the value of human life and activity; but Goethe has in his old age become more fully aware of the price which has to be paid for the realisation of that value. And so the ending cannot be 'fine and grandiose' in quite the same way as Goethe would have intended in 1800. In the Prologue in Heaven the Lord had confidently, even blandly, asserted that though the devil might do his worst, Faust would win through in the end. So indeed it proves; but it needs a rather drastic intervention of heavenly grace to snatch Faust, literally, from the jaws of Hell. Mephistopheles, who in the course of the last two acts has come to appear rather less of a comedian and more of a traditional devil, finally stands revealed in the figure of the 'Nordic phantom' which he was so anxious to repudiate in the Witch's Kitchen, and summons up the hosts of Hell in all their various shapes and sizes – fat devils and thin ones, devils with straight horns and devils with curly ones – to help him seize Faust's soul. Just as in a medieval morality-play, performed on a stage divided into various 'mansions', Hell gapes at stage left, belching fire and brimstone, while hosts of angels enter from above right, strewing roses of heavenly love which burn Mephisto and his allies with unbearable pain (and inflame him with appropriately diabolical lust for the cherubs' chubby backsides). Faust's 'immortal part', as the stage direction calls it (l. 11933), is borne aloft by angels, acclaimed by mystical anchorites, welcomed by transfigured penitents – one of them, we are told, 'formerly known as Gretchen' (stage direction at l. 12069) – and escorted out of our sight under the benevolent gaze of the Mater Gloriosa. The love which had inspired Faust's first earthly adventure here returns to redeem him, perhaps, from the consequences of the others. Though Faust is saved rather than damned, the poem has formally returned to its origins in a matrix of Christian legend.

It is in fact grandiose in its mystery, although, or perhaps because, it is suffused with an irony lacking in Schiller's not totally dissimilar flirtation with Romantic neo-Catholicism at the end of *Die Jungfrau von Orleans*. And the Mater Gloriosa, here apostrophised as 'highest mistress of the world', is a figure on a different plane of poetic seriousness from the benign theatre-director–God of the Prologue in Heaven. Like Schiller, Goethe is using Christian imagery to convey what is not really a Christian meaning (and has been similarly castigated by both Christians and non-Christians for so doing). Faust regrets his association with the devil and seeks, unsuccessfully, to repudiate his aid; but there is no question, no mention even of the possibility, of his turning to God. The faith which sustains Faust from beginning to end, in which he never wavers even in those moments when he despairs of earthly life, and by virtue of which (if not exclusively because of which) he appears at the end to be saved, is in fact a faith in *himself* alone. But Faust's faith in himself corresponds to the faith expressed by the Lord in the Prologue in the essential goodness of his creation, and with it of man. Mephistopheles tells the Lord that he finds life on earth a thoroughly poor affair; he introduces himself to Faust as 'the spirit that denies' (l. 1338), as a nihilist who believes that all that exists deserves only to be destroyed; and he comments at the end of Faust's earthly life that '"finished" is as good as "never was"' (ll. 11600f), and that 'eternal emptiness' is to be preferred to the senseless and illusory round of existence. Such radical nihilism could only be denied, and Faust's salvation symbolically betokens its denial.

This does not mean that *Faust* does not deserve its designation 'tragedy', as Erich Heller argued.[4] Goethe affirms the value of life and human striving while fully recognising the tragic impermanence of all human achievement. Three times Faust believes that he is about to grasp eternity: in the consummation of his love for Gretchen, in his union with Helen, and in the creation of his colony on land reclaimed from the sea. Each time the belief is shown to be, if judged in literal terms, an illusion. Gretchen is abandoned and destroyed; Helen returns to the shadowy underworld from which she was conjured up; Faust himself sinks into the grave which his own diabolical workmen have dug for him. Faust's illusory achievements also bring suffering, death and destruction upon others. His love for Gretchen kills her, her mother, her brother and her child. Faust's colonial scheme can only be begun on the basis of ruthless military aggression, his technological triumphs achieved only at the price of human lives. Even the aesthetic experience of the Helen episode involves the imaginative acceptance of destructive violence, as Faust uses military force to protect Helen from her husband Menelaus. But in spite of all this, we are not allowed to believe that it would have been better for Faust never to have left the confines of his Gothic study – or, in the terms of the Prologue, for the Lord to have left man uncreated. Faust does indeed achieve what he had envisioned in that very first scene, just before the conjuration of the Earth Spirit:

> Courage I feel to face the world at last,
> In all earth's joys and sorrows to stand fast,
> In storms to nail my colours to the mast
> And not to falter in the shipwreck's blast! (ll.464ff)

In Goethe's treatment Faust has become a kind of Everyman. Naturally enough, as a figure of German origin and as the hero of the life's work of Germany's greatest poet, he has been seen as embodying – for good or ill – the essence of the German spirit; but if the work does seem at last to return to the Nordic origins from which it had sought to escape, it nevertheless remains far wider in intention and significance. The three great tragedies of Faust's life, assigned respectively to his (restored) youth, his manhood and his old age, symbolically encompass the whole range of human experience and endeavour: the realm of private, individual relationships and passions, the realm of artistic experience and creation, and the realm of public affairs and action in the outside world. But Faust is also, specifically, modern European man: a figure of the first Renaissance, re-created in the second, and living forward, with his creator, into the new and still unknown world of the nineteenth century. His career can be seen as demonstrating how the progressive realisation of the characteristic modern desire for 'life, liberty and the pursuit of happiness' leads inevitably to the transformation – intellectual, emotional, artistic, political, technological – of the whole world.

As has already been seen, *Faust* is formally and stylistically extremely complex and heterogeneous. The division into two parts marks a thematic and stylistic transition: Part I deals with private, Part II with public worlds, and there is between them a corresponding difference of register, of poetic and intellectual character, to which Goethe himself repeatedly drew attention. One would also expect some such difference from the mere fact that the second part was completed almost thirty years after the first. But the division into two parts was in origin only an expedient: it tells us more about the genesis of the work than about the structure and meaning of the completed text, and it has encouraged too many critics to look for more disunity and disparity than in fact there is. For many years, Part I having established itself in the general consciousness of the reading public (and given rise to sundry offspring in the realm of romantic opera), Part II was judged a failure or even 'an elaborate mistake',[5] or simply regarded with blank incomprehension. In the twentieth century, and particularly since 1945, the second part has come into its own with academic critics, who have traced the patterns of its symbolism with ever-increasing elaboration. Others have denied that the work has any unity of theme, of characterisation or of design, and have seen it as a mere collection of poetic fragments, indelibly marked with the irreconcilable characteristics of the different periods of Goethe's life at which they were written. Some attempts have, however, been made to see Goethe's design as the artistic whole which it surely is.

If we set aside the division into two parts, we can see the whole poem as containing three principal tragedies: the Gretchen tragedy of Faust's youth, the Helen tragedy of his manhood, and the colonial tragedy (the 'Herrschertragödie' or 'ruler's tragedy' as German

critics have called it) of his old age. These are set in an elaborate but
not incomprehensible framework. The inner frame is constituted by
the 'scholar's tragedy' of Part I, the pact with the devil, and a
number of later scenes bearing directly upon this, culminating of
course in the scene of Faust's death and Mephistopheles' final
discomfiture. To the Prologue in Heaven corresponds the final
scene, 'Mountain Chasms', in which Faust's soul is borne aloft;
before the whole stand the Dedication and the Prologue. It is, like
Schiller's *Wallenstein* trilogy, not simply a sequence of action but a
grand architectural composition which has to be appreciated, as it
were, spatially as well as in the linear way more generally characteristic of drama.[6] The 'fungoid growths' certainly stretched the
framework which Goethe had about 1800 devised to contain them.
They certainly caused the work to outgrow the dimensions of a
normal drama, but they did not destroy its essential shape or
proportions. These remain determined by that intellectual and
artistic framework devised by Goethe, in collaboration with
Schiller, at the height of their classical period.

Neo-classic drama, with its limitations, its unities and proprieties,
its austerity of stage presentation, Goethe's *Faust* certainly is not.
Nor is it really a character drama or chronicle play in the manner of
Shakespeare, the 'Nordic' genius, as conceived by the 'Stürmer und
Dränger'. But it is not totally unlike Marlowe's *Doctor Faustus*
(which Goethe appears, incidentally, not to have known before
1818), in which a loose sequence of episodic and masque-like scenes
is contained within a framework of conjuration, compact, death and
damnation – though Goethe's work has more internal structure and
proportion than Marlowe's. Much of it does indeed have the
character of masque or revue, evoking such diverse models and
analogies as the carnival plays of Hans Sachs, the Roman carnival
which made such a powerful impact on Goethe when he was in
Italy, the courtly *trionfi* of the Renaissance,[7] Goethe's own symbolical or allegorical masques like *Des Epimenides Erwachen*, and
modern satirical revue. In this *Faust* points both backwards and
forwards to a long theatrical tradition – albeit a very different one
from that of the mainstream of 'straight' literary drama from the
Renaissance to the 'well-made play' of nineteenth-century middle-
class realism.[8] These and other heterogeneous elements are often

presented in the form of self-conscious pastiche or even parody. Goethe had realised that Schiller was right in observing that the modern poet could no longer be 'naive'. He could not simply translate into the present the forms of the past, whether those of popular German tradition, as he had imagined in his 'Sturm und Drang' years, or those of classical antiquity, as he had later believed. The forms of art were subject to the same laws of growth and change as life itself. Indeed, Goethe cannot have failed to become aware of how the changing forms of his own artistic life – of his own youth, manhood and old age – had expressed themselves in the three principal episodes of the Faust drama: it had become a life's work in a unique sense, a unique kind of spiritual and artistic autobiography. And the essential modernity of *Faust* lies in the self-awareness with which these different artistic elements are combined. All this is formally summarised in the Helen tragedy of Act III: beginning in Greek trimeters, it moves through blank verse and rhymed exchanges to a final scene with full musical accompaniment, thus enacting before our eyes and ears the history of tragic drama from its origins in ancient Greece to its 'rebirth' (as Nietzsche was later to propound) in modern opera.

The operatic element in the mature Weimar theatrical style has already been touched upon. Goethe once in his later years expressed the wish that Mozart could have written music for *Faust*, in the style of *Don Giovanni*. (He was a conservative in musical taste too, and did not appreciate the radicalism of Beethoven.) Mention of opera also reminds us that the operatic, as opposed to what we generally regard as the 'straight' literary, stage was by no means unfamiliar with elaborate spectacle. It is often said that *Faust*, particularly Part II, pays no regard to the practical exigencies of the stage. But it would be more appropriate to regard the work as representing an imaginative extension of the possibilities which the Weimar stage had in fact possessed and which Goethe and Schiller had, as we have seen, sought to exploit during the years of their collaboration. In the light of what happened in 1817, it is unlikely that Goethe would have wished Mephistopheles on his first appearance to be played by a real poodle; on the other hand, Goethe was well acquainted with the enchanted menagerie of the *Magic Flute*, and would no doubt have been fascinated by the mechanical ingenuities with which Wagner

11  *Faust II* on the modern stage: the Euphorion scene in Act III at the Lyric Theatre, Hammersmith, 1988. The ladder-arch was a permanent feature of the set, of which (as here) much effective use was made; ... from Faust and Mephistopheles, the multitudinous other parts were all played by a team of five actors.

succeeded in giving physical embodiment to his supernatural imaginings at Bayreuth later in the century. (Wagner, for his part, speculated a great deal on how *Faust* might appropriately be staged.) In our own day a number of directors have essayed *Faust*, Part II, or even the whole work, using the still more highly developed technical resources of the modern theatre; it seems that at last Goethe's great dramatic vision is beginning to gain the theatrical acceptance which it richly deserves.

# CHAPTER IX

# A Prussian meteor: Heinrich von Kleist

In the Weimar theatre Goethe had attempted to follow the Horatian precept of mixing instruction, or improvement, with pleasure, giving the public some (but not too much) of what it wanted while trying to educate its taste to higher things. He also sought to discover and encourage congenial talent amongst the rising generation of German writers, the young men who were beginning to call themselves 'Romantics'. From the beginning, however, relations between Goethe and, particularly, Schiller and the Romantics were tense. In any case, these writers made no lasting original contribution to the German drama. The Schlegel brothers – August Wilhelm and Friedrich, nephews of the eighteenth-century playwright Johann Elias – are principally remembered as critics and literary theorists. In 1802 tragedies by both of them were performed at Weimar: August Wilhelm's *Ion*, an imitation of Euripides, and Friedrich's *Alarcos*, an 'honour tragedy' in the Spanish style, reflecting the increasing vogue for the drama of that country (the plot somewhat resembles that of Calderón's *El médico de su honra*). Their distinguished pedigrees notwithstanding, both works were disastrous failures, provoking such noisy ridicule (no doubt in part organised by the supporters of Kotzebue) that Goethe was forced to rise from his seat in the balcony to quell the uproar. Much more successful in their day, in Weimar and elsewhere, were the historical dramas of Zacharias Werner (1768–1823) and his 'fate tragedy' *Der 24. Februar*; but they are nowadays scarcely read and never performed. The same is true of sprawling, lyrico-dramatic legendary or pseudo-historical farragos like Ludwig Tieck's *Leben und Tod der heiligen Genoveva* (*Life and Death of St Genevieve*, 1799) or Clemens Brentano's *Die Gründung Prags* (*The Foundation of Prague*, 1814). Of considerably more interest is Tieck's fairy-tale comedy *Der gestiefelte Kater* (*Puss in Boots*, 1797), with its surrealistic treatment of the theatre and its blurring of the boundaries between role and actor, stage and audience; but this too found little favour at the time and has since fallen into general neglect, despite occasional revivals.

Though works such as these were probably not seriously intended for the stage, Tieck undoubtedly had a strong practical interest in the theatre. He later became one of the first to investigate the original conditions of performance of Shakespeare's plays, and played an important role as 'Dramaturg' or adviser to the Saxon court theatre in Dresden. He also presided over the completion of the one lasting monument of German Romanticism in the theatre, the 'Schlegel–Tieck' translation of Shakespeare's works. August Wilhelm Schlegel translated seventeen of Shakespeare's plays between 1797 and 1810; under Tieck's editorship, a revised version appeared from 1825 to 1833, with the remaining plays translated by Wolf Heinrich Graf Baudissin and by Tieck's daughter Dorothea. The Schlegel–Tieck Shakespeare soon supplanted all earlier versions, and despite the subsequent appearance of many other translations still holds its own as something of a German classic.[1]

The other great German poet of the age, Friedrich Hölderlin (1770–1843), stands apart both from Weimar classicism – though ancient Greece was one of the prime sources of his inspiration – and from Romanticism. In his lyrical tragedy *Der Tod des Empedokles* (*The Death of Empedocles*), on which he was working just before the turn of the century, he attempted to grapple with the same contemporary themes which were beginning to concern Goethe and Schiller at the same time – the conflict of the old order with the new, the need for regeneration, and the figure of the charismatic leader. He too adopted, as was natural to him, an elevated, poetic form, and he chose a subject from classical antiquity – the death of the ancient Greek philosopher, prophet and demagogue Empedocles, who had sacrificed himself by leaping into the crater of Mount Etna. Three fragmentary versions of the play, containing passages of great beauty and power, survive, together with a theoretical essay, the *Grund zum Empedokles* (*Foundation of Empedocles*), of fearsome intellectual complexity, in which Hölderlin seeks to relate the drama to the movement of history. But Hölderlin was unable to give his work convincing dramatic shape. The death of Empedocles seems undoubtedly to have a kind of poetic or even philosophical inevitability, but it was necessary to find a comprehensible dramatic motivation for it; the three successive versions approach the problem in different ways, but evidently none of them satisfied Hölderlin, for he abandoned work on the drama about 1800 and returned to lyric poetry. Soon afterwards he succumbed to the insanity which enveloped the remaining forty years of his life.[2]

There was, however, one writer of uniquely dramatic genius among Goethe and Schiller's younger contemporaries. He was personally acquainted with some of the Romantics and shared some of their characteristic preoccupations, but in his work as in his life he remained, like Hölderlin, essentially a solitary figure. Today he is regarded as one of the greatest German dramatists, though in his life-time his work met largely with indifference, incomprehension and hostility. Heinrich von Kleist was born in 1777 into an old aristocratic Pomeranian–Prussian family which for generations had supplied officers to the Prussian army. At least one member of the family had, however, also achieved literary fame, the melancholy soldier-poet Ewald Christian von Kleist, friend of Lessing and part-model for Lessing's Tellheim, who died as a result of wounds received at the battle of Kunersdorf in 1759. Heinrich was also destined for a military career, and entered the army at sixteen; but seven years later he resigned his lieutenant's commission to devote himself to the study of literature, philosophy and science. In 1800–1 he suffered what is commonly referred to as his 'Kant crisis', when his reading of contemporary German philosophy destroyed his belief in the sense and order of the universe, or at any rate in its accessibility to human reason and understanding. The reverberations of this intellectual shock are evident in the plays and short stories which he produced in the remaining few years of his life. In May 1807 Goethe read his comedy *Amphitryon* and described it as 'the strangest of signs of the times, a portentous and displeasing meteor in a new literary heaven'. His dislike of *Amphitryon* notwithstanding, Goethe accepted Kleist's other comedy *Der zerbrochne Krug* (*The Broken Jug*) for performance at Weimar the following year. But the performance was a failure, and Goethe rejected Kleist's tragedy *Penthesilea* as unplayable. Kleist's career was indeed meteoric. In 1811 he made a suicide pact with a young woman suffering from inoperable cancer and, on the shores of the Wannsee just outside Berlin, shot her and himself. He was suffering from no comparable physical malady, but 'the truth was', as he wrote in his last letter of farewell to his half-sister Ulrike, 'that there was no helping me in this world'.

Kleist began his career as a playwright with a bloodthirsty tragedy, *Die Familie Schroffenstein* (*The Schroffenstein Family*, 1803) – originally conceived with a Spanish setting, perhaps reflecting the general interest in Spanish drama at the time, but translated to Swabia in its final published version. Another tragedy, *Robert Guiskard, Herzog der Normänner* (*Robert Guiscard, Duke of the Normans*), was apparently completed soon after this, but in October 1803, in one of his many crises of depression and self-doubt, Kleist destroyed the manuscript, though he later rewrote or reconstructed the opening scenes and published them as a fragment. The years 1806–8 saw the completion of no less than five plays, some of which at least must have been germinating in his mind in the intervening period: the two comedies and the tragedy *Penthesilea*, already mentioned, the spectacular medieval extravaganza ('großes historisches Ritterschauspiel' or 'grand historical chivalric play') *Das Käthchen von Heilbronn, oder die Feuerprobe* (*Kate of Heilbronn, or the Ordeal by Fire*), and the patriotic drama *Die Hermannsschlacht* (*The Battle of Hermann*). His final masterpiece, *Prinz Friedrich von Homburg*, was completed in the year of his death, though with *Die Hermannsschlacht* it had to wait another ten years for publication. The plays have all received a bewildering diversity of interpretations, more violently conflicting than in the case of almost any other playwright: plainly they are exploratory dramatisations of the profound uncertainties and contradictory apprehensions of life experienced by their creator, but they seem to reach no definitive conclusion. Critics have tried to trace a thematic or philosophical development in them,[3] but this seems a doubtful enterprise, particularly since they were all conceived and composed within the same short span of years. Kleist went through no definable stylistic evolution, as did Goethe and Schiller in their separate but parallel developments from 'Sturm und

Drang' to classicism; and he seems to have felt little or no need to theorise, as in particular Schiller did, about his dramatic intentions. His work certainly shows an advance in stylistic mastery, but even this is not without its lapses and regressions.

Kleist's 'Kant crisis' was probably no sudden reversal of firmly held beliefs, but the culmination of a process of steadily mounting doubt and despair. His temperament was one of extreme intensity, aggravated by what appears to have been a powerful, but heavily repressed sexuality. He was a man satisfied with nothing but absolutes. Even the outward course of his biography is not without its mysteries, and his inner life is ultimately as inaccessible as that of his most characteristic protagonists. As a Prussian, indeed a member of the Prussian ruling class, he was also more keenly exposed to the turmoil of those 'high, momentous times' than were Goethe and Schiller in provincial Weimar. Schiller's words in the *Wallenstein* Prologue of the crumbling of the old order had proved even truer than he could have anticipated in 1798. The Napoleonic tide flowed over the whole of central Europe and engulfed all the German states. Prussia, chief of the northern states and from the mid-eighteenth century apparently the rising power in Germany, collapsed after the battle of Jena in 1806, to be followed in due course by Austria, the traditional political leader of the 'German nation'. Kleist's world was a world in chaos, both without and within. And philosophy could offer no certainty to counter it. Kant taught that we live in a world of sensory manifestations or 'phenomena' ('Erscheinungen'); our minds impose order on these phenomena and assume behind them a stable world of 'noumena' or things as they 'really' are ('Dinge an sich'), but the latter are and remain of necessity totally inaccessible to us. Kant's 'critical' philosophy aimed to establish the limits of reason in order to put a stop to what he regarded as unprofitable speculation about what lay beyond those limits – the 'illusions of metaphysics', as he called them. But Kleist interpreted this philosophy (or its more radical development in the work of Fichte) as meaning that the phenomenal world accessible to our senses and our understanding is nothing but an illusion ('Schein'), a fabric of essentially misleading appearances behind which lies a reality ('Sein') of a totally different kind. This reality may at any time break in upon our illusory world with irresistible disruptive force.

Schiller had been drawn to Kant's moral and aesthetic philosophy, to his doctrines of the moral autonomy of man, of sublimity, and of the high seriousness of art which mediates between the sensory and the moral world, between the realms of 'nature' and 'freedom'. In his theoretical essays he had worked out his own reformulations of Kantian doctrine, and in his plays he had sought to present, in forms of appropriate dignity and elevation, the struggles of characters faced with momentous moral decisions. Kleist's concerns are more basic and elemental. Rarely do his characters rise above the reality which confronts them: often it is more than they can do merely to understand their own destinies and to come to some kind of terms with the unknown powers which control them. In Schiller as in Kleist we encounter the opposition of 'Schein' and 'Sein', of illusion and reality, but for Schiller as for Kant the nature of reality is, if not indubitable, confidently to be assumed for practical or moral purposes; if his characters are the victims of illusion it is usually because they deceive themselves. Kleist's characters live in a world which is deception itself, and reality is for them radically unknowable. They are beset with riddles and confusions, with misleading evidence, with the shattering of the assumptions upon which their lives are based. Nor can they rise above their circumstances with Schillerian sublimity, for the unknowable powers which rule their lives may always intervene – fate or apparent chance, arbitrary human authorities or mythical gods whose benevolence, unlike that of the gods in *Iphigenie auf Tauris*, cannot be assumed, still less guaranteed. 'It cannot be an evil spirit', Kleist wrote to a friend in August 1806, 'that presides over the world, it is only one we do not comprehend.' But the reassurance rings hollow. More characteristic is the note struck by Sylvester's anguished plea in *Die Familie Schroffenstein*:

> God of justice!
> Speak clear to man, that he may see and know
> What he must do! (v, i)

*Schroffenstein* is a family tragedy of intrigue and revenge. With its pervading atmosphere of illusion, deception, suspicion, and hideous retributive violence, it is perhaps the most 'Jacobean' of German tragedies. The two branches of the Schroffenstein family, Rossitz and Warwand, are locked in deadly feud. A gleam of peace and reconciliation appears in the love of Ottokar, son of Rupert of Rossitz, and Agnes, daughter of Sylvester of Warwand; but this love, needless to say, is doomed. In a cave in the forest, Ottokar and Agnes exchange clothes in token of the merging of their identities in love. But they are discovered and killed by their fathers – each killing his own child in mistake for the other's. A blind man, a witch and a madman reveal the truth. In the closing lines of the play, Ottokar's crazy half-brother Johann describes the whole action as a satanic conjuring trick on the part of the witch Ursula:

> Away with you, old witch. You conjure well.
> I'm satisfied with your performance. Go.     (v, i, end)

The description is apt: by classical standards *Die Familie Schroffenstein* is not so much a tragedy as a kind of grisly farce. Indeed, it is reported that when Kleist first read the work to a group of friends, he and they alike were seized with hysterical laughter, and the reading had to be abandoned. Some of the crudities may be excused, like those of *Die Räuber*, as natural in the work of a young writer who has yet to learn artistic discipline. But very similar elements of violence and excess are apparent in Kleist's other completed tragedy, *Penthesilea*, together with a similar pattern of oppositions and a plot-mechanism similarly founded upon misunderstanding, deception and illusion – even though all this is here submitted to a rigid classical discipline in external form. The subject-matter is also, of course, classical in provenance, the love of the Greek hero Achilles and the Amazon queen Penthesilea. The vision of ancient Greece which we are offered here is, however, to use the terms later coined by Nietzsche, very much a 'Dionysian' rather than an 'Apolline' one: not the Winckelmannian 'noble simplicity and calm grandeur' of *Iphigenie auf Tauris*, but the dark savagery of Euripides' *Bacchae*.

It is not surprising that Goethe was horrified by it. He may even have thought (for there are obvious echoes of his *Iphigenie* in the work) that Kleist was trying deliberately to 'revoke' his own humanitarian message, rather as the composer Adrian Leverkühn, in Thomas Mann's *Doktor Faustus*, sets out to 'revoke' the humanitarian optimism of Beethoven's Ninth Symphony. At all events,

*Penthesilea* (written seventeen years before the Ninth Symphony, and at about the time when Beethoven was working on *Fidelio*, another eloquent celebration of the triumph of humanity) seems to offer little hope or comfort, save the ecstasy of the very passion which proves its own destruction. As in *Die Familie Schroffenstein* Kleist presents two groups of characters in conflict – here, Greeks and Amazons – and two individuals whose love seems to transcend the enmity of their nations. But Achilles and Penthesilea are destroyed not by that national enmity as such, nor by the conflict which arises between the two of them as individuals and their duty to their respective nations, but by the intensity and the paradoxical nature of the irresistible force which draws them together, and in which love and hate, tenderness and extreme violence, the desire to possess and the desire to destroy, are inextricably combined. The battle of the sexes, embodied in the war of Greek against Amazon, serves as background to the inner conflict of sexuality itself. A series of encounters, complicated by deceptions and misunderstandings, reaches a horrific climax when Penthesilea, enraged at her latest supposed humiliation by Achilles, challenges him to single combat, sets her dogs on him and joins them in tearing him limb from limb. (In the myth as usually related, it was Achilles who killed Penthesilea.) When she realises what she has done, she resolves to join him in death: she takes farewell of her people, renouncing the Amazon state and its sacred laws, and, in a conclusion as extraordinary as what has led up to it, kills herself – not with any real weapon, but with a visionary dagger forged, as she describes it, from the hammered passions of her own breast.

Both Kleist's tragedies, despite the violence of their content, are constructed with great formal care and symmetry. We have already observed their similar use of opposed blocks of characters; but this underlying pattern is given totally different scenic form in the two plays. In *Die Familie Schroffenstein* the scene changes frequently between Rossitz, Warwand and the open countryside where the lovers meet, and as in *Die Räuber* or *Maria Stuart* the different scenes are associated with different characters. In *Penthesilea* a single, unchanged setting is occupied by Greeks and Amazons in turn as the tide of battle surges back and forth across the stage, in a kind of Dionysian equivalent of the Apolline choreography of Goethe's

*Iphigenie*. *Die Familie Schroffenstein* is divided into the usual five acts; *Penthesilea*, in authentically Greek fashion, has no act-divisions (there are occasional 'choric' effects too, though nothing as systematic or deliberate as in *Die Braut von Messina*) and the twenty-four scenes ('Auftritte') are marked only by entrances and exits. Yet it seems intended to be no less spectacular in the theatre than *Schroffenstein*. Though most of the actual battle scenes take place offstage and are reported or narrated to us, Kleist also calls for such striking visual effects as the appearance of Achilles in his chariot with horses, the pursuit of Greeks by Amazons in a hail of arrows, and Penthesilea setting out for her final encounter with Achilles accompanied by dogs, elephants and scythed chariots, with the dogs howling and the thunder rolling in sympathy. Both plays also exhibit a remarkable combination of violence and control in their language. From the beginning Kleist writes in blank verse,[4] but in a verse very different from the polished instruments of the classical Goethe and Schiller. With its roughness, its frequent enjambements, breaks and pauses, and changes of speaker in mid-line, which seem at times designed purposely to disrupt its verse structure, it is technically speaking more like Lessing's blank verse in *Nathan der Weise*, though the techniques are applied to a totally different expressive purpose. There is also, in *Penthesilea* in particular, a tortuousness of syntax and word-order which seems partly intended actually to imitate the surface structure of ancient Greek, praised by Lessing in *Laokoon* for its expressive superiority to German in this respect. Whether this is so or not, such language is supremely dramatic, or 'gestural' ('gestisch'), to use the word favoured by Brecht. It is also essentially poetic, if rarely (though on occasion) self-consciously lyrical: meaning is sought and grasped *in* language, even at times wrested *from* it, rather than pre-formed in thought and then expressed *through* language, as is often the case, for example, with the more rhetorical Schiller.

If in the case of *Die Familie Schroffenstein* we may feel inclined to make allowances for a beginner, in *Penthesilea* the polarities have become not less but more exaggerated, the violence even more extreme. It is beyond doubt a *tour de force* of amazing virtuosity, in which Kleist has welded together various stylistic elements, some of ancient Greek and some of more modern provenance, with what often looks like reckless daring. He steers a perilous course between the sublime and the grotesque, between poetic intensity and bathos. Ultimately, as with *Die Räuber*, the sheer power of the work compels us to ignore or to forgive its imperfections.

Savage violence is also present, in what may seem even less readily forgivable form, in the patriotic drama *Die Hermannsschlacht*, in which Kleist strikes again a note both atavistically primitive and (more disturbingly) prophetically modern. We seem here to be even further removed from the triumph of humanity. The work can indeed be seen as deliberately anti-classical in more senses than one. The defeat of the Romans by Hermann (Arminius) in AD 9 had already been dramatised by J. E. Schlegel and by Klopstock, in the course of the eighteenth-century quest for patriotic subject-matter; but once again a historical subject had acquired a new topical urgency, now that Germany was under the domination of Napoleon and the Roman rhetoric of the Revolution was being pressed into the service of the recently proclaimed French Empire. Kleist's play seems to have been intended to appeal directly to a German patriotism of the kind which Goethe (cosmopolitan and admirer of Napoleon) had explicitly repudiated. He hoped to have it performed in Vienna, to encourage the Austrians to stand firm against Napoleon and to assume the leadership of Germany after the collapse of his own native Prussia; but after the Austrian defeat at Wagram in July 1809 all such hopes were dashed. Schlegel and Klopstock in their Hermann dramas had depicted the German tribesmen as 'noble savages' in the eighteenth-century style, exemplars of manly uprightness and simplicity. Kleist's Hermann, however, lures the Romans to their defeat by treachery and deceit, angrily repudiating their claims to superior civilisation, refusing to obey the 'rules' for the proper treatment of prisoners-of-war and hurling them back in the face of his captive Septimius:

> You say you know what right is, cursed villain,
> And came to Germany all unprovoked,
> Here to oppress us?
> – Go, take a club of double weight,
> Beat him to death! (v, xiii)

The play includes other shock effects, some of them almost anticipating those of Howard Brenton's *Romans in Britain*. Kleist's play is a disturbing document in the evolution of modern nationalism; but if it is itself fiercely, even rabidly nationalistic, it is also (like Brenton's) anti-imperialist – Germany being at the time the victim, and not yet even capable of being the perpetrator, of imperialistic aggression. And perhaps too there is something tragic, or potentially so, about Kleist's Hermann, triumphant though he appears at the end of the play, something in his lonely fanaticism of the 'raging melancholy' of Lessing's Prince Philotas, or of the hubris of the charismatic war-lord who dreams of his own imperial mission, like Wallenstein or like Guiskard, the hero of Kleist's own abandoned tragedy of hubristic ambition. The play has rarely been seen on the German stage since 1945; but Claus Peymann's production at Bochum in 1982 sought to bring out these and other undertones which sound beneath its apparent chauvinism.

Kleist's most superficial and least disciplined play is *Das Käthchen von Heilbronn*, but this romantic fairy-tale has nevertheless been one of his most popular and successful works on the stage. Nor does it lack authentically Kleistian features. Kleist described its heroine as the polar opposite of Penthesilea, related to her as are plus and minus in algebra: a woman who pursues her love in total devotion and submission, even when spurned and threatened with violence. Her rival for the love of the hero, Graf Wetter vom Strahl (Count Storm-and-Lightning) is the wicked Kunigunde, a hideous enchantress disguised by cosmetic witchcraft as a beautiful young woman. On briefly glimpsing Kunigunde unadorned, the hero enquires of her maid,

> Who was that strange lady
> Who passed us now, just like the Tower of Pisa? (v, v)

But he persists in his misguided affection for Kunigunde until it is revealed that not she but Käthchen is the Emperor's daughter whom he is destined to wed. All this is played out against a colourful romantic medieval background of forests and castles, with secret courts meeting in underground caves, a castle destroyed by fire with the heroine escorted through the flames by an angel, and a dream-vision narrated by Käthchen as she lies asleep beneath an elder-bush. In a spectacular final tableau the mysterious truth is at last revealed, and Wetter and Käthchen are betrothed before the Emperor as music plays, bells ring and Kunigunde impotently swears 'plague, death and revenge'. It is Kleist's most operatic work, and seems at times to sound a note almost of self-parody. Goethe is said to have criticised its forced, unnatural character and the 'hypochondria' or pathological streak which it revealed in its creator – qualities which Goethe described as typically 'Nordic'. Again the adjective is for the Goethe of 1810 no longer the term of commendation which it is, for example, in the Shakespeare essay of 1771. *Käthchen* is, of course, one of the Romantic progeny of *Götz von Berlichingen*, a progeny which Goethe was in his later years at pains to disown. It can also be seen, like *Götz* itself, as a nostalgic evocation of the vanished order of the medieval German Empire.

All these works in their different ways reveal Kleist's predilection for the extreme and the bizarre. But in his best works extremism yields to a subtle, elusive blend, an often precarious balance of paradoxical elements. Remarkably, though Kleist can perhaps be said to have possessed a more authentically or thoroughgoingly tragic view of life than any of the other dramatists we have so far considered, none of his greatest plays (unless we include *Penthesilea*) actually ends tragically. Indeed, apart from the fairy-tale happy ending of *Käthchen* and the dubious nationalistic triumph of *Die Hermannsschlacht*, he wrote two plays which are actually designated comedies, and his final drama ('Schauspiel') *Prinz Friedrich von Homburg* again ends on a note of apparent triumph and apotheosis. All these works do indeed skirt the brink of tragedy, and disturbing questions remain unanswered to darken the optimistic or conciliatory tone of their conclusions. Their avoidance of tragic bloodshed may, however, be considered a sign not only of the range and variety of Kleist's talent, but also of superior artistic self-discipline.

*Der zerbrochne Krug* is generally regarded as one of the few great or classic German comedies, with witty dialogue, a teasing and amusing basic situation, and a memorable central comic character whom we can laugh both at and with. It is a courtroom drama, set in a humble Dutch milieu which is designed to recall the homely, even earthy realism of Dutch painting. It begins with Licht, the clerk to the village magistrate Adam, finding his master lamenting certain

mysterious injuries – a sprained foot and wounds about the head –
together with the loss of his wig:

LICHT Why, what the devil, tell me, Master Adam!
    What has become of you? How do you look?
ADAM Yes, look! To stumble, all you need is feet;
    Here on this plain smooth floor, is there a stump?
    I stumbled here; for every one of us
    Bears his own stumbling-block about with him.
LICHT No, tell me, friend! You say each bears his block –
ADAM About with him!
LICHT              Be damned!
ADAM                    What do you say?
LICHT You had a wild old ancestor, you know,
    Who fell like that, when first the world was made,
    And earned a reputation by his fall;
    You're sure you've not – ?
ADAM              What?
LICHT                 Likewise – ?
ADAM                       I? I tell you – !
    Believe you me, here was the place I fell.
LICHT Not figuratively?
ADAM           Figuratively, no.
    It was no pretty figure that I cut.           (Scene i)

But as the action unfolds from the barbed exchanges of this opening,
it soon becomes apparent that the old Adam has been up to no good,
and that we are indeed witnessing a kind of burlesque re-enactment
of that original Fall, of the temptation of Adam by Eve – or, as it
seems here, of the temptation of Eve (daughter of Frau Marthe,
owner of the eponymous jug) by Adam. And when Marthe brings a
suit before Adam for compensation for the breakage of her jug, the
judge is trying a case in which he himself is the guilty party. Adam
sets about using the machinery of justice not for its ostensible
purpose, to bring the truth to light, but to try to hide it; only the
chance intervention of the visiting Judge Walter ensures that Adam's
purposes are foiled, his guilt and Eve's innocence established, and
Eve and her fiancé Ruprecht reconciled and reunited. At the end
only Marthe is left unsatisfied, still bemoaning the loss of her jug:
object of sublime beauty, priceless family heirloom, document of
Dutch history –

Here, right upon this hole, where now there's nothing,
All the United Provinces were handed down
To Philip, King of Spain. Here in his robes
Of state stood Charles the Fifth, the Emperor;
Now nothing but the legs of him is left.
Here Philip knelt, and took from him the crown;
He's fallen through, except his hinder parts,
And even they have taken quite a knock . . .          (Scene vii)

– symbol of Eve's innocence, or even of a whole shattered Kleistian world – or perhaps at last only a jug after all. Adam dominates the proceedings not only verbally, with his constant stream of lies and blusterings, of threats and ingenious excuses, but also as a physical presence, from his bald head (bereft of the wig which would have given it the semblance of judicial dignity, but which has been left hanging in the bushes outside Eve's window) to the club-foot which recalls not only the devil, but also Oedipus the swollen-footed, another judge who was condemned to preside over the revelation of his own guilt. He is an uncouth and threatening presence, but for all his villainy a richly comic and even sympathetic figure, a veritable Lord of Misrule. Kleist has constructed his play skilfully around this dominating central figure. The play raises familiar Kleistian issues – of truth and illusion, of trust between human beings as their only hope of avoiding error, of the imperfection of human institutions such as the law. The conclusion is not one of unqualified optimism – the reconciliation of the lovers has a bitter taste, Adam may yet return to continue his misdeeds, and the jug is still broken. But for all this, *Der zerbrochne Krug* affirms the traditional wisdom of comedy – that to seek perfection in this imperfect world is to invite disaster. It is a highly accomplished dramatic creation; and with its economical composition, its rigorous observance of the unities (like *Penthesilea*, it has no act-divisions, but unfolds in a single unbroken sequence of scenes) and its employment of blank verse, Kleist demonstrates that comedy no less than tragedy can aspire to the formal perfection of classical drama.

Kleist's other comedy, *Amphitryon*, is doubly classical in intention: not only is the subject taken from Graeco-Roman mythology, but, as the subtitle 'A Comedy after Molière' proclaims, it is closely modelled upon a work by the greatest comic playwright in the

European neo-classic tradition. Much of Kleist's play is in fact translated directly from Molière's *Amphitryon* of 1668, though he substitutes the uniform discipline of blank verse throughout for Molière's varied rhyming verse. But he makes a number of significant changes, ranging from slight textual modifications to the insertion of whole new scenes, including a new finale, which shift the emphasis of the work considerably. The subject is one with a long history in dramatic literature, from classical antiquity to the twentieth century, when it has been treated by Jean Giraudoux (*Amphitryon 38*, 1929) and by the East German playwright Peter Hacks (1968). Zeus or Jupiter, king of the gods, takes on the shape of Alkmene's husband Amphitryon and makes love to her, knowing that she is too pure to yield to any temptation of infidelity. If the cuckolding of Amphitryon has comic possibilities, the deception of the virtuous Alkmene is at least potentially tragic; and if Molière stresses the former aspect, Kleist brings out the latter, developing Alkmene's character far more than Molière had done and making the testing of her feelings, of her love and loyalty to her husband, the focus of his play. In doing so he has stretched the limits of comedy much further than in *Der zerbrochne Krug*.

The plot is, of course, a comedy of errors; and as in Shakespeare's play of that name, we have two pairs of characters of indistinguishable physical appearance, in each case a master and a servant – the 'lower' characters re-enacting the 'serious' plot at a more basic, farcical level. Here we have the added piquancy that the 'double' is in each case a god, deliberately imitating his human counterpart. Jupiter takes on the likeness of Amphitryon, Mercury that of Amphitryon's servant Sosias. Amusing though this may be for the audience with its detached overview, for the person thus cheated of his identity it is, of course, no joke. Mercury simply forces the wretched Sosias to hand over his identity by threats and violence; Jupiter, more insidiously, not only makes love to Amphitryon's wife, but forces her to choose between him and her husband and to declare, confronted with the two of them, that it is Jupiter who really 'is' Amphitryon. And in doubting her husband's identity, she comes perilously close to losing her own. The problem of identity is one which occurs elsewhere in Kleist's work (notably in some of his short stories, where the motif of the 'Doppelgänger' or double is again employed). Molière treats it in a more straightforwardly comic manner; though here too philosophical undertones have been detected, for his play has been interpreted as a burlesque on the philosophy of Descartes – one of the ancestors of that Kantian theory of knowledge which had so disturbed Kleist.[5] Descartes had taught that in order to attain certain knowledge of the world, we had to assume (though we could not prove) the existence of a truthful God (a 'Dieu véridique') rather than of an evil spirit ('mauvais génie') who deceives our senses with illusory impressions. And Kleist himself had written that 'it cannot be an evil spirit who presides over the world, it is only one we do not comprehend'. But if his Jupiter is not positively malign, his capricious intervention in the lives of his mortal creatures is all the more disturbing because his motives are inscrutable: a mixture, it seems, of genuine love for Alkmene, of jealousy of Amphitryon, and of the desire to show the mortals his omnipotence, to expose the human self-sufficiency of their love as an illusion, and so to teach them a lesson (the phrase may literally imply enlightenment, but also suggests punishment for their presumption). Kleist's most important additions to Molière's play are two scenes of intense cross-examination of Alkmene by Jupiter, in which riddles are answered with riddles as Alkmene struggles to preserve her own integrity in a situation increasingly incomprehensible to her, and the final scene in which she is forced to choose between her husband and the god (in Molière's play, Alcmène does not appear in the last act at all). She chooses the god, as she must; but Amphitryon himself now saves the situation by a moving affirmation of his faith in her absolute purity and fidelity. The god at last reveals his identity and the mortals prostrate themselves before him, before he returns to Olympus and they are left to themselves again; but Alkmene can utter nothing but a sigh ('Ach!'), a brief, mysterious syllable with which the play ends. It has been variously interpreted as an expression of joy, of relief, of bewilderment, of horror, of despair; and Kleist's 'comedy after Molière' has correspondingly been described as 'serious comedy', as tragi-comedy, even as tragedy. It is a rare blend of tenderness and cruelty, of farce, philosophical wit, and profound emotion. The mysterious poignancy of its ending makes all traditional generic labels inadequate.

Kleist's last play, *Prinz Friedrich von Homburg*, is the summation of all his dramatic work, and almost all his favourite themes and motifs are combined in it. As in *Die Familie Schroffenstein*, we witness a complex action with repeated reversals and changes of fortune, in which characters act precipitately upon the flimsiest of evidence. As in *Penthesilea* (and *Guiskard*) the protagonist is a military leader seemingly at odds with the national community whose spirit he nevertheless seems to embody in his own person. As in *Das Käthchen von Heilbronn*, we have a fairy-tale in which dream proves truer than apparent reality; as in *Die Hermannsschlacht*, a patriotic history play which for all its apparent nationalistic fervour goes far beyond this in its deeper meanings; and as in *Amphitryon*, a mysterious relationship between a mortal protagonist (the Prince) and a superior authority (the Elector of Brandenburg) who, if not divine, has a number of divine attributes including a degree (to be paradoxical) of omnipotence. Like *Amphitryon*, the play ends with the protagonist seemingly triumphant, but bewildered and inwardly disoriented. And as in *Der zerbrochne Krug*, the outcome hinges upon a juridical question – though here it is not the judge who is the guilty party, but the guilty one who is made his own judge. All this is presented with extraordinary terseness and economy, for *Homburg* is the shortest of Kleist's completed plays – five acts, with eleven changes of scene, taking up less than 2,000 lines of blank verse, shorter than the one-act *Krug* and not much more than half the length of *Penthesilea*. (It is shorter even than the classically simple *Iphigenie auf Tauris*, and less than half as long as *Maria Stuart*.)

Kleist takes his subject from another episode in German history when national forces rallied to defeat a foreign invader – the defeat of the Swedes by the 'Great Elector' Frederick William of Brandenburg at the battle of Fehrbellin in 1685. During the battle Prince Frederick of Hessen-Homburg earned the Elector's displeasure by charging without waiting for the order to do so, but was pardoned on account of his patriotic zeal and his contribution to the victory. In Kleist's play, however, the Elector actually has the Prince court-martialled and sentenced to death for insubordination, and only pardons him at the very last minute before execution, after pleas and protests verging upon mutiny from his other officers and from his niece the Princess Natalia – but also after having obtained from the

Prince himself the recognition that his condemnation was just. The Prince is portrayed as a visionary, lost to the world in romantic dreams of love and military glory. We see him first in a somnambulistic trance, weaving himself a victor's laurel wreath in the garden of the Elector's palace at night; then preoccupied and absent-minded, failing to listen to his orders at the briefing before the battle; dashing into the fight, returning triumphant, then dumbfounded when the Elector orders his arrest; reduced to a pitiful wreck, trembling with physical fear at the prospect of death; then regaining his self-possession and courage, facing his execution with equanimity and even joy, resolved (rather like Melville's Billy Budd) to die for the greater glory of the law, his country and his commander. But if the Prince's progress is clearly charted for us, the role of the Elector is more mysterious. Some interpreters of the play have seen him as an ideal ruler, all-wise and benevolent, systematically educating the headstrong young Prince to a true, almost Kantian, sense of duty, and resolved all along to pardon him in the end. Others, however, have seen him in a more problematic light, as capricious, arbitrary, jealous of the younger man's fame and glory and of the love he sees growing between him and Princess Natalia; on this reading the play depicts not a process of education but an Oedipal conflict in which the younger man struggles to assert his own autonomy against the jealous anger of the older one, who ultimately gives way only because he is forced to. Kleist probably did see the Elector as the representative of an ideal, whether as ruler or father-figure, but the relationship between him and his subordinates remains ultimately as mysterious as that between Jupiter and the mortals in *Amphitryon*. In the final scene, set like the first in the palace garden at night, the Prince is spared before the very muzzles of the firing-squad; he faints – like Alkmene when Jupiter reveals his identity – and recovers consciousness to a storm of acclamation, with cannon firing a salute, a march playing and the palace, as if by magic, illuminated in the background. He seems bewildered, but his old friend Colonel Kottwitz seeks to reassure him:

KOTTWITZ Salute the Prince of Homburg!
THE OFFICERS                           Hail! Hail! Hail!
ALL The victor on the field of Fehrbellin!

(*A moment's silence*)
HOMBURG No, speak, is it a dream?
KOTTWITZ                          A dream, what else?
SEVERAL OFFICERS To battle!
COUNT TRUCHSS                 To the field!
FIELD MARSHAL                              To victory!
ALL Death to all enemies of Brandenburg!                    ˙ (v, xi, end)

The Prince's dream, with which the play began, has, it seems, proved truer than the intervening reality of arrest and condemnation. If the dénouement of *Die Familie Schroffenstein* was a satanic conjuring trick, that of *Prinz Friedrich von Homburg* is a sublime one, even if we remain ultimately unconvinced of the benignity of the magician who performs it. In Peter Stein's production at the Schaubühne in Berlin in 1972, both the intensity and the fragility of the dream-vision were strikingly conveyed. The Prince who was carried off shoulder-high by the officers was only a dummy, and the real Prince was left alone on the stage in a trance, as in the opening scene: we were back, it seemed, exactly where we had started.[6]

The note of patriotism is also, as we see, sounded strongly in the play and echoes loudly at its conclusion. Kleist may well have intended the work principally as a patriotic rallying call, a plea for national reawakening and resistance to the foreign oppressor, even an appeal to the over-cautious Prussian king Frederick William III to sever the ties that bound him to Napoleon and to risk the political upheavals that a national uprising might bring in its wake. (Kleist wished to dedicate the play to Princess Amalia of Hessen-Homburg, the King's sister-in-law and a descendant of its hero, but the dedication was refused.) But it has many other layers of meaning – metaphysical, psychological, even autobiographical. In the romantic figure of the Prince – soldier and visionary, whose dreams could perhaps find their ultimate fulfilment only in death – there is undoubtedly much of Kleist himself. No one had sought more ardently than he to rouse the nation with his art, to win fame and acclamation, to be rewarded with the victor's laurel crown. And in the work's technical mastery, as well as in the numerous unmistakable echoes of the recognised masterpieces of the German drama of its day – of *Egmont* and *Tasso*, of *Wallenstein* and of *Maria Stuart* – and

12  Kleist's *Prinz Friedrich von Homburg* on the modern stage. Peter Stein's production at the Schaubühne, Berlin 1972: the opening scene, with the Elector (right) observing the sleepwalking Prince with his laurel wreath.

of other models such as *Measure for Measure* or Calderón's *Life is a Dream*, we can see Kleist staking and proving his claim to rank with the acknowledged masters, to rank with Goethe or to take the place which Schiller's death had left vacant beside him.[7]

The play also represents the summation of Kleist's stagecraft. Its concision has already been noted. Within a brief compass Kleist presents a great deal of action, both outward and inward: the battle of Fehrbellin and its aftermath, the inner evolution of the Prince and the unfolding of his relationship with the Elector, the turmoil of the army, the threatened mutiny and its suppression. There is much varied spectacle: the torchlit opening and closing scenes in the garden, the presentation of the captured Swedish standards, the final gathering of the whole court and army. The actual battle takes place offstage, but is vividly re-created for us in the excited commentaries of the watching generals, as well as in the noise and smoke of the artillery. The language encompasses a great variety of tone, and the verse ranges from characteristically Kleistian broken lines and 'gestural' speech to set-pieces of considerable eloquence, including monologues (a rarity in Kleist's work) for both the Prince and the Elector. Full and elaborate stage directions show that Kleist has truly conceived his work in the three dimensions of theatrical space. Even the dialogue has spatial depth: to most remarkable effect in the briefing scene in Act I, with its different groups of characters – the officers taking down their orders, the Elector with his wife and niece preparing for their departure, and the distracted Prince in between – all following their own separate courses, rather like the three simultaneous stage bands in *Don Giovanni*. The rhythm of blank verse is maintained, yet the speech is convincingly colloquial; words and actions, and the interplay between them, convey a great deal of important information; the scene has great tension, but also a strong admixture of comedy. There is nothing more intensely dramatic, or quintessentially theatrical, in all the plays of Goethe or Schiller.

Goethe, however, claimed to find Kleist's work not only displeasing but unplayable. He did make some effort to understand and even to encourage the young rival whose work so plainly represented a new and alien world, in accepting *Der zerbrochne Krug* for performance in Weimar. But the production in March 1808 was a disaster, and this must, it seems, be attributed in considerable measure to Goethe's own lack of sympathy for the play and for its theatrical style, so different from that cultivated in Weimar. Though he had complained that it was a piece of 'invisible theatre', static and lacking in visual interest, these supposed defects can only have been exaggerated by the slow pace of the Weimar production and by Goethe's arbitrary division of Kleist's unbroken sequence of scenes into the three acts traditionally thought proper for comedy. Kleist

sent Goethe an extract from *Penthesilea* 'on the knees of my heart',
claiming that the play was not written for the stage, that the present
circumstances of the German theatre were 'neither before the curtain
nor behind it' such as to encourage hopes of a successful production,
and that he preferred to wait for the future rather than make
concessions to vulgar public taste – but obviously hoping that
Goethe would be interested in performing it. But if his remarks
were intended to earn Goethe's goodwill, in fact they provided him
with the opportunity to deal Kleist a stinging rebuff:

> Allow me also to observe (for if one is not to be frank, it would be better to
> remain silent) that it never ceases to disturb and distress me to see young
> men of spirit and talent waiting for a theatre that has yet to appear. . .I
> believe I could take the plays of Calderón to any country fair, perform them
> on bare boards nailed on barrels, and give the greatest pleasure both to the
> educated and to the uneducated members of the public. . .

Goethe's remarks even here are not simply hostile or condescending, but reflect, like those of the Director in the Prelude to *Faust*,
years of practical concern with the theatre. But they were still unfair
and unjustified, and indicate a profound and possibly wilful incomprehension of Kleist's work. Kleist was deeply wounded. In his
journalistic essays of the following years he frequently attacks
Goethe in return, sometimes with veiled hints, sometimes with
satire of savage directness – as in the essay *Unmaßgebliche Betrachtung*
(*A Casual Observation*), in which he suggests that the only way to
make Goethe's plays theatrically viable would be by some sensational gimmick, such as having all the men's parts played by
women and vice versa. But the majority of Kleist's own plays
remained unperformed in his life-time. *Die Familie Schroffenstein* and
*Das Käthchen von Heilbronn* were both first performed in Austria, the
former at Graz as early as 1804, the latter in March 1810 at the
Theater an der Wien in Vienna, where its spectacular effects were
well calculated to appeal – though Iffland in Berlin had rejected it as
unplayable. It was also seen at Graz later in the same year, and at
Bamberg in September 1811, not long before Kleist's death. It was
even performed in Weimar, in 1822, some years after Goethe's
resignation as theatre director. But *Die Hermannsschlacht* and *Prinz
Friedrich von Homburg* were not even published until 1821, when
Tieck (another of his claims to the gratitude of posterity) first edited

Kleist's posthumous works. *Penthesilea* was not performed on stage until 1876, *Amphitryon* not until 1899. In the twentieth century, however, the plays have established a secure place in the classical German repertory, and some of them have been seen outside Germany too: *Homburg*, which might be thought one of the most intransigently 'German' of plays, was successfully produced in Paris in the 1950s, with Gérard Philipe playing the Prince as a hero in the existentialist mould, and this play has also been seen a number of times in Britain. In Germany in recent years Kleist's work has often received more sympathetic theatrical treatment than that of Goethe and Schiller, no doubt in large measure because of that very modernity which so disturbed Goethe – a telling instance of the fluctuating and problematic relationship between literary drama and the stage.

# CHAPTER X

# Classicism in Vienna (i): Grillparzer

Though Vienna, nominal capital of the Holy Roman Empire, was a major European metropolis with a metropolitan culture, Austrian writers had played little part in the German literary renaissance of the eighteenth century. The later Habsburg Emperors had shown on the whole less interest in the affairs of the 'German nation' than in consolidating their multinational hereditary dominions in east-central Europe, and the Emperor Francis II had set the seal on this development in 1804 by proclaiming himself Emperor Francis I of 'Austria', that is of a territory embracing present-day Austria, Hungary and Czechoslovakia together with large areas of Poland, Romania, Yugoslavia and northern Italy. The Holy Roman Empire itself was formally dissolved in 1806; however, the Congress of 1815 not only revived the Empire under the name of the German Confederation, but itself made Vienna the headquarters of the post-Napoleonic European restoration. From 1815, at any rate until the revolutions of 1848, Vienna had more claim to be considered the effective capital of the German-speaking world than at any time in the previous century.[1] And at the same time, appropriately enough, the Burgtheater in Vienna under the directorship of Josef Schrey-vogel was establishing its reputation as the foremost serious German theatre, with a repertory which included works by Lessing, Goethe, Schiller and even Kleist, together with Shakespeare, Calderón and the French classics. There was also a flourishing popular theatre, with a tradition embracing a wide range of comedy – from senti-mental plays of moral improvement to sharp satire and lively farce – and musical plays. This tradition produced two dramatists of genius in Ferdinand Raimund (1790–1836) and Johann Nepomuk Nestroy (1801–62); the latter in particular, with his scintillating and often abrasive wit, is still a theatrical favourite, whose reputation is by no means confined to Austria, despite the very local flavour of much of his work.[2]

There were, however, two dramatists working in Vienna during this period who aspired to far more than local or provincial status, seeing themselves as the heirs to the classical German tradition which Goethe and Schiller had sought to establish in Weimar. Franz Grillparzer (1791–1872) and Friedrich Hebbel (1813–63) were in many ways natural antipodes, and both were men of difficult, even neurotic temperament: their mutual hostility is unsurprising. Nowadays Grillparzer's critical stock stands higher than Hebbel's and his disparaging comments on his younger rival are often quoted with approval, but the two dramatists nevertheless have a good deal in common.

Grillparzer was a native Viennese, and a professional civil servant; he came from a cultured middle-class background (his maternal uncle Josef Sonnleithner was co-author of the libretto of *Fidelio*), but there was also a family history of mental instability. Hebbel was a native of the far north of Germany, from Wesselburen in Holstein, who settled in Vienna in 1845 and married the Burgtheater actress Christine Enghaus (also a northerner by birth); he had made his own way from very humble origins and had the characteristic fierce pride, even arrogance, of the autodidact. Both regarded their art with great seriousness, though Grillparzer acknowledged the value of the popular theatrical tradition and drew on it in his work, while Hebbel generally regarded it with contempt (he once said that Nestroy was so vulgar that he would make a rose stink by sniffing at it). Grillparzer saw the theatre, as Goethe and Schiller had done, as an institution of educative or civilising potential: the audience, he wrote, go in just as people ('Leute'), but come out as human beings ('Menschen'). Hebbel, though not unconcerned with theatrical performance – several of his most memorable roles are those he wrote specifically with Christine in mind – is more interested in the drama as a literary and philosophical art-form, as the symbolic representation of a 'world-historical process' very like that described in the philosophy of Hegel. Grillparzer detested the slightest whiff of Hegelian philosophy; his interest in history was of a much more concrete and political kind. Yet Hebbel too had a practical concern with politics; indeed, he was actually nominated (unsuccessfully) as a liberal deputy to the Frankfurt Parliament in 1848. Both men were liberals, of a sort, during the years of the so-called 'Vormärz' or 'pre-March', the period before the uprisings of March 1848; but both were horrified by the spectacle of revolutionary violence and the threat of popular democracy and communism, and after 1848 both espoused increasingly conservative, even reactionary views, which naturally find expression in their dramatic work.

Grillparzer and Hebbel are obviously inhabitants of the same post-Napoleonic Restoration Europe: they share a desire to find some kind of meaning in history, and increasing concern for order in a threateningly unstable world, and a fascination with the psychology or even (particularly in Hebbel's case) the psychopathology of power. Both are also concerned with the psychology of sex and the relationship between the sexes – one usually of tension and often (again particularly in Hebbel) of hostility and mutual incomprehension. In both the philosophical and the psychological aspects of their work we see the expression of new and characteristically nineteenth-century concerns. They also both seek to broaden the stylistic range of classical drama, Grillparzer by incorporating Romantic, Spanish and popular elements, Hebbel in some of his plays by abandoning blank verse for prose. Yet both retained a classical ideal of form and beauty, and a traditional regard for tragedy as the highest and most dignified dramatic form – in marked contrast, for example, to their radical young contemporary Büchner. The result is a drama which has often been criticised, in both their cases, as an unhappy combination of traditional and more modern elements, but which at its best achieves a genuine synthesis of them.

Grillparzer made his debut as a playwright at the Theater an der Wien in 1817 with *Die Ahnfrau* (*The Ancestress*), a Gothic melodrama featuring ruins, robbers, incest, and the family ghost of the title, who finally clasps the doomed hero Jaromir to her icy bosom. It obviously owes much to Romantic 'fate' drama and also to *Die Räuber*, but if Jaromir is something of a reincarnation of Karl Moor he is also a very characteristic Grillparzerian figure, driven by a restless, blind will. Schiller had seen the will of man, as had Kant, as a rational faculty by which man could overcome the irrational, animal side of his nature, rise above material circumstances and assert his moral worth. Grillparzer sees the will rather as itself irrational, itself part of man's animal rather than his spiritual nature (to use Schiller's terms), embroiling him in the world rather than enabling him to rise above it. The essentially evil nature of the will, of ambition, even of all practical action, is a recurrent motif in Grillparzer's work. His pessimistic views have much in common with those of another contemporary philosopher, Schopenhauer, whose major work *Die Welt als Wille und Vorstellung* (*The World as Will and Representation*) appeared in 1818. *Die Ahnfrau* employs a good many of what Grillparzer himself called the 'noisy and sensational effects' ('Schall- und Knalleffekte') of the popular theatre, but its most interesting stylistic feature is its adoption of the four-beat trochaic metre of Spanish drama, which gives the dialogue a hurried, hectic character; for most of his later work Grillparzer reverted to the more classical form of blank verse.

*Die Ahnfrau* enjoyed a considerable success on the stage. In the course of the next twenty years, seven more works by Grillparzer were performed at the Burgtheater and other Viennese theatres. First came two tragedies on subjects from Greek legend, in which the theme of love plays a major part: *Sappho* (1818), on the unhappy love of the poetess for an ordinary young man, and *Das goldene Vlies* (*The Golden Fleece*, 1821), a dramatic trilogy concerned principally with the tragic relationship of Jason and Medea. Grillparzer then produced two historical tragedies, both on subjects from the thirteenth century: *König Ottokars Glück und Ende* (*The Fortune and Fall of King Ottokar*) deals with the defeat of Ottokar of Bohemia and the foundation of the Habsburg dynasty by Rudolf I, *Ein Treuer Diener seines Herrn* (*A Faithful Servant of his Master*) with the civil disturbances in Hungary under the regency of the Palatine Bancbanus. In these plays Grillparzer presented his ideal of kingship and empire, and expounded his views on a question of continuing and crucial importance in the history of nineteenth-century Austria – the relations between the various subject nations of the Habsburg Empire. The predictable result was trouble with the rigorous official censorship, which was concerned to suppress any work dealing with political issues, even from what Grillparzer claimed (in the case of *Ein treuer Diener*) was an 'excessively loyal' point of view; and he retreated to the safer ground of Greek legend and the unpolitical subject of love in his next tragedy, *Des Meeres und der Liebe Wellen* (*The Waves of the Sea and of Love*, 1831), on the story of Hero and Leander. Political ambition and action in the public realm are explicitly renounced in the exotic fairy-tale play *Der Traum ein Leben* (*A Dream for a Life*) of 1834, in which Grillparzer reverts to the mixture of popular Viennese style and Spanish verse which had proved so successful in *Die Ahnfrau*. *Der Traum ein Leben* was indeed Grillparzer's greatest theatrical success: the original Burg-theater production of 1834 remained in the repertory for sixty years. But his comedy *Weh dem, der lügt!* (*Woe betide the Liar!*) of 1838 was a disastrous failure, after which Grillparzer retired, embittered, from further active involvement with the stage; he later claimed (though it was not strictly true) that after 1838 he had never set foot in a theatre again. In three more, posthumously published tragedies, however, *Die Jüdin von Toledo* (*The Jewess of Toledo*), *Libussa* and *Ein Bruderzwist in Habsburg* (*Fraternal Strife in Habsburg*), he gathered up all his most characteristic themes: the dangers of ambition and passion, of the active as opposed to the contemplative life, and above all the ideals of kingship and empire as a focus of unity and stability in a world increasingly threatened by the disruptive forces of revolution and nationalism. All three plays were probably completed by the middle of the century, and bear the mark of the events of 1848. In a will of that year he ordered the destruction of 'the two seemingly finished tragedies' *Libussa* and *Bruderzwist*, but later relented. At the end of his life he finally consented to their performance, and two rival productions of *Bruderzwist* were actually in preparation in Vienna when he died; they opened within days of each other in September 1872.

Grillparzer's output is substantial, varied, and uneven in quality. Even his best work is not without its flaws. But in the very different forms of the *Golden Fleece* trilogy and the two Habsburg plays, at least, he scaled considerable tragic heights, and in *Der Traum ein Leben* achieved a remarkable combination of serious and popular elements.

The trilogy is the first work in which Grillparzer's dramatic style reaches maturity. Many other dramatists, from Euripides onwards, had treated the tragic story of Medea, the barbarian princess from Colchis, on the far shore of the Black Sea, who helped the Greek hero Jason to steal the Golden Fleece, and became his wife; on their return to Greece she found herself rejected, and avenged herself upon Jason by murdering their children and the new bride who had supplanted her in his affections. Lessing had even produced a modern-dress version of the story in *Miss Sara Sampson*. But no other playwright had treated the relationship of Jason and Medea from its first beginnings, the birth as well as the death of their love, the power of Jason's personality which had compelled Medea to abandon and betray her father and her country and to follow him. Grillparzer felt this to be necessary in order to establish the extremity of his subsequent betrayal of her and so to motivate and even justify the extremity of her revenge. But in doing so, he broadened the thematic scope of his work beyond the merely psychological. It is no longer simply the tragedy of Medea. It is also the tragedy of Jason: the story of the rise and fall of a hero, a man who confidently and successfully pursues a heroic goal, only to find that his achievements ultimately bring him nothing but rejection and misery. At the end of the trilogy the wretched Jason, now himself an outcast, knocks on the door of a peasant's hut:

PEASANT Who knocks? Who are you, stranger, tired to death?
JASON Only a drink of water! – I am Jason!
    The hero of the Fleece! A prince! A king!
    Jason, the leader of the Argonauts!
PEASANT Are you that Jason? Then be off with you!
    You shall not enter and pollute my house!

(Medea, v, ll. 2292–7)

The pervading symbol of heroic striving is, of course, the Golden Fleece itself, the fatal talisman which brings tragedy upon all who become involved with it. Grillparzer in a working note states that 'the Fleece *accompanies* the action throughout, but does not actually *cause* it', but this is hardly true, for it is men's desire for the Fleece which motivates them throughout the work, from Medea's father Aietes in the first part, *Der Gastfreund* (*The Guest*), through Jason in *Die Argonauten* (*The Argonauts*) to King Creon in the final part,

*Medea*, and it is the magic powers associated with the Fleece which enable Medea to carry out her revenge. The dramatic function and the symbolic meaning of the Fleece are in fact very similar to those of the Nibelung's ring in Wagner's operatic tetralogy. Both represent the object of a driving, ruthless ambition which is identified as the principal source of evil in the world, and which in both cases – in Grillparzer implicitly, in Wagner explicitly – involves the renunciation of love and humanity. Both are stolen goods, and the world will know no peace until they are returned to where they belong: the ring to the depths of the Rhine, the Fleece to the temple at Delphi. At the end we see Medea setting off for Delphi, after her last bitter farewell to Jason, the Fleece no longer flying proud like a banner, but wrapped around her shoulders like a cloak:

> Look: here is what you fought for. Do you know
> It still? It seemed to offer fame and fortune.
> What is it men call fortune? Idle shadows!
> What is it men call fame? An idle dream!
> You foolish man! Your dreams were all of shadows.
> Your dreams are over, but the night not yet.
>
> (*Medea*, v, ll.2364–9)

(This is, incidentally, a tragedy in which both the principal characters remain alive at the end.) Like Wagner after him, Grillparzer has impressively adapted an ancient myth to represent an abiding truth. Indeed, both men identified ambition and the quest for power, which lies at the heart of both their myths, as a particular characteristic of their own age – an eternal human failing, no doubt, but one which was taking on new, more ruthless and ever more menacing forms in nineteenth-century Europe.[3]

The opposition of Greek and 'barbarian' worlds is another important thematic and structural element in *Das goldene Vlies*, and here too Grillparzer touches upon issues which were beginning to take on new and more sinister significance for the modern world. The dark and wild atmosphere of Colchis is well evoked in the opening scenes of *Der Gastfreund*. The Colchians speak in jagged, irregular verse forms to which the smooth, flowing blank verse of the Greek Phryxus makes a striking contrast: 'He speaks and speaks', observes Medea, 'How horrible!' (*Der Gastfreund*, ll.366–7). For here, as in Kleist's *Hermannsschlacht*, the comparison of 'civilisation' and 'barbarism' is by no means to the former's advantage. Phryxus in *Der Gastfreund*, Jason and his men in *Die Argonauten*, King Creon in *Medea* all regard themselves as superior to the Colchians, but by this superiority the 'barbarians' are abused, exploited and ultimately driven to their terrible revenge. Like Kleist, Grillparzer was a committed patriot, but his patriotism was of a very different kind. The Austrian Empire of the post-Napoleonic era claimed his loyalty precisely because it represented, however imperfectly, an ideal of civilisation which stood above petty nationalisms. He regarded the idea of 'nationality' as another of the curses of the modern world, looked with suspicion and contempt upon the aspirations of the subject nationalities – Czechs, Magyars and so on – within the Habsburg Empire, and wrote bitterly in a famous epigram that

> The way of modern culture, we see,
> Leads from humanity
> Through nationality
> To bestiality.

But if Grillparzer thought that Habsburg Austria had a civilising mission, in *Das goldene Vlies* he shows the Greeks, long regarded as the ideal exemplars of civilisation, in a very unfavourable light. Where Goethe's *Iphigenie auf Tauris* celebrated the emergence of humanity from barbarianism, Grillparzer has no such optimistic message. In Goethe's play the 'rough Scythian' Thoas proved himself the moral compeer of the Greeks; in Grillparzer's, Jason and Creon in their unscrupulous greed prove themselves no better than the frankly savage Aietes.

Grillparzer's handling of the trilogy form has its weaknesses. He adopted the form with considerable reservations, despite the precedents furnished by Greek drama and by Schiller's *Wallenstein*. He regarded it as essentially epic rather than dramatic, involving lengthy narration rather than that concentrated, immediate presentation which to him was the essence of drama and of theatre. The length and pacing of the three parts of *Das goldene Vlies* is very uneven, and from the purely psychological point of view – though it was specifically from this aspect that Grillparzer chose to justify his extended treatment of the subject – the final part, *Medea*, is virtually self-sufficient and can be performed on its own – which it usually is, despite Grillparzer's express wish that it should not be. The confrontation of Greek and barbarian worlds is also powerfully evident in *Medea* by itself; the latent themes of racial hostility and colonial exploitation were powerfully exploited in an English-language production by the South African director Barney Simon in the early 1980s. But this and the other broader themes undoubtedly gain from their fuller exposition and development in the trilogy, and it is these broader themes, symbolically implicit in the motif of the Fleece, which make the work more than merely the proto-Strindbergian tragedy of a broken marriage. The antique setting also contributes to some effective visual drama, with the contrast of Greek and Colchian landscape and costume, and the striking recurrent appearances of the Fleece itself, which fully satisfy Grillparzer's criterion for the highest theatrical effect – 'word and image ('Bild') at the same time'.[4]

Grillparzer's first historical tragedy, *König Ottokars Glück und Ende*, completed in 1823, shows him at the height of his powers (indeed, almost all his subsequent plays were originally conceived in the early 1820s, their completion delayed by his ever-increasing hesitation and loss of confidence). It is one of the most genuinely Shakespearian of German historical tragedies; this is to some extent unfortunate, for its obvious indebtedness to Shakespeare may seem to diminish its originality and the significance of its subject-matter. The rise and fall of King Ottokar of Bohemia had been treated by other dramatists as diverse in style and talent as Lope de Vega and Kotzebue,[5] but Grillparzer's principal model is plainly *Richard III*. His play, however, recalls Shakespeare's not merely in dramatic terms but also in its historical and political significance, for it too celebrates the founding of the dynasty which was ruling in the playwright's own day and the consequent establishment – so we are asked to believe – of order, justice and peace after a period of chaos, tyranny and bloodshed. Rudolf I, the first Habsburg Emperor, had been elected to office in 1273; by 1823, his dynasty had already lasted a good deal longer than the Tudors, and it was to last nearly a hundred years more. The reconstitution of the Empire under Francis II/I in 1804, and the rise and fall of Napoleon, added further contemporary significance to the story, and Grillparzer in his diary noted, and indeed exaggerated, parallels between the characters and careers of Ottokar and Napoleon, notably their divorces and subsequent remarriages, which he identified as fatal turning-points in their lives. But Ottokar is not portrayed as an evil man: he can be rough and brutal, but he is not a self-consciously melodramatic villain like Shakespeare's Richard. He seeks, albeit mistakenly, the greater glory of the Bohemian nation. Again, Grillparzer strongly disapproved of Czech nationalism, but nevertheless resists any temptation to caricature Ottokar or to set Bohemian against Austrian as such in the play. Against Ottokar's mistaken conception of monarchy in terms of personal and national aggrandisement, Rudolf represents the ideal of Empire as a quasi-divine mission, transcending all personal and national goals. The 'Germany' he invokes is a supra-national entity, as was the Habsburg Empire of the nineteenth century:

> I am not he whom you have known of old!
> Not Habsburg am I, no, nor even Rudolf;
> Through my veins runs the blood of Germany,
> The pulse of Germany beats in my heart.
> All that was mortal I have cast from me,
> And am the Emperor, who never dies.     (III, ll. 1785–90)

Rudolf has been criticised, rather like Richmond in *Richard III*, as a rather flat character who commands little truly dramatic interest, though in fact his importance is established in the very first scene of the play, the contrast between the two men is emphasised throughout, and in Act III he dominates the proceedings. He has also been seen as simply too good to be true, though Grillparzer tries to give him some psychological depth by presenting him as a man with a wild, 'heroic' youth which he has deliberately put behind him. Grillparzer is undoubtedly playing (as did Shakespeare in the figure of Richmond) upon the expectation of certain ready-made patriotic responses in his audience.[6] At the same time, he may be doing so with a certain degree of irony. The play ends with cries of 'Hail Habsburg! Austria! Habsburg for ever!', which recall the end of *Prinz Friedrich von Homburg*. But the Austria which is here invoked is, like Kleist's Brandenburg, an ideal rather than a direct reflection of contemporary reality. Grillparzer's play, like Kleist's, or like

Schiller's *Wallenstein*, has more than merely local or patriotic significance, though it may be that it is less readily detachable from its national and historical context.

The action of *König Ottokar* is complex, with several strands of interest all maintained from the first act to the last: the fall of Ottokar from the summit of power on which we see him standing in Act I, and his progressive eclipse by Rudolf; his divorce of Queen Margareta, her death and their posthumous 'reconciliation', as the defeated Ottokar prays at her coffin; Ottokar's wronging of the Rosenberg family, their plans for revenge, and the seduction of his new queen Kunigunde by Zawisch von Rosenberg (a smooth and self-confident villain, and one of Grillparzer's most memorable characters); and Ottokar's vindictive treatment of Merenberg and the revenge of Merenberg's son Seyfried, by whose hand Ottokar is eventually slain. This complexity is well handled, indeed Grillparzer seems to revel in it – notably in Act I with its continuous arrival of messengers and delegations adding more and more to Ottokar's store of power and good fortune, up to the climactic reversal when we hear that not he but Rudolf has been elected Emperor. This is stagecraft of a high order. Grillparzer never again succeeded in imposing such dramatic unity upon complex historical material. Or perhaps it is rather the case that, excepting *Des Meeres und der Liebe Wellen* with its return to Greek simplicity, none of his later tragedies aspires to quite the same kind of conventional dramatic unity. They all tend to be episodic, and despite their carefully visualised theatricality they contain a strong admixture of that 'epic' quality which Grillparzer in theory deplored as undramatic.

The apparently optimistic note on which *König Ottokar* concludes is also untypical of Grillparzer. Certainly his other Habsburg play *Ein Bruderzwist in Habsburg* is altogether darker in import. Whereas the earlier play dealt with the founding of the Habsburg dynasty and the consequent stabilising of the Empire, the later one portrays the chaos and dissension of the reigns of Rudolf II and Mathias in the early years of the seventeenth century, the period of personal, political and religious rivalry which led to the outbreak of the Thirty Years' War. Once again there are obvious specific parallels with Grillparzer's own times, with the rise of popular and national movements which threatened the unity of the Empire and even in

1848 its very existence. But the play is also a vision of history. It is the most anti-Hegelian (and perhaps also deliberately anti-Hebbelian) of historical dramas, in which the 'world-historical process' is seen as one not of dialectical advance to some certain, if remote, state of future perfection, but of collapse, disintegration and decay. Like *König Ottokar*, the play is a complex interweaving of many strands of action, each in this case carried forward by a particular member of the Hasburg family: the Emperor Rudolf II, his vain, ambitious but ineffectual brother Mathias, his ruthless, fanatical nephew Ferdinand (whose election as Emperor in succession to Rudolf and Mathias was actually to trigger off the war), his other nephew Leopold, loyal and warm-hearted but dangerously impulsive, and his illegitimate son Cäsar, 'this time's rude son' as Rudolf calls him in Act III, another of those figures in whom Grillparzer has embodied all the destructive tendencies of human nature in general (including, not least, sexuality) and of the modern world in particular. While the other characters embody various forms of activity, Rudolf remains passive, seeking by deliberate inaction and withdrawal to delay the onset of the catastrophe which he himself sees as ultimately inevitable. Rudolf II has generally been seen by historians as an ineffectual ruler, eccentric to the point of madness, neglecting his duties in favour of astrological and alchemical speculation, allowing the Empire to fall into decay and thus becoming himself as responsible as anyone for the eventual outbreak of the war – even though this did not happen until six years after his death, not almost immediately thereafter as Grillparzer seems to imply (for with the traditional licence of the historical dramatist, he compresses the events of some fifteen years into a more or less continuous sequence). Grillparzer himself does not entirely absolve Rudolf of responsibility, but he makes his inactivity the result of a deliberate political decision, of a profound, if deeply pessimistic historical wisdom (he is also something of a self-portrait of the withdrawn and incommunicative dramatist). His study of the stars is not an idle fantasy, nor are the constellations for him, as for Schiller's Wallenstein, a projection of his own delusions of grandeur. They represent an image of divine order and harmony to be contrasted with the futile world of human ambition and activity:

> Man fell from God, the stars above did not . . .
> So in the stars is truth, in rocks and stones,
> In plants and beasts and trees, but not in man.     (I, ll. 407–12)

And whereas Schiller's Marquis Posa had urged King Philip to see the natural world as the embodiment of the principle of liberty, Rudolf urges his discontented subjects, concerned with the formulation and recognition of their 'rights', to see it as the embodiment of order and hierarchy:

> Behold the world, so plain for all to see,
> How hill and vale, how field and river lie.
> The mountains, bare themselves, attract the clouds
> And send them down as rain into the valleys.
> The forest checks the wild, destructive storm,
> The springs flow fruitless, but they nourish fruits,
> And from this interplay of high and low,
> Of fruit and shelter, is brought forth this whole,
> Whose right and ground is simply that it is.
> Oh, do not seek to judge these sacred bonds
> Which all unconscious, from our very birth,
> Beyond all proof, for proof they are themselves,
> Unite what reason parts in enmity.     (III, ll. 1608–20)

In the last act, when Rudolf is dead, and his successor Mathias already being threatened by Ferdinand as Rudolf was threatened by Mathias in Act I (history repeats itself, even to the configuration of characters on the stage), there appears the last and most frankly brutal of all Grillparzer's embodiments of the will in the person of Wallenstein, evil genius of the Thirty Years' War. For Schiller Wallenstein, whether traitor or misguided idealist, was still a figure of tragic grandeur. For Grillparzer – and the allusion not only to the historical Wallenstein, but also to Schiller's portrayal of him, is unmistakable – he is simply the embodiment of violence, welcoming war – 'Let it last thirty years!' – as his natural element.

*Ein Bruderzwist in Habsburg* is undoubtedly a rich and profound work. It touches upon almost all Grillparzer's most characteristic concerns; it has been called his political testament, and some regard it as his greatest play. It is, however, considerably more diffuse and episodic than *König Ottokar*, and with its passive central figure it lacks the dynamism of the earlier work. Furthermore, though it demonstrates Grillparzer's continued concern for visual effect, for setting and for grouping of characters, for costume, mime and gesture (indicated, as in all his plays, in precise and elaborate stage directions), it does not always achieve the fusion of the theatrical with the truly dramatic, which was his artistic ideal.

The work in which those elements are perhaps most successfully fused is his greatest popular success, *Der Traum ein Leben*. It is also a work in which serious themes are successfully treated in a relatively light-hearted manner. The title is adapted from that of Calderón's *La vida es sueño* (*Life is a Dream*), one of the Spanish playwright's most popular works in Germany, and the 'awakening' of the hero to a truer realisation of his own nature and of the proper moral course of his life recalls the *desengaño* or disillusionment which is a recurrent motif of Spanish Golden Age drama. But the use of dream or supernatural agency (or both) to teach the hero a lesson and to give him the chance of mending his ways is also typical of the 'Besserungsstück' or play of moral improvement, one of the favourite forms of the Viennese popular theatre, brought to artistic perfection by Raimund – and often parodied by Nestroy. The same formula had also been adopted by Lessing for one of his abortive attempts to dramatise the Faust legend: Faust was to dream his temptation and his pact with the devil, and to awaken resolved to pursue knowledge and wisdom only by legitimate means. Grillparzer himself had sketched, before the second part of Goethe's *Faust* had appeared, a projected continuation of his own, in which Faust, after the destruction of Gretchen, was to repent of his Promethean striving and to realise that true wisdom lay in 'self-limitation and spiritual peace'. And this is indeed the conclusion reached by Rustan, the hero of *Der Traum ein Leben*, the simple Persian peasant youth whom Heinrich Laube (liberal critic and after 1848 director of the Burgtheater) was to dub 'the Austrian Faust'. Bored by the homely monotony of his humble life, the never-changing cycle of sunrise and sunset, the virtuous but unexciting company of his uncle Massud and his cousin and prospective fiancée Mirza, Rustan dreams of adventure, power and glory. Tempted by the black slave Zanga, he embarks on a career of escalating dishonesty, treachery and crime: making his way through trickery into the favour of the King of Samarkand (not unlike Goethe's Faust with the Emperor!), he murders and supplants the King and marries his daughter, the Princess Gülnare. But the fulfilment of his ambition brings him to the brink of disaster and death, upon which he wakes up, gives thanks for his deliverance and praises the very monotony of existence which had formerly provoked his discontent – the familiar scene, the morning, the 'eternal sun' and the 'blest Today' ('Ew'ge Sonne, sel'ges Heut'!' IV, l.2621). The final moral is pronounced in words which recall Medea's bleak farewell to Jason:

> Earthly greatness is but danger,
> Earthly fame an idle play.
> What they bring are idle shadows,
> But so much they take away.     (IV, ll.2653–6)

Here the moral seems somewhat trite, even complacent; if Medea may be felt to have earned by her suffering the right to speak as she does, Rustan has only been dreaming, at home in his comfortable if modest bed. The verse at the end of *Der Traum ein Leben* also seems correspondingly flat and unadventurous. But the dream-scenes, in which Rustan acts out his fantasies ('an exercise in depth psychology', in the words of one critic),[7] are gripping, fast-moving and colourful. The sequence of events, though bizarre and even surrealistic, seems more convincing than the drab reality within which the work is framed; likewise the King and Gülnare, flat characters who might have stepped out of a fairy-tale picture-book, seem nevertheless more convincing than Massud and Mirza, their drab everyday equivalents. The trochaic verse is often lively and exciting, even appropriately hectic, and in the mouth of Zanga, the Mephistopheles of Rustan's Faustian dream, takes on a sardonic quality not unworthy of Goethe's Mephisto himself. Grillparzer makes full and effective use of theatrical resources, including magical transformations. The work's popular success is readily understandable – but again its homely message takes on further significance in the atmosphere of the 'pre-March' years. Rustan, in his fabulous dream-world, is acting out not only his own fantasy, but those of his creator and their audience. Perhaps this acting-out of fantasy helped creator and audience, as it enables Rustan, to accept the message of resignation, of the abrogation of Faustian ambition or even of fantasy, which is the work's official moral.[8] Despite its portrayal of the assassination of a king, *Der Traum ein Leben* seems not to have worried the ever-vigilant censor. But perhaps, as Grillparzer's twentieth-century compatriot, the satirist Karl Kraus, observed, 'satire that the censor understands deserves to be forbidden'.

Grillparzer's other works can be more briefly surveyed. *Sappho*, though it aroused Byron's enthusiasm, is not free of sentimentality, and the rather over-decorative Viennese theatrical style of the time, with its elaborate use of costume, decor and studied tableau, is not very successfully combined with the Greek setting or with the very evident intention to emulate Goethe at his most scrupulously neo-classical. *Tasso* is Grillparzer's obvious, at times too obvious, model for the dramatic treatment of a conflict between the demands of art and of life: between Sappho's consciousness of her poetic vocation and the sacrifices which it enjoins upon her, and her desire to share the pleasures of ordinary life, notably love. Both here and in *Des Meeres und der Liebe Wellen* Grillparzer uses a setting of classical antiquity with the evident intention of conferring a degree of universality upon a conflict between duty and desire – a common theme in his work. In both plays, however, the duty involved is a personal, private, even esoteric concept – Sappho's poetic vocation, Hero's vow of chastity as a priestess of Aphrodite – rather than a public and immediately recognisable one such as we find in his political plays. The treatment in *Des Meeres und der Liebe Wellen* is more successful, with duty embodied in the stern figure of Hero's uncle, the priest, who puts out the lamp intended to guide Leander across the Hellespont to an assignment with his love. Grillparzer said that he had given the play its 'somewhat pretentious' (but untranslatably mellifluous) title, rather than calling it simply 'Hero und Leander', in order to draw attention to the combination of romantic with more strictly classical elements. The play was and has remained one of Grillparzer's most successful works on the stage, and has been described by some critics as his dramatic masterpiece. It contains much that is genuinely touching: the lovers' first meeting, with Hero inadvertently catching sight of Leander as she turns on her way to the temple to swear her vows, and their second, when Leander swims across the Hellespont and climbs to Hero's window. Here again, however, there is perhaps too much of the picturesque tableau, and the conduct of the action in the intervening scenes is not always persuasive. The last act, however, rises to a moving climax in Hero's lament for the dead Leander – a gentler version of Penthesilea's lament for Achilles in Kleist's play. Again a Shakespearian comparison suggests itself to Grillparzer's disadvantage: *Des Meeres und der Liebe Wellen* is a *Romeo and Juliet* transported to the paler and less convincing setting of classical antiquity. Ultimately it seems a sad, even a sentimental, rather than a truly tragic story, a 'tale of private woe' lacking in the wider resonances that are present in Grillparzer's best work.

Even this is often characterised by a certain diffuseness, and in works such as *Ein treuer Diener seines Herrn* and the posthumous plays, notably *Libussa*, Grillparzer's searching analysis of psychological processes, notably of sexual psychology, is not always successfully combined with his treatment of political themes, or with the rather unreal, pageant-like treatment of history or historical legend and the rather flat, picture-book characterisation which this involves. Grillparzer's attempt to combine such heterogeneous elements is itself of considerable interest, however. Both *Ein treuer Diener* and *Libussa*, though designated tragedies, are very unconventional examples of that genre. *Ein treuer Diener* includes violence and death, but as in *Das goldene Vlies* both the titular hero Bancbanus and his principal antagonist Duke Otto remain alive at the end of the play, though the former is bereaved of his young wife, and the latter – the agent of her death – broken to the verge of madness. The basic dramatic formula – the moral testing of a regent in the absence of his sovereign – recalls that of *Measure for Measure*, and the play has the similar general character of a dark 'problem play', with the King returning at the end to provide a rather ambiguous conclusion. *Libussa* is a combination of romantic comedy and tragic historical myth. The courtship of the fairy-tale princess Libussa and the ploughman Primislaus is treated in a spirit of high comedy (there are even echoes of Gozzi's *Turandot* and the *commedia dell'arte*), with riddles, reversals and moments of pure farce as well as genuinely touching and tender episodes. Their marriage marks the establishment of the Bohemian royal dynasty, the founding of the city of Prague – and the emergence of the people of Bohemia from pre-historic innocence into the unhappy state of modern nationhood. The play ends with Libussa dying after uttering a visionary prophecy of the alienated course of modern history, with only the faintest glimmer of hope that one day the Golden Age may be restored. Grillparzer may have intended this strange work to some extent as a deliberate counter to the Romanticism of Brentano's treatment of the same subject in *Die Gründung Prags*: he certainly regarded literary Romanticism, Czech nationalism and theories of historical 'progress' with equal disfavour, and *Libbussa* seems to be designed to attack all three.

Surprisingly, it is perhaps the element of comedy in *Libussa* which is most successful. This is not a common feature in Grillparzer's work, and as we have mentioned, his one attempt at the comic genre, *Weh dem, der lügt!*, was at its first performance a disastrous failure; though the work has been successfully revived, it has generally proved more popular with literary critics than with theatrical audiences. As contemporaries such as Laube observed, it is in fact a very literary comedy. Leon, the wily kitchen-boy, offers to free Atalus, nephew of Bishop Gregor of Chalons, who is being held captive by a heathen German tribe. As we see, the confrontation of civilisation and barbarism recurs here too; and the plot is a kind of comic variation on that of *Iphigenie auf Tauris*. The puritanical bishop orders Leon to tell no lies, so he tells Atalus's captors the truth – that he intends to run away with Atalus – knowing full well that they will not believe him. The character of Leon has something of the cheeky resourcefulness of a Spanish *gracioso*, at times even of the abrasive obstinacy of a Nestroy hero; but on the whole the characters are neither attractive enough to be sympathetic nor foolish enough to be merely risible, and the wit is often forced and ponderous, and unhappily combined with the more farcical elements. More characteristic and more convincing is the frank, bitter pessimism of *Die Jüdin von Toledo*. Based upon a play by Lope de Vega, *Las Paces de los Reyes* (*The Royal Reconciliation*), it tells of the infatuation of King Alfons of Castille for the beautiful Jewess Rahel, her brutal murder by the disaffected nobility at the instigation of the Queen, the King's disillusionment or *desengaño* and his subsequent return to the paths of duty. Esther, sister of the murdered Rahel, who throughout the play acts as a kind of chorus, ends it with a moral and a prayer: may God forgive us all, for we are all miserable sinners. Grillparzer, though a nominal Catholic, was not a conventionally religious man; he seems to have believed in some kind of ultimate divine order, but he saw man as living in a fallen state with little if any hope of redemption.

Grillparzer once characteristically described himself as 'the sort of cross between Goethe and Kotzebue that the theatre needs'. By this he meant that the classical German drama had suffered, in his view, from its excessively literary character, and while remaining loyal to the ideals of the classical writers, he sought to remedy this deficiency in his own plays. He prided himself on his roots in a metropolitan theatrical tradition; visiting Weimar in 1826, and unimpressed by a performance of Schiller's *Wallenstein*, he wrote in his diary: 'How much greater the great dramatist would have been if he had ever known a real public and real actors.' He himself, even after his withdrawal from active theatrical involvement in 1838, always attached great importance to the visual as well as to the verbal aspect of his work, and this has generally been counted in his favour as a playwright. Yet though his critical standing is currently high, he is not much played on the modern German stage; and one may hazard the suggestion that this is not only because of the conservatism of his views, but because of his theatricality itself, or of its specific character. His work is too much rooted in a particular theatrical style, too specifically conceived in terms of the Viennese stage of the early nineteenth century, in which elaborate visual effects carry a great deal of a play's meaning. In the theatre of our own times, with its very different visual conventions, his work is difficult to realise appropriately.[9] This stylistic limitation prevents him from being a dramatist of the very first order. But he is certainly to be accounted a major writer in his often highly successful combination of acute psychological probing with a broad philosophic or historical vision. The failure to achieve a convincing blend of these elements is the criticism which has most frequently been levelled at his younger rival Hebbel.

# CHAPTER XI

# Classicism in Vienna (ii): Hebbel; the end of the tradition

In 1845 Hebbel, then aged thirty-two, arrived in Vienna for what was intended to be only a short visit, on his way back from Italy to his home in the north. He had obtained a travelling bursary from the King of Denmark (as a native of Holstein, Hebbel was a subject of the Danish crown) and was supposed to return to Copenhagen to report to his patron. But after being lionised by some admirers of his work, and, most importantly, after meeting and falling passionately in love with Christine Enghaus – for whom he was to abandon Elise Lensing, the mistress who had been loyal to him for ten years and borne him two children – he decided to stay. He paid a call on Grillparzer and was courteously received; Grillparzer was of course by this time no longer actively involved with the theatre, and it was only in the 1850s, when Laube had begun to revive Grillparzer's earlier works at the Burgtheater, that he began to see the younger man as a dangerous rival. But Hebbel's ambitions as a dramatist were already plain enough by 1845.

He had already by that date completed three tragedies and had one of them successfully performed. *Judith*, published in 1840 and produced in both Berlin and Hamburg in that same year, is based upon the Apocryphal story of the Jewish heroine who kills the Assyrian general Holofernes, *Genoveva* (1842) on the medieval legend of the sufferings of St Genevieve of Brabant and her persecution by the diabolical Golo, which had previously been dramatised by Tieck and before him by the 'Sturm und Drang' writer 'Maler' Müller. His third play, *Maria Magdalena*, was a realistic 'bürgerliches Trauerspiel' with a contemporary setting, partly autobiographical in content. It was published in 1844, with an important preface in which Hebbel grandly expounds his own dramatic intentions and his views on the art of tragedy. The heroine Klara, the Mary Magdalene of the title – a 'fallen woman' in the eyes of the world who may nevertheless hope to find favour in the sight of God – is a carpenter's daughter, who, pregnant and abandoned by the father of her child, drowns herself to avoid social disgrace, not so much for her own sake as for that of her bitter, tyrannical and uncomprehending father. Totally different in setting and style (*Genoveva* is in blank verse, the other two in prose), the three plays all show a preoccupation with sexual conflict and with the psychological reactions of men and, especially, women in situations of extreme stress. The continuing exploration of this subject-matter in a variety of settings, historical and legendary, characterises the remainder of Hebbel's dramatic work. *Herodes und Mariamne* (1849) is set at the court of Herod the Great in Jerusalem just before the birth of Christ; *Agnes Bernauer* (1853) in fifteenth-century Bavaria; *Gyges und sein Ring* (*Gyges and his Ring*, 1856) in a world of pre-classical Greek legend; *Die Nibelungen* (*The Nibelungs*, 1861) in a legendary Germanic world. Only in one or two minor pieces, however, including a bitter satirical comedy, *Der Diamant* (*The Diamond*, written in 1841 though not published till 1847) did he employ a contemporary setting as in *Maria Magdalena*.

In the light of Hebbel's quasi-Hegelian theories of the relationship between drama and history, it would seem that we are intended to see the plays principally as representations of world-historical turning-points or moments of crisis, when an established system of social or moral values is being challenged or supplanted by a new one: thus *Judith* portrays the clash of Judaism and paganism, *Herodes und Mariamne* the dawning of the Christian era, *Die Nibelungen* the end of Germanic paganism and the prospect of its supersession by Christianity, and *Agnes Bernauer* the challenging of the rigid class divisions of the feudal system by the first stirrings of modern egalitarianism. But the most memorable feature of Hebbel's plays is the series of remarkable, even extraordinary heroines who dominate the dramatic proceedings, whether they are at the forefront of the action like Judith or Mariamne, remain in the background but still actively influence the course of events like Kriemhild in *Die Nibe-*

*lungen*, or form a passive centre about which the dynamic action turns, like Genoveva or Agnes. If the purity and innocence of the last-named make them close dramatic kin to Kleist's Käthchen, then Mariamne, Kriemhild and Rhodope (in *Gyges und sein Ring*) are more like Penthesilea in the passion, even ferocity, with which they respond to male violation of their integrity. Their male antagonists represent a variety of types of male aggression and domination, whatever their supposed historical significance. Appropriately enough the most substantial recent German study of Hebbel's work locates him 'between Hegel and Freud'.[1]

Perhaps the most passionate of all, and the most complex in her sexual psychology, is Hebbel's first heroine, Judith. She vows to save the city of Bethulia and the Jewish nation by killing Holofernes, but in order to do so she has, unlike her biblical prototype, actually to give herself to him: 'The way to my deed lies through sin' (III). Yet she is plainly also drawn to him by sexual desire. In another, somewhat bizarre modification of his biblical source, Hebbel has made the young widow Judith a virgin, her marriage unconsummated, her late husband sexually impotent just as the men of the Jewish nation are, in a wider sense, impotent to resist the Assyrian conqueror. In contrast to this nation of eunuchs, Holofernes appears as the only real man, and Judith longs to meet him for that reason. But when he has taken her virginity Holofernes simply goes to sleep and ignores her: she is for him not another human being, but only an object. And so she takes his sword and decapitates him, not so much in accordance with her original intention as in revenge for his spurning her womanly feelings. On her return to Bethulia, received by the people with jubilation, she begs the priests to kill her if she should prove to be pregnant by Holofernes, for she will not bear his child. The psychological reasoning here is extraordinarily modern.

If Judith is the prototype of Hebbel's heroines, Holofernes is similarly the model for many of his subsequent male protagonists, though also drawn with features more exaggerated than most of his successors. He is not merely the embodiment of masculine self-confidence like Kleist's Achilles, in whom unthinking self-assertion and even brutality go hand in hand with genuine affection. He is a titanic egotist, even a solipsist, for whom no other

human being truly exists; he is like Grillparzer's Jason as Medea
describes him:

> He, he alone exists in all the world,
> And nothing else but stuff for his own deeds.
>
> (*Medea*, ii, ll.630–1)

Holofernes himself expresses this in posturings which recall and
surpass those of the 'Kraftkerls' of the 'Sturm und Drang'; indeed,
'Kraft' is one of his own watchwords, here perhaps best rendered
simply as 'strength': 'Strength! strength! that is all. Let the man
come who will stand up to me, who will cast me down. I long to
meet him! It is so empty to have nothing to admire but oneself' (v).
(When *Judith* was performed at the Burgtheater in 1849, with
Christine Hebbel in the title role, these and other exaggerations
were gleefully seized upon in a hilarious parody by Nestroy: 'I'd like
to set me on myself one day,' cries Nestroy's Holofernes, 'just to see
who's stronger, me or me.') This titanic egoism easily slips into
nihilism, into a desperate challenge to God to prove His existence:
'This world seems to me contemptible, I believe I was born to
destroy it, so that something better can take its place. . .I bore
deeper and deeper with my sword; if the howls of agony wake no
deliverer, then there is none there' (v). A similar challenge to
creation and creator is hurled down by Golo in *Genoveva*. Tor-
mented by his lust for the saintly heroine, Golo ponders whether a
mere everyday villain might by the intensification of his crimes
become a 'world-murderer, murderer of God' (iii, x). To avenge
himself on Genoveva he denounces her to her too credulous
husband Siegfried as an adulteress. Siegfried's reply reminds us of
Sylvester Schroffenstein's anguished questioning of God:

> What think you, Golo, does God have the right
> To let things happen that no man can grasp?     (iv, vi)

From the beginning, Hebbel's work strikes a note of pessimism and
despair deeper than that of Grillparzer or even Kleist. And this
remains constant, though never again quite so frenetically expressed
as in these first two plays.

In *Genoveva* the heroine retains her purity and integrity inviolate,
despite the assaults of Golo and despite the sentence of banishment

203

pronounced by her credulous husband. In *Herodes und Mariamne* and *Gyges und sein Ring* the heroines, Mariamne and Rhodope, feel themselves debased and defiled by husbands who treat them as mere possessions, unable to return or even adequately to comprehend their love and devotion. Mariamne swears to herself that she would rather die than outlive her husband Herod; but when he *asks* her to swear to *him* that she will kill herself if he should fail to return from his dangerous mission to Mark Antony in Egypt, she refuses. He leaves, ordering his sister's husband Joseph to kill Mariamne if he does not come back. Joseph boasts of his office to Mariamne herself; Herod returns, Mariamne upbraids him, and Herod has Joseph executed. Once again Herod is summoned to Mark Antony, this time to aid him at the battle of Actium – and the story repeats itself. Discovering that she has again been left to 'live beneath the sword', Mariamne resolves that if he does return this second time Herod shall find what he evidently wants to find – her celebrating the report of his death, in apparent proof of her infidelity:

> You shall destroy the wife you saw in me
> And then in death behold me as I am. (v, vi)

She stages a great feast; at its climax, Herod returns. He orders her death, and, as she had foretold, discovers her innocence too late. She has forced him to be her executioner, to destroy the precious possession whose real value he did not understand. In *Gyges und sein Ring* Rhodope, the Indian consort of the Lydian king Kandaules, insists on living in strict purdah, allowing no man but her husband even to see her. But when Gyges arrives with the magic ring which makes its wearer invisible, Kandaules makes him accompany him into Rhodope's bedroom. For Kandaules is, like Herod, funda-mentally insecure in his relationship to his wife: he needs, as he tells Gyges,

> a witness who can prove I am
> No fool who idly boasts if he would claim
> To kiss the fairest woman on this earth,
> And I have chosen you! (I, iii)

Gyges knows that what he is doing is wrong, but agrees to Kandaules' request. Discovering her husband's betrayal of her, Rhodope forces him and Gyges to fight to the death for the right to

13  Christine Hebbel as Brunhild in *Siegfrieds Tod* at the Burgtheater, Vienna in 1863, the year of her husband's death. Photograph by Carl Mahlknecht. The complete *Nibelungen* trilogy had been premiered in Weimar two years previously, with Christine playing Brunhild in *Siegfrieds Tod* and Kriemhild in the final part, *Kriemhilds Rache* – which was not seen in Vienna until 1871.

possess her, and when Gyges is victorious she kills herself. Communication and community between man and woman have become totally impossible. Sexual rivalry and antagonism seems also to have been the theme which attracted Hebbel to the medieval German epic of the Nibelungs, rather than the national or legendary qualities which had appealed to others such as Wagner. (Wagner had written the text of his tetralogy between 1848 and 1853, though the musical composition of the whole cycle was not completed until the 1870s.) Hebbel seized upon the rivalry of Brunhild and Kriemhild for the love of Siegfried, and in particular upon the terrible and long-meditated revenge which Kriemhild, after Siegfried has been murdered by Hagen at Brunhild's instigation, wreaks upon Hagen, Gunther and all their kinsmen. Wagner ignored completely the story of Kriemhild's revenge, reduced Kriemhild (or Gutrune, as he renames her) to a minor figure and concentrated on developing the mythical and symbolic elements in the earlier part of the Siegfried story; what interested Hebbel above all – and it must be admitted that in this he shows himself far more faithful to the medieval poem – was the transformation of the character of Kriemhild from tender, loving woman to vengeful fury.

The sexual psychology of Hebbel's plays is certainly extreme: the relationship between the sexes is usually one of uncompromising antagonism. (Interestingly enough, though Hebbel obviously feels deep sympathy and even admiration for the victims of male aggression whom he depicts in his plays, he was in real life vehemently opposed to the emancipation of women: his ideal of womanhood was one of virtuous passivity.) Whether this is necessarily implausible, as is often claimed, and the plays fundamentally flawed on this account, is another question. Kleist's portrayal of the battle of the sexes in *Penthesilea* has also been criticised, but not usually from the standpoint of realistic psychology: it seems to be recognised that realistic psychology was not Kleist's intention. And after Hebbel, Strindberg portrayed sexual antagonisms every bit as fierce and extreme as those of Hebbel's plays in a convincingly realistic style. The trouble seems to be that Hebbel falls between two stools, between myth and metaphysics on the one hand and realistic psychology on the other. We have noted a similar problem in relation to *Die Jungfrau von Orleans*, but in Hebbel's work the conflict is all-pervading. Even if he may have been drawn to choose his plots by the element of sexual confrontation which he found in them, he seeks at the same time to present them as the embodiment of universal, metaphysical forces. Indeed, the actual characters present themselves in this way: Kleist's Penthesilea destroys Achilles because he has spurned *her* love, but Mariamne tells Herod: 'In me you have affronted all humanity' (III, iii). This is another aspect of Hebbelian hyperbole. The characters in their own utterances raise themselves to a level of abstraction at which they leave behind the very real psychological conflicts in which they are embroiled. In the failure of the characters to understand or communicate with each other, another motif which recalls Kleist, we also sense in Hebbel's case the dramatist's manipulating hand. Just as in Judith's account of her wedding-night some supernatural force seems to put forth its hand to prevent her husband from consummating their marriage, so again and again in the plays Hebbel seems to put forth his hand to prevent his characters from speaking to or understanding each other: the dialogue, particularly in the early plays, bristles with asides, semi-asides, and speeches delivered in complete disregard of the presence of other characters on the stage. Even Mariamne seems positively determined to be misunderstood by her husband, while having at the same time to explain her actions to other characters – notably the Roman captain Titus, who functions as a kind of neutral observer of the action – for the audience's benefit, which increases still further the sense of contrivance.

A similar process of abstraction affects Hebbel's treatment of history and his choice of historical subjects and settings. The conception of history which informs his plays and his sense of the historical mission of the tragic dramatist are not derived immediately from his experience of the history of his own times, as is the case with Schiller and with Grillparzer. His own sense of living in a period of change, of actual or impending social and political upheaval, undoubtedly affects his portrayal of similar periods of crisis in the past. *Herodes und Mariamne*, for example, was actually written during the revolutions of 1848, and this can, with hindsight, be felt in Hebbel's depiction of Herod's political situation, menaced both at home – by internal conspiracy and dissension in Judaea – and abroad – by the instability of the Roman Empire and the power struggle between Mark Antony and Octavian. But Hebbel's perception of the historical movements of his own times, far more than Grillparzer's or even Schiller's, is filtered through a philosophy of history, and one of a highly abstract and schematised nature. Kant, who had proved such an important influence on Schiller, is described as an idealist philosopher, but in his essay on Universal History he had seen historical processes as motivated by real conflicts of interest between men living in a real, material world. Hebbel's philosophical mentor Hegel, however, sees history as the 'phenomenology of spirit' (*Phänomenologie des Geistes*, the title of his principal philosophical work, dating from 1806), that is as the record of the successive manifestations in the real world of the workings of a cosmic Mind, the progressive unfolding of a universal Idea. This Idea, or Mind, or Spirit, is the nineteenth-century philosopher's substitute for Lessing's divine providence: whatever it decrees, is by definition right, and process is by definition progress. The conflicts of the real world are seen in ideal or mental terms as a 'dialectic', as the successive resolutions of 'contradictions' as in a logical argument: a 'thesis' generates an 'antithesis' and their conflict is resolved in a 'synthesis' which then becomes the 'thesis' of the next stage of the argument. One day all the contradictions will be resolved, and the historical process will reach its consummation. Perhaps, Hegel suggests, this is already happening, for he seems at times to be implying that his own philosophy is itself the final, definitive manifestation of the Idea, or of Mind in a state of complete self-realisation;[2] in a rather similar vein Hebbel argues in the Preface to *Maria Magdalena* that the task of dramatic art is nothing less than 'to help to bring to its conclusion the world-historical process of our times'. It is to do this by demonstrating the working of the dialectic.

A dialectical pattern can certainly be detected in some, at any rate, of Hebbel's plays. In *Herodes und Mariamne*, for example the underlying pattern seems to be that of a conflict between traditional Judaism and the Roman world giving rise to the emergence of Christianity, heralded by the appearance at the end of the play of the Magi seeking the new-born Christ. In *Gyges und sein Ring* thesis, antithesis and synthesis are represented by the ultra-conservative Rhodope, the over-hasty innovator Kandaules, and Gyges, the catalyst and survivor of their conflict. Such a reading however, runs

against the emotional grain of the plays, which directs our sympathies strongly, if not exclusively, towards Mariamne and Rhodope;
and it is very hard to see how the moral progress of the world is in
any way advanced by their deaths. The truth seems to be that
although Hebbel may have sought comfort or the reassurance of
meaningfulness in a Hegelian philosophy of history, the plays
themselves convey no such optimistic view. They are as profoundly
pessimistic at the universal level, in their depiction of the human
situation, as they are at the individual level, in their depiction of
human nature. History appears in them not as a process, certainly
not as a progress, perhaps not even (as in *Ein Bruderzwist in
Habsburg*) as a falling-away from a divine origin which still,
however, retains its truth and validity as a moral standard, but
rather as what Nietzsche, a great denigrator of Hegelian and all
other systems of historical optimism, was to call an 'eternal recur-
rence', an ever-turning wheel (the image is one which recurs a
number of times in Hebbel's plays and other writings) beneath
which individual lives are inexorably crushed. Despite the Hegelian
patterns evident in Hebbel's theoretical writings and his attempt to
impose a Hegelian framework upon the dramatic conflicts of his
plays, the true philosophical kinship of Hebbel the poet is rather
with the great pessimist, Schopenhauer.

Like his predecessors whom we have considered in these pages,
Hebbel set the highest possible value on the art of drama, and
regarded it with the utmost seriousness, as something to be kept
distinct from the mere representation of contemporary reality. With
few exceptions, his choice of subject-matter and style accordingly
conforms to the classical principle of *éloignement*. Frequently his
plays were conceived in direct rivalry with predecessors whose
work he considered to be inferior, whereas Grillparzer's frequent
echoes of Goethe and Schiller are rather to be taken as complimen-
tary allusions to the works of the acknowledged masters of the
tradition in which he wished his works to be seen – even where such
allusions serve, as we have noted, to express a very different
message or attitude on Grillparzer's part. *Judith* was intended
specifically to rival *Die Jungfrau von Orleans* in its portrayal of the
psychological conflict undergone by a woman entrusted with a
historic mission. *Maria Magdalena* was written, or so the Preface

claims, to demonstrate that the 'bürgerliches Trauerspiel' was capable of high artistic seriousness and not necessarily doomed to the triviality manifested, in Hebbel's view, by most previous examples of the form. These of course included such works as *Kabale und Liebe*, which Hebbel later described, in a diary entry of March 1847, after seeing a performance of the piece, as a work of 'infinite nullity' ('grenzenlose Nichtigkeit'). In *Genoveva* Hebbel vies with Tieck and Müller, in *Agnes Bernauer* and *Die Nibelungen* respectively with August von Törring and Ernst Raupach – dramatists who are today indeed quite forgotten, but whose treatments of these subjects had enjoyed considerable success in their own day. Curiously enough, Hebbel seems not to have known that the story of Herod and Mariamne had been treated by many dramatists before him, including such varied figures as Hans Sachs, Calderón, Voltaire and Christoph von Schönaich (a protégé of Gottsched's);[3] at all events, he appears not to have known any of their works at first hand, but the choice of such a long-established tragic subject is characteristic of him. Hebbel's last tragedy was again conceived in direct rivalry with Schiller, but like Schiller himself he died before his *Demetrius* was completed. Though he experimented a number of times with prose, and even with satirical 'Knittelverse' in a couple of minor pieces, he reverted again and again, and finally definitively, to the discipline and elevation of blank verse, and he eschewed any such variations as the quasi-lyrical ornamentations of the Romantics or the Spanish metres of Grillparzer. In all this his aspiration to classical style and classic status is unmistakable.

There is undoubtedly a sense of strain in Hebbel's work. His metaphysics, his searching and often very modern psychology, and his historical settings are rarely harmoniously integrated. The intense self-awareness of his characters has been repeatedly criticised, by his contemporaries and by successive generations of critics, as standing out anachronistically from the historical backgrounds to which he seeks with such insistent symbolism to relate them. Though the rhetorical posturings of a Holofernes or a Golo are extreme even by Hebbel's standards, hyperbole is rarely absent, even in his best work. And although the plays are not without moments of striking theatrical effectiveness – Herod's two sudden reappearances in Acts III and IV of *Herodes und Mariamne*, for example

– their overall character is very literary. His language holds its meaning like a clenched fist, from which it can often only with difficulty be prised. And though Hebbel was by no means indifferent to theatrical success, and undoubtedly conceived his later heroines very much as parts for Christine, he was of no mind to compromise with public taste. Neither in his life-time nor since has any of his plays enjoyed the stage success of Grillparzer's. In this respect it is Grillparzer who appears the more convincing heir of Weimar classicism. And whereas Grillparzer continues to prove attractive to academic criticism, and a good deal of interesting work has appeared on him in recent years, Hebbel's critical stock remains low, and attempts to revive interest in him have met with little success. Fashions change, of course, and it may be that he is simply taking a long time to recover from the odium of having been in favour (largely, like Nietzsche, for mistaken reasons) during the Nazi era. But it seems more likely that in his work Hebbel will remain, as he was in his life, an awkward and difficult man to deal with.[4]

Hebbel's art is at its grandest in *Herodes und Mariamne*, a work in which the collision of two strong-willed protagonists is powerful and moving even if it strains our credulity, and which deserves to be seen more often. It is at its most austerely refined in *Gyges und sein Ring*, a play which Hebbel declared to be fit for the Théâtre français in its neo-classic purity and economy of form – and the clash of cultures which is here portrayed, whatever its world-historical significance in Hebbel's eyes, has perhaps other and more immediate meanings for a multicultural civilisation. But Hebbel is at his least forced, and most convincing, in *Maria Magdalena* and perhaps in *Agnes Bernauer*. Both these plays are in prose, and in them Hebbel shows a considerable gift for dramatic realism. This is particularly so in *Maria Magdalena*, with its many direct reminiscences of Hebbel's life in Wesselburen and in Munich. The claustrophobic atmosphere of the artisan's household, the stifling force of the petty-bourgeois code of social respectability, the fierce pride and at the same time the intense vulnerability of Meister Anton the carpenter, and the helplessness of Klara, the victim upon whom all these environmental, social and family pressures come to bear, are conveyed with force and conviction. In the Preface Hebbel claims that his aim was not to depict social reality as such, still less to point, as earlier authors of 'bürgerliche Trauerspiele' had done, to remediable – and therefore untragic – problems such as class conflict or economic deprivation, but to demonstrate that even the realistic depiction of such humble characters and the milieu in which they live can rise to the heights of tragedy. In theory, the wheel has come full circle, back to Lessing's introduction of the 'bürgerliches Trauerspiel' with *Miss Sara Sampson*. And Hebbel's play, with its careful integration of character and environment, plainly represents a similar development. Like Lessing, Hebbel had aimed at the restoration and purification of a classical literary tradition; but again like Lessing, he had in fact taken a major step towards the social realism which was to supplant the classical tradition in the drama of the later nineteenth century. Ibsen was indeed much impressed by *Maria Magdalena*, and it may well have influenced his own turning-away from poetic and historical drama to the contemporary social realism of his middle years.

*Agnes Bernauer*, despite its medieval setting, has some of the same virtues. It is not such an innovatory play as *Maria Magdalena*, but it successfully combines elements of the 'bürgerliches Trauerspiel' with the historical realism Goethe had introduced into the drama with *Götz von Berlichingen*. Duke Albrecht, heir to the Bavarian throne, loves and insists on marrying Agnes, the beautiful daughter of a barber-surgeon in Augsburg; but Agnes is abducted and executed by the reigning Duke Ernst, Albrecht's father, who regards his son's action as a danger to the state and the social order. Albrecht rebels, but is finally forced to submit, to accept the duties of his station and to acknowledge that his attempt to override the class barriers of feudal society was premature, if nothing worse. Like Grillparzer's *Die Jüdin von Toledo*, with which it has much in common in both plot and theme, *Agnes Bernauer* has been criticised as an unsuccessful combination of a love-tragedy and a tragedy of political necessity, the two elements each taking up its own part of the play with insufficient structural links between them. It has also been attacked for its apparently reactionary political stance, as a dramatised version of Hegel's idealisation of the State and of the existing social order, though this interpretation has been disputed; it has even been criticised for lacking the passion, however exaggerated, which inspires Hebbel's other tragedies. There is some justice in all these criticisms. But the creation of historical atmosphere, and the integration of the main protagonists and their relationship with the historical background, is much more convincing than in Hebbel's other historical tragedies, where the background detail, as in so many nineteenth-century historical works, both plays and novels, often seems gratuitous, merely picturesque, or self-consciously symbolic. Particularly in the first three acts, a complex world of social and environmental relationships is created: Augsburg with its patrician families, jealous of their privileges, and its rising guilds of craftsmen and artisans; the chivalric world of the late medieval nobility; and the relations of the Duchy of Bavaria with the Empire and the Papacy. Together with the successful portrayal of a very different, modern social world in *Maria Magdalena*, this suggests that Hebbel's real talent lay in just this kind of realism. The individual fates of Albrecht and Agnes are also much more closely and convincingly related to Hebbel's theme of historical transition: the hero Albrecht, very much like Ferdinand in *Kabale und Liebe*, is plainly a man ahead of his time, whose insistence on the immediate fulfilment of his ideal leads only to the destruction of what he holds most dear. *Agnes Bernauer* also conveys much more directly than any of Hebbel's other plays a sense of his response to the political events of his own day: the risings of 1848, the frustration of the liberals' hopes of a united Empire with a parliamentary constitution, their resignation and turning to conservatism in the face of the threat of more radical revolution. In his other plays Hebbel deliberately turned his back on directness and realism in favour of abstraction and classical stylisation. It may be that in so doing he prevented what was undoubtedly a formidable talent from achieving its full potential, and from making a major contribution to the development of German and indeed European drama.

# Epilogue

Grillparzer and Hebbel had inherited the tradition of poetic drama from Goethe and Schiller. Like Kleist, they modified that tradition in their own ways, developing in particular a concern with the dramatic presentation of psychology and of history in new forms, in the light of their own experience and thought. But they remained true to its essential spirit, rather than rebelling against it.

Rebellion was the course chosen by their young contemporary Georg Büchner, with his vehement anti-idealism, his deliberately anti-Schillerian historical drama *Dantons Tod* (*Danton's Death*, 1835), his turning-back to the social realism of the early 'Stürmer und Dränger', especially Lenz, in protest against the whole classical movement, and his radical development of the Lenzian manner in his posthumous, fragmentary *Woyzeck*. Büchner died of typhus in 1837 at the age of twenty-three, almost unknown as a playwright; had he lived, he would undoubtedly have set the German drama on a different course, and one wonders whether Hebbel would have remained uninfluenced by his radicalism. Büchner did not begin to come into his own until the 1880s, when he was discovered by another generation, that of Hauptmann and the Naturalists. The only other dramatist of the first half of the century who rose above mediocrity was another north German, Christian Dietrich Grabbe (1801–36). In his also relatively short life Grabbe produced a number of historical dramas, not unlike Hebbel's in their strident pessimism, his last play being yet another dramatisation of the Hermann story. He also wrote an anarchic, very amusing but also deeply pessimistic comedy, *Scherz, Satire, Ironie und tiefere Bedeutung* (*Jest, Satire, Irony and Deeper Meaning*, 1822, revised for publication 1827), whose title gives a good indication of its surrealistic, self-reflective character (Grabbe himself appears on stage at the end of the play; the schoolmaster tries to prevent his entry, but is rebuked by the heroine Liddy for being 'so ungrateful to the man who has written you'); and a poetic drama, *Don Juan und Faust*, performed in his native town of Detmold in 1829, in which with typically exaggerated ambitiousness (another characteristic in which he resembles Hebbel) he vies with Goethe, Mozart and Byron, bringing together on stage the two characters whom he regarded as the great mythical heroes of modern times. His most challenging work is his *Napoleon oder die Hundert Tage* (*Napoleon or the Hundred Days*, 1831), in which the return of Napoleon from Elba, the reactions of the French people and the representatives of the restored Bourbon regime, and the final defeat of Waterloo, are portrayed in an 'epic' style which demands the techniques of the cinema for its effective realisation. If Grillparzer's work remains firmly anchored to the past and Büchner's looks resolutely to the future, Grabbe (again rather like Hebbel) is caught between the two, anxious to challenge his dramatic predecessors on their own ground while also initiating developments which only come to fruition long after his death. There has been something of a revival of interest in Grabbe in Germany, both in literary studies and on the stage, but his place in the history of German drama is far from assured.[1]

With Grillparzer and Hebbel the classical age of German drama finally comes to an end. Indeed, after their deaths there is something of a hiatus in the history of German drama, which resumes only with the beginnings of Naturalism in the 1880s – though Ibsen, the principal progenitor of the new movement as far as the drama was concerned, was actually living and working in Germany from 1864 to 1891, when he at last returned to Norway. The greatest and most important German writer for the stage in these years was, of course, not a literary dramatist, but the composer Richard Wagner. Wagner – born in 1813, the same year as Hebbel and Büchner – saw himself as a poet as well as a musician; his principal operas all have texts of his own composition, and he aimed to make his music subservient to the words and the drama. He was deeply involved in the events of 1848, and was influenced by them in his conception of the historic mission of the artist. In his essays of 1849–51 he sets out his ideal, echoed in his young disciple Nietzsche's *Die Geburt der Tragödie aus dem Geiste der Musik* (*The Birth of Tragedy from the Spirit of Music*) of 1872, of modern opera or 'music-drama' as a renewal of Greek tragedy, and he and Nietzsche (though Nietzsche was soon enough to become disillusioned with his idol) undoubtedly saw the opening of the Festspielhaus or Festival Playhouse in Bayreuth in 1872 as the latest, perhaps the concluding chapter in the long story of the struggle to establish a German National Theatre.[2] (The German nation, minus Austria, had of course at last achieved political unity under Prussian leadership in the previous year.) Posterity has not seen Wagner's work in quite the same light. Up to about 1820 most German theatre companies had performed both spoken drama and opera. Many actors, actresses and actor-managers had also been noted as singers, including Corona Schröter, Goethe's first Iphigenie; Karoline Jagemann, the bane of his final years as director in Weimar, who sang Leonore in *Fidelio*; and Nestroy, an accomplished bass, whose repertoire included Rocco in *Fidelio* and Sarastro in *The Magic Flute*. Goethe himself had written texts for 'Singspiele', and there was, as we have observed, much that was 'operatic' in the dramatic and theatrical style of classical Weimar, where a heightened, stylised form of expression began to leave behind all pretence at mimetic realism. In the nineteenth century, however, opera and serious spoken drama began more and more to diverge, and it became clear that the future of the latter lay after all in the direction of realism. Wagner tried to bring the two together again, but since his day they have again generally followed separate paths. And if Wagnerian opera is to claim the dubious title of German national drama, then it is in a very different sense from that envisaged by the cosmopolitan humanitarianism of Goethe and Schiller.

The tradition of verse drama in German has, however, never been completely lost. Some twentieth-century attempts at verse drama strike one as conscious revivalism, with its attendant artificiality. This is plainly the case, despite their very real merits, with the poetic dramas of Hugo von Hofmannsthal, designed as they are to embody the call for a 'conservative revolution' and a return to the cultural and spiritual values of the past. It is even more strongly felt in those of Gerhart Hauptmann (more successful in his Naturalist manner), from the early neo-Romantic *Die versunkene Glocke* (*The Sunken Bell*, 1896) to his last work, the *Atridentetralogie* of the 1940s, in which the legend of Iphigeneia and the Atrides is used again to symbolise the course of human and perhaps in particular German history, but to show it in a light very different from that of Goethe's optimism. Brecht, the dominant figure of twentieth-century German drama, was of course a conscious enemy of the classical tradition, parodying the blank verse of Schiller (and others) in *Die heilige Johanna der Schlachthöfe* (*St Joan of the Stockyards*) and *Arturo Ui*, where along with other 'ideologies' it is 'unmasked' as a rhetorical device serving to conceal motives of exploitation and domination. But Brecht himself employs heightened forms of speech, broken into lines of verse, for serious expressive purposes in some of his later plays such as *Der gute Mensch von Sezuan* and *Der kaukasische Kreidekreis*; and Brecht's brand of theatrical 'realism' is as fiercely opposed to the Naturalism of Hauptmann as was the classicism of Goethe and Schiller to the 'naturalism' prevalent in the theatre of their own day. Even in the period since 1945, various forms of verse have been employed in the serious dramatic treatment of historical and political subject-matter by dramatists as diverse as Weiss and Hochhuth, though again their employment is often parodistic or 'alienating' in the Brechtian sense of the word: thus in Weiss's famous *Marat/Sade*, 'Knittelverse' are used for the play within the play, with its puppet-like figures and deliberately simplistic manner. And Peter Hacks's *Amphitryon*, though it has little else in common with Kleist's, is again in blank verse.

The classics of the German drama are still regularly performed on the German stage, chiefly Lessing, Schiller and Kleist, together with *Faust*, while Grillparzer has maintained his status as the classical Austrian dramatist. The heritage of Weimar classicism has, however, been subjected to a searching revaluation in both West and East Germany, for the catastrophic course of German history has created for present generations of Germans a uniquely problematic relationship to the German culture of the past, notably to the literary products of Weimar classicism. After 1945 these seemed to represent a 'better Germany', an ideal from which German history had tragically fallen away, but which offered a model for future regeneration.

Some saw them – a natural enough approach in the immediate post-war period, when the forcible politicisation of culture in the cause of National Socialism was all too fresh in the memory – as the repository of a philosophical wisdom which evolved according to its own immanent laws, but was scarcely if at all affected by the material events of history.[3] More recently, however, others – taking up a political stance already occupied by writers such as Büchner and Heine in the nineteenth century – have seen Weimar classicism as itself setting German culture on a false course. The deliberate abandonment by Goethe and Schiller, in the works of their maturity, of the radical, liberated manner of their youth in favour of the formal order and discipline of the essentially courtly classical style has been interpreted not, as Schiller had argued, as an attempt by art to meet in an appropriately serious manner the challenge of those 'high, momentous times', but on the contrary as a failure of nerve in the face of the Revolution, or even as signifying an actual capitulation to the forces of feudal reaction and the *ancien régime*. It has been argued that the Weimar programme of 'aesthetic education' not only failed in its ostensible purpose of preparing men through civilisation for social and political maturity, but if anything actually achieved the opposite end, preventing the cultured classes of the German nation from achieving political maturity by cocooning them in artistic illusion and thus effectively contributing to the disasters of German history – the failure to achieve any form of democratic national unification in 1815 and again in 1848, and hence, indirectly, the catastrophically different forms which unification did take in the Second Reich and even more so in the Third. This can be seen as the peculiar German variety of the radical, sociologically based literary and cultural criticism which has gained a good deal of currency in other Western countries in recent years, and which sees all forms of culture which are not specifically popular or oppositional as essentially instruments of repression, serving to maintain existing systems of social and political domination. (Lessing and the 'Stürmer und Dränger' have generally escaped this kind of criticism, being regarded as essentially 'progressive' writers; Kleist's credentials are rather more dubious in this respect, but perhaps Goethe's hostility to Kleist has served his reputation as an enemy of the establishment.) Goethe and Schiller were certainly in their later years supporters of order rather than of revolutionary upheaval, but they were not reactionaries (as might more accurately be maintained of some of the Romantics, or possibly even of Kleist) and they continued to hope for the eventual triumph of humanity. But to the radicals of West Germany in the years after 1968 they were the perpetrators (even if perhaps also the victims) of a 'legend' which had to be demolished and 'de-mystified'.[4] Criticism of this kind persists under various ideological labels, whether overtly political or post-structuralist. A similar kind of debate, if generally in less strident tones, has been conducted in East Germany. Here the official Marxist view has been that the cultural 'heritage' which in the past was monopolised by a few has to be made available for positive appreciation by all; that the products of Weimar classicism, like all truly great works (for established Marxist criticism has tended to retain the kind of hierarchical value-judgements which many Western Marxists have rejected as 'mystification'), are essentially progressive in spirit, and that it is the task of the critic to reveal this. But the nature of this 'heritage' and of the proper relation of present-day culture to it has nevertheless been the subject of a good deal of discussion, and a certain amount of irreverence has manifested itself in the German Democratic Republic too – following the example set by Brecht, the *enfant terrible* of German Marxism, whose own disrespectful attitude towards the classics drew from paladins of Marxist criticism such as Georg Lukács the rebuke of 'ultra-leftism'.[5]

The existence of these debates shows that the classical writers are at the very least a real presence in German cultural history, whose significance for the present demands constant reassessment with an urgency which is perhaps not felt in the case of other national literatures. The most useful recent criticism has taken this into account; it has reasserted that Goethe and Schiller were, after all, men of formidable intellectual and artistic powers with an insight into the human condition which has by no means lost its validity for us today – but it has recognised that their works cannot simply be regarded as timeless masterpieces transcending any historical context, but stand in a complex and often contradictory relationship to the unprecedentedly disorientating social and political upheavals of the times in which they lived.[6] Goethe himself was fully aware of these contradictions, even ten years before the Revolution: 'It is a cursed business,' he wrote to Charlotte von Stein as he was working on the first version of *Iphigenie*, 'the King of Tauris has to speak as if there were no stocking-weavers going hungry in Apolda' (the neighbouring town to Weimar).

The controversies voiced by the literary critics have also made themselves felt in the German theatre. Here directors and 'Dramaturgen' of left-wing political persuasion, trained in Brechtian forms of theatre, have been zealous in playing the classics 'against the grain', in the attempt to force their audiences to critical awareness, to shake them out of their alleged bourgeois complacency, or simply to shock them. King Thoas has appeared on a bicycle, Maria Stuart in the nude, and German theatre festivals have often been occasions on which 'fashionable directors overtake each other in calculated displays of irreverence towards the classics'.[7] The stylistic disciplines of classicism have been studiously disregarded. One of the pioneering works in this respect was Hansgünther Heyme's Cologne production of *Wallenstein* in 1966, which 'freed the work from the formal conventions which Schiller believed himself obliged to observe'.[8] The development of reception studies in literary criticism has also had its parallel in the theatre, with directors attempting to build into their productions allusions to a whole history of interpretation and of alleged ideological appropriation, as in Heyme's production of *Wilhelm Tell* in Stuttgart in 1984 as a 'tragedy of German history'. Brecht objected to what he called 'intimidation by the classics', but the effect of this kind of intrusive directorial interpretation can itself be intimidating to a theatre audience. The insistence of directors on engaging, as it were, in political debate with their playwrights as well as with their audiences often means that the plays appear reduced to a merely German, even parochial significance, and are denied the universal human appeal to which they aspired and which they undoubtedly still possess.

Goethe and Schiller would themselves have been the first to agree that it is legitimate, even necessary, to adapt literary dramas to the needs of the public, the theatre and (in the case of works from the past) the age for which they are to be performed; such was indeed their own practice, and it remained normal theatrical practice until the nineteenth century introduced the dubious and probably impossible demand for 'authenticity' and faithfulness to authorial intention. It has been argued that the liberties that, for example, Heyme has taken with Schiller are no greater than those taken by Schiller with *Macbeth* – or even with *Egmont*. Goethe and Schiller would, however, probably have been shocked by a subversion of the proprieties more radical than that of their own 'Sturm und Drang' period. They would certainly have been shocked to hear their verse deliberately mutilated, and to discover that 'rhythmophobia', as they called it, now affects a majority not only of actors but also of directors. At the same time, they would have recognised that many modern productions – calling as they do upon the rich resources of a theatre enjoying generous public subsidy – have been very exciting in purely theatrical terms: Heyme's spectacular *Tell* itself, for example, with its extravagant scenic effects and huge numbers of extras, or Peter Stein's magical *Prinz Friedrich von Homburg*.[9] And at their best these have brought genuinely illuminating insights, revealed rarely seen aspects of familiar works, or even made works theatrically accessible which are all too rarely seen on the stage, as was the case with Heyme's *Wallenstein*, which incorporated substantial parts of the whole trilogy, including *Wallensteins Lager*, in a single evening. With its tradition of 'director's theatre' – to which itself, as we have seen, Goethe in Weimar made a major, perhaps the decisive contribution – the present-day German stage can boast some formidable interpretative talent; and the work of directors such as Stein, Heyme and others has at all events shown that the German classics are still very much alive, presenting a theatrical and intellectual challenge which is constantly taken up and constantly renewed.

# Notes

## Classicism and neo-classicism: Germany and the European tradition

1 On the social and political background of eighteenth-century German literature, see A. Menhennet, *Order and Freedom: German Literature and Society, 1720–1805*, London 1973.

2 Walter Benjamin argued in his *Ursprung des deutschen Trauerspiels*, Berlin 1928 (translated into English as *The Origins of German Tragic Drama*, London 1977) that the seventeenth-century German Baroque 'Trauerspiel' was an autonomous form having little or no real relation to the Greek, Renaissance or neo-classic 'Tragödie'. Most German writers, whether playwrights or critics, have used the terms more or less interchangeably.

3 For further discussion of the meaning of 'classicism' with reference to German literature, see T. J. Reed, *The Classical Centre: Goethe and Weimar 1775–1832*, London and New York 1980 (reprinted Oxford 1986). The notion of 'classicism' has been the subject of lively, often fierce debate in Germany itself (see above, pp. 217ff): a variety of viewpoints is represented in K. O. Conrady (ed.), *Deutsche Literatur zur Zeit der Klassik*, Stuttgart 1977. See also Dieter Borchmeyer, *Die Weimarer Klassik. Eine Einführung*, Königstein 1980.

4 For a fuller account of Gottsched's reforms, and a discussion of the drama of the period in relation to its social and theatrical background, see W. H. Bruford, *Theatre, Drama and Audience in Goethe's Germany*, London 1950. See also H. Kindermann, *Theatergeschichte der Goethezeit*, Vienna 1948; and H. Knudsen, *Deutsche Theatergeschichte*, Stuttgart 1959.

5 The origin of this curious term appears to be the practice of performing a play depicting kings and affairs of state ('Staatsaktion') as the main part ('Hauptaktion') of a theatrical entertainment, followed by a comic after-piece or some form of musical number.

## Classicism in modern dress: Lessing and the beginnings of realism

1 Characteristically, though the form originated in England and its first English practitioners were plainly aware of the innovatory nature of their work, the English did not in fact have a generic term for it at the time. Johnson describes some of Shakespeare's plays which do not deal with affairs of state, such as *Othello* and *Timon of Athens*, as 'domestic tragedies', but the particular application of the term to the eighteenth-century middle-class form seems to be the work of later critics. Goldsmith, who did not approve of the innovation, calls it a 'Tradesman's Tragedy'.

2 For vivid impression of the history of Lessing's plays in performance since the Second World War, see D. Diederichsen and B. Rudin (eds.), *Lessing im Spiegel der Theaterkritik 1945–1979*, Berlin 1980.

3 J. G. Robertson's *Lessing's Dramatic Theory*, Cambridge 1939 (reprinted New York 1965), gives a very full account of the *Dramaturgie* in relation to the European tradition of dramatic criticism, though in demonstrating how much he drew from other writers, Robertson does less than justice to the originality and coherence of Lessing's own thought.

4 The extent to which Lessing's interpretation of Aristotle is distorted by his own presuppositions and those of his age is still the subject of controversy. See Stephen Halliwell, *Aristotle's Poetics*, London 1986, pp. 312ff.

5 For a fuller account of Lessing's work, see my *Lessing and the Drama*, Oxford 1981. Of more recent German studies, G. Ter-Nedden, *Lessings Trauerspiele. Der Ursprung des modernen Dramas aus dem Geist der Kritik*, Stuttgart 1986, stresses the intellectual nature of the plays and their critical relationship to earlier drama, while Peter Pütz, *Die Leistung der Form. Lessings Dramen*, Frankfurt 1986, considers the plays in their own right and emphasises Lessing's mastery of theatrical technique.

## The revolt of Prometheus (i): Goethe and the 'Sturm und Drang'

1 See the informative survey by R. R. Heiter, *German Tragedy in the Age of Enlightenment*, Berkeley and Los Angeles 1963.

2 See E. A. Blackall, *The Emergence of German as a Literary Language*, Cambridge 1959, pp. 482ff.

3 Aristotle, *Poetics*, ch. 6. See also John Jones, *On Aristotle and Greek Tragedy*, London 1962; and Halliwell, *Aristotle's Poetics*, pp. 138ff.

4 F. Gundolf, *Shakespeare und der deutsche Geist*, 2nd edn, Berlin 1914, pp. 226f.

5 See Benjamin Bennett, *Modern Drama and German Classicism*, Ithaca and London 1979.

6 See Herbert Lindenberger, *Historical Drama: The Relation of Literature and Reality*, Chicago and London 1975, pp. 114f. See also C. E. Vaughan, *Types of Tragic Drama*, London 1908, p. 199: 'the historical play, as essayed by Goethe and Schiller . . . forms a wholly new departure in the history of the drama'.

7 R. Peacock, *Goethe's Major Plays*, Manchester 1959, p. 12.

8 See, for example, the discussion in Bennett, *Modern Drama and German Classicism*. See also E. M. Wilkinson, 'The Relation of Form and Meaning in Goethe's *Egmont*', in E. M. Wilkinson and L. A. Willoughby, *Goethe, Poet and Thinker*, London 1962.

9 For a representative selection of recent German critical viewpoints on Goethe's plays, see Walter Hinderer (ed.), *Goethes Dramen. Neue Interpretationen*, Stuttgart 1980. Hinderer has also edited similar volumes on Schiller (1979) and Kleist (1981).

## The revolt of Prometheus (ii): Schiller's prose plays

1 The modified acting version (or rather a further revision based upon it) was itself subsequently published, under the designation 'Trauerspiel', and this version is found in a few modern reprints; but the original printed version, subtitled 'Schauspiel', is generally regarded as the authentic one. The prompt copy used for the first production has been reprinted in an edition by H. Stubenrauch and G. Schulz, *Schillers Räuber. Urtext des Mannheimer Soufflierbuchs*, Mannheim 1959. Apart from substantial cuts, the most radical changes made by Schiller were in the fate of Franz (see note 3 below) and in the backdating of the action from the original middle of the eighteenth century to the sixteenth, the period which *Götz von Berlichingen* had made so popular. This latter change was made at Dalberg's insistence, but Schiller objected to it strongly, claiming that the characterisation, thought and language of his play were essentially modern.

2 See E. L. Stahl, *Friedrich Schiller's Drama: Theory and Practice*, Oxford 1954. Though Stahl's extrapolation of Schiller's theoretical concepts in particular to the early plays is questionable, his book is still the best general introduction to Schiller's dramatic work in English.

3 In the 'Trauerspiel' Franz is captured, and is hurled into the dungeon from which his dying father has just been released; but this is much less effective than his suicide in the 'Schauspiel'. When the original version gained acceptance on the stage, the two parts were sometimes played by

the same actor: a feat of theatrical bravura calling for exceptional physical, vocal and expressive resources. Traditionally, the actor wore a dark wig for the part of Karl and a red one for Franz: stage villains conventionally had red hair – like Schiller himself.

4 On the development of Schiller's dramatic language, see H. B. Garland, *Schiller the Dramatic Writer: A Study of Style in the Plays*, Oxford 1969.

5 For an account of the original production, with much interesting information on contemporary theatrical practice, see the essay by O. Schmidt in the reprint of the *Soufflierbuch* (see note 1 above).

6 Erich Auerbach, 'Miller the Musician', in his *Mimesis: The Representation of Reality in Western Literature*, Princeton 1953 (German original, 1947), ch. 17.

7 For a translation of this work, and a discussion of the significance of Schiller's medical studies for his general intellectual and artistic development, see Kenneth Dewhurst and Nigel Reeves, *Friedrich Schiller: Medicine, Psychology and Literature*, Oxford 1978.

## *The triumph of humanity:* Nathan der Weise, Iphigenie auf Tauris, Don Carlos

1 See Menhennet, *Order and Freedom*.

2 Erich Heller, 'Goethe and the Avoidance of Tragedy', in *The Disinherited Mind*, Cambridge 1952.

3 'Verdirb uns – wenn du darfst': the literal meaning hovers between 'must' and 'may'.

4 The role of Thoas is rather like that of the non-singing Pasha Selim in Mozart's *Seraglio*, the basic 'rescue' plot of which is very similar to that of *Iphigenie auf Tauris*: after all ruses and stratagems have failed, Belmonte and Constanze obtain their liberty by telling the Pasha the truth.

5 On the Germans' view of Greece, see E. M. Butler, *The Tyranny of Greece over Germany*, Cambridge 1935; and H. Trevelyan, *Goethe and the Greeks*, Cambridge 1941 (new edn 1981).

6 See Lindenberger, *Historical Drama*, p.139. Though Lindenberger discusses Schiller at some length, he fails to my mind do justice to *Don Carlos*, either intrinsically or to its importance in Schiller's dramatic development: he seems unwilling to take seriously the optimistic philosophy which informed Schiller's view of history in the late 1780s. For a very positive assessment of *Don Carlos*, see Vaughan, *Types of Tragic Drama*, pp. 201ff.

7 Translation is of little use here, particularly on account of the total strangeness of the alexandrine in English. But here are first Schlegel's,

then Goethe's version of Pylades' opening speech, in which he attempts to encourage the downcast Orest:

> Zwar weichen werd ich nicht. Ich bin mir nicht so lieb
> Als du, dein Glück, Orest, und unser Freundschaftstrieb.
> Doch laß dich nicht zu bald von deinem Schmerz bezwingen.
> Ihn sollst du stillen, Freund, nicht nach dem Tode ringen.
> Gedenkst du, daß du so des Himmels Wort erfüllst,
> Wenn du die Raserei durch Sterben schließen willst?
> Vielleicht gibt dieser Tag uns Mittel in die Hände,
> Dadurch dein Kummer sich zu deinem Besten wende,
>
> (Schlegel, i, iii)

> Ich bin noch nicht, Orest, wie du bereit,
> In jenes Schattenreich hinabzugehn.
> Ich sinne noch, durch die verworrnen Pfade,
> Die nach der schwarzen Nacht zu führen scheinen,
> Uns zu dem Leben wieder aufzuwinden.
> Ich denke nicht den Tod; ich sinn' und horche,
> Ob nicht zu irgendeiner frohen Flucht
> Die Götter Rat und Wege zubereiten.　　　　(Goethe, ii, i)

## Crisis and response: the beginnings of Weimar classicism

1 See W. Hinck, 'Man of the Theatre', in E. M. Wilkinson (ed.), *Goethe Revisited*, New York and London 1983/4. For a much fuller account, see Marvin Carlson, *Goethe and the Weimar Theatre*, Ithaca and London 1978; and W. Flemming, *Goethe und das Theater seiner Zeit*, Stuttgart 1968.

2 See the essay of this title by E. M. Wilkinson, in Wilkinson and Willoughby, *Goethe, Poet and Thinker*.

3 As quoted in D. McLellan, *The Thought of Karl Marx*, London 1971, p. 217. The point, of course, is not so much that Goethe anticipated Marx's sociological insights but that Marx's view of man and society was profoundly coloured by the intellectual heritage in which he was steeped, and in which the German classics played a major part.

4 See Peacock, *Goethe's Major Plays*, p. 96.

5 See H. W. Sullivan, *Calderón in the German Lands and the Low Countries: His Reception and Influence, 1654–1980*, Cambridge 1983, esp. pp. 185ff, 244ff.

6 See Stahl, *Friedrich Schiller's Drama*; and for a good brief survey of the aesthetic essays S. S. Kerry, *Schiller's Writings on Aesthetics*, Manchester 1961.

7 Reproduced in Carlson, *Goethe and the Weimar Theatre*, pp. 309ff.

## The high tide of Weimar classicism: Schiller and Goethe, 1798–1805

1 See Lindenberger, *Historical Drama*, pp. 9ff.

2 See Golo Mann, *Wallenstein*, London 1976 (German original, 1971).

3 Coleridge, in his translation of *Wallenstein*, which appeared as early as 1800, omitted the *Lager* altogether, put much of the banquet scene into prose, and made a number of stylistic emendations – several of them, interestingly enough, because he found Schiller *too* earthy and insufficiently decorous: the 'lax verses' of the *Lager* he thought would be quite unacceptable to 'the present taste of the English Public'. Had he intended his version for actual stage performance, Coleridge would no doubt have treated *Wallenstein* as freely as Schiller did *Macbeth*.

4 Others who had dramatised the story before, including the English Restoration dramatist John Banks (*The Island Queens*, 1684), had also found it necessary to engineer a meeting between the two queens on stage. Schiller may well have known some of these earlier treatments.

5 G. Steiner, *The Death of Tragedy*, London 1961, p. 181. Vaughan in *Types of Tragic Drama* firmly assigns the whole German tradition to the romantic rather than the classical type.

6 See M. H. Abrams, *Natural Supernaturalism: Tradition and Revolution in Romantic Literature*, Oxford 1971.

7 'Hamlet' (1919), in *Selected Prose of T. S. Eliot*, ed. Frank Kermode, London 1975, p. 48.

8 No fewer than six of Schiller's plays served as the bases for opera libretti: *Die Räuber* (*I Masnadieri*), *Kabale und Liebe* (*Luisa Millerin*), *Don Carlos* and *Die Jungfrau von Orleans* (*Giovanna d'Arco*) for Verdi (*La Forza del Destino* also borrows, very interestingly, from *Wallenstein*), *Maria Stuart* for Donizetti and *Wilhelm Tell* for Rossini.

9 See Stahl, *Friedrich Schiller's Drama*; and for more extreme examples Ilse Graham, *Schiller's Drama: Talent and Integrity*, London 1974, and much recent German criticism. For a more empirical appraisal of the historical plays in particular, see W. F. Mainland, *Schiller and the Changing Past*, London 1957; and Lesley Sharpe, *Schiller and the Historical Character*, Oxford 1982.

## Nordic phantoms: Goethe's Faust

1 On the Faust legend and its various literary treatments from Marlowe to Thomas Mann, see E. M. Butler, *The Fortunes of Faust*, Cambridge 1952

(reprinted 1979); and J. W. Smeed, *Faust in Literature*, Oxford 1975. The critical literature on Goethe's *Faust* is, of course, of immense extent. J. R. Williams in *Goethe's 'Faust'*, London 1987, summarises the main lines of interpretative controversy and offers a convincing overview of his own. See also N. Boyle, *Goethe: 'Faust, Part One'*, Cambridge 1987; and the introduction and bibliography to David Luke's translation of *Faust Part I*, Oxford 1987.

2 The name appears in various forms, the earliest being 'Mephostophilis' (thus in Spies, and in Marlowe), which could be construed as 'me-Fausto-philis', dog-Greek for 'no friend of Faust'; various other etymologies have been suggested – Greek, Hebrew and even Celtic – but none of them totally convincing. Goethe also uses the abbreviation 'Mephisto'.

3 I quote the opening lines in their original form, corresponding to ll. 354ff. of the finished work, where they appear slightly modified.

4 Heller, 'Goethe and the Avoidance of Tragedy'.

5 G. H. Lewes, *The Life and Works of Goethe* (1855), book 7, ch. 7 (Everyman edn, p. 557).

6 For a somewhat over-fanciful development of this 'architectural' approach, see Harold Jantz, *The Form of 'Faust': The Work of Art and its Intrinsic Structures*, Baltimore and London 1978.

7 The carnival at the Emperor's court in Part II, Act I appears to have been inspired in some of its details by prints based on Mantegna's *Triumph of Caesar*, the originals of which can be seen at Hampton Court. This is one of many instances in which Goethe derived inspiration from the visual arts.

8 See Jane K. Brown, *Goethe's 'Faust': The German Tragedy*, Ithaca and London 1986, in which the work is seen as a deliberate attempt by Goethe to reintegrate German drama into a non-Aristotelian tradition of 'world theatre'.

## A Prussian meteor: Heinrich von Kleist

1 See R. Paulin, 'The Drama', in S. S. Prawer (ed.), *The Romantic Period in Germany*, London 1970, pp. 173–203; and for further details of Tieck's work the same writer's *Ludwig Tieck. A Literary Biography*, Oxford 1985.

2 See D. J. Constantine, *Hölderlin*, Oxford 1988, pp. 131–51.

3 See, for example, E. L. Stahl, *Heinrich von Kleist's Dramas*, Oxford 1960; and J. Gearey, *Heinrich von Kleist: A Study in Tragedy and Anxiety*, Philadelphia 1968. Much previous criticism is usefully summarised in R. E. Helbling, *The Major Works of Heinrich von Kleist*, New York 1975.

4 In *Die Familie Ghonorez*, the 'Spanish' version of *Schroffenstein*, and in *Das*

*Käthchen von Heilbronn* the blank verse is interspersed with prose, but Kleist never wrote a play entirely in prose.

5 See L. Gossman, *Men and Masks. A Study of Molière*, Baltimore 1963. Whether or not this is a plausible reading of Molière's intentions in the play, Kleist may very well have read it in a similar sense. It has more usually been seen in a much less metaphysical light, as a satire on the amorous escapades of King Louis XIV.

6 For an account of this production, see Michael Patterson, *Peter Stein: Germany's Leading Theatre Director*, Cambridge 1981, pp. 90ff.

7 For a characteristic reading of the play as a 'drama about drama', see Bennett, *Modern Drama and German Classicism*, pp. 22–56.

## Classicism in Vienna (i): Grillparzer

1 See Stella Musulin, *Vienna in the Age of Metternich: From Napoleon to Revolution 1805–1848*, London 1975.

2 See D. Prohaska, *Raimund and Vienna*, Cambridge 1970; and W. E. Yates, *Nestroy*, Cambridge 1972. For an extensive discussion of the work of these and other Austrian dramatists of the time, including Grillparzer, as embodying a continuing Baroque, Catholic and counter-Reformation culture, see R. Bauer, *La Réalité, royaume de Dieu. Études sur l'originalité du théâtre viennois dans la première moitié du xix$^e$ siècle*, Munich 1965.

3 The similarity of the two works has been observed by a number of critics, though Grillparzer's has rarely if ever been cited as an actual source for Wagner's. Wagner professed a low opinion of Grillparzer, but this need not, of course, have prevented his borrowing from him. It is well known that Wagner was profoundly influenced by Schopenhauer, unlikely that Grillparzer had already read him at the time of composition of *Das goldene Vlies*. All three, philosopher and artists, articulate a pessimism which was profoundly characteristic of the age; we shall encounter it again in Hebbel.

4 The phrase occurs in a diary entry referring to the dramatic character of Cromwell's gesture in dissolving the Long Parliament. On his own visit to England in 1836, Grillparzer was a keen attender at the House of Commons; the Irish leader Daniel O'Connell he noted as a particularly impressive 'performer'.

5 Kotzebue, after writing a large number of successful plays, had by his death in 1819 earned another kind of fame, or notoriety. He had entered the Russian service during the Napoleonic wars, and returned to Germany afterwards as an agent of the Tsar; he was assassinated by a

member of one of the liberal student movements of the time. The event provoked a tightening of the counter-revolutionary screw in the so-called Karlsbad Decrees of the same year.

6 See Lindenberger, *Historical Drama*, p. 82.

7 Bruce Thompson, *Franz Grillparzer*, Boston 1981, p. 72. This and W. E. Yates, *Grillparzer: A Critical Introduction*, Cambridge 1972, are the best works on Grillparzer in English.

8 See H. Politzer, *Grillparzer oder das abgründige Biedermeier*, Vienna 1972, perhaps the most generally interesting of recent German books on Grillparzer. Politzer's chapter on *Der Traum ein Leben* is entitled 'Verdrängter Vormärz', 'Repressed Pre-March'.

9 For a history of Grillparzer's work in performance, see Norbert Fürst, *Grillparzer auf der Bühne*, Vienna and Munich 1958.

### Classicism in Vienna (ii): Hebbel; the end of the tradition

1 Birgit Fenner, *Friedrich Hebbel zwischen Hegel und Freud*, Stuttgart 1979. The best book on Hebbel in English is still Edna Purdie, *Friedrich Hebbel: A Study of his Life and Work*, Oxford 1932. Mary Garland, *Hebbel's Prose Tragedies*, Cambridge 1973, discusses only these, but stresses their poetic qualities.

2 See Peter Singer, *Hegel*, Oxford 1983, p. 71.

3 See M. J. Valency, *The Tragedies of Herod and Mariamne*, New York 1940. Schönaich's dramatic works were the subject of a devastating review by Lessing in 1755.

4 It is noteworthy that in Walter Hinck's *Handbuch des deutschen Dramas*, Düsseldorf 1980, Hebbel is the only dramatist who receives a second chapter on his work, devoted specifically to the difficulty of performing it appropriately for a modern audience.

### Epilogue

1 See R. A. Nicholls, *The Dramas of Christian Dietrich Grabbe*, The Hague 1969; and R. C. Cowen, *Christian Dietrich Grabbe*, New York 1972. The best of many books on Büchner is M. B. Benn, *The Drama of Revolt: A Critical Study of Georg Büchner*, Cambridge 1976.

2 See H. F. Garten, *Wagner the Dramatist*, London 1977; M. S. Silk and J. P. Stern, *Nietzsche on Tragedy*, Cambridge 1981; and D. Borchmeyer, *Das Theater Richard Wagners. Idee, Dichtung, Wirkung*, Stuttgart 1982.

3 See Benno von Wiese, *Die deutsche Tragödie von Lessing bis Hebbel*,

Hamburg 1948, and several subsequent editions, long influential and still well worth reading.

4 See Reinhold Grimm and Jost Hermand (eds.), *Die Klassik-Legende*, Frankfurt 1971.

5 A useful impression of the East German debate is conveyed by Philip Brady, 'On not being Intimidated: Socialist Overhauling of a Classic', in Wilkinson, *Goethe Revisited*.

6 See the volumes of essays edited by K. O. Conrady and Walter Hinderer; and W. Hinck's very useful *Handbuch des deutschen Dramas*. One might observe that the approach of such transatlantic critics as Benjamin Bennett (*Modern Drama and German Classicism*) and Jane Brown (*Goethe's 'Faust'*), different though it is from, say, Benno von Wiese's, is at least as unconcerned with the European political and social realities which confronted Goethe and his contemporaries.

7 Ronald Hayman, *The Times Literary Supplement*, 18 June 1982, on the Berlin 'Theatertreffen' of that year.

8 Volker Canaris, note to Schiller/Heyme, *Wallenstein, Regiebuch der Kölner Inszenierung*, Frankfurt 1970, p.170. It has become increasingly common practice for German theatre directors to publish the texts of their performances, often in the form of a reprint of the author's original text with all the director's cuts and alterations incorporated.

9 Patterson, *Peter Stein: Germany's Leading Theatre Director*, gives an excellent impression of the character of modern German 'director's theatre', including its pretentious and questionable aspects. See also Volker Canaris, 'Style and the Director', in Ronald Hayman (ed.), *The German Theatre: A Symposium*, London 1975.

# Bibliography

The bibliography lists all principal secondary sources referred to in the text, plus a few other works which may be of use to the reader seeking further information.

Abrams, M. H. *Natural Supernaturalism: Tradition and Revolution in Romantic Literature*, Oxford 1971

Auerbach, E. *Mimesis: The Representation of Reality in Western Literature*, Princeton 1953 (German original: *Mimesis. Dargestellte Wirklichkeit in der abendländischen Literatur*, Bern 1947)

Bauer, R. *La Réalité, royaume de Dieu. Études sur l'originalité du théâtre viennois dans la première moitié du xix$^e$ siècle*, Munich 1965

Benjamin, W. *The Origins of German Tragic Drama*, London 1977 (German original: *Ursprung des deutschen Trauerspiels*, Berlin 1928)

Benn, M. B. *The Drama of Revolt: A Critical Study of Georg Büchner*, Cambridge 1976

Bennett, B. *Modern Drama and German Classicism: Renaissance from Lessing to Brecht*, Ithaca and London 1979

Blackall, E. A. *The Emergence of German as a Literary Language*, Cambridge 1959

Borchmeyer, D. *Die Weimarer Klassik. Eine Einführung*, Königstein 1980
*Das Theater Richard Wagners. Idee, Dichtung, Wirkung*, Stuttgart 1982

Boyle, N. *Goethe: 'Faust, Part One'*, Cambridge 1987

Brown, J. K. *Goethe's 'Faust': The German Tragedy*, Ithaca and London 1986

Bruford, W. H. *Theatre, Drama and Audience in Goethe's Germany*, London 1950

Butler, E. M. *The Tyranny of Greece over Germany*, Cambridge 1935
*The Fortunes of Faust*, Cambridge 1952 (reprinted 1979)

Carlson, M. *Goethe and the Weimar Theatre*, Ithaca and London 1978

Conrady, K. O. (ed.) *Deutsche Literatur zur Zeit der Klassik*, Stuttgart 1977
Constantine, D. J. *Hölderlin*, Oxford 1988
Cowen, R. C. *Christian Dietrich Grabbe*, New York 1972
Dewhurst, K. and Reeves, N. *Friedrich Schiller: Medicine, Psychology and Literature*, Oxford 1978
Diederichsen, D. and Rudin, B. (eds.) *Lessing im Spiegel der Theaterkritik 1945–1979*, Berlin 1980
Fairley, B. *Goethe's 'Faust': Six Essays*, Oxford 1953
Fenner, B. *Friedrich Hebbel zwischen Hegel und Freud*, Stuttgart 1979
Flemming, W. *Goethe und das Theater seiner Zeit*, Stuttgart 1968
Fürst, N. *Grillparzer auf der Bühne*, Vienna and Munich 1958
Garland, H. B. *Schiller the Dramatic Writer: A Study of Style in the Plays*, Oxford 1969
Garland, M. *Hebbel's Prose Tragedies*, Cambridge 1973
Garten, H. F. *Wagner the Dramatist*, London 1977
Gearey, J. *Heinrich von Kleist: A Study in Tragedy and Anxiety*, Philadelphia 1968
*Goethe's 'Faust': The Making of Part One*, New Haven and London 1981
Graham, I. *Schiller's Drama: Talent and Integrity*, London 1974
Grimm, R. (ed.) *Deutsche Dramentheorien*, 2 vols., Frankfurt 1971
Grimm, R. and Hermand, J. (eds.) *Die Klassik-Legende*, Frankfurt 1971
Gundolf, F. *Shakespeare und der deutsche Geist*, 2nd edn, Berlin 1914
Halliwell, S. *Aristotle's Poetics*, London 1986
Hayman, R. (ed.) *The German Theatre: A Symposium*, London 1975
Heitner, R. R. *German Tragedy in the Age of Enlightenment*, Berkeley and Los Angeles 1963
Helbling, R. E. *The Major Works of Heinrich von Kleist*, New York 1975
Heller, E. *The Disinherited Mind*, Cambridge 1952
Hinck, W. (ed.) *Handbuch des deutschen Dramas*, Düsseldorf 1980
Hinderer, W. *Schillers Dramen. Neue Interpretationen*, Stuttgart 1979
*Goethes Dramen. Neue Interpretationen*, Stuttgart 1980
*Kleists Dramen. Neue Interpretationen*, Stuttgart 1981
Jantz, H. *The Form of 'Faust': The Work of Art and its Intrinsic Structures*, Baltimore and London 1978
Jones, J. *On Aristotle and Greek Tragedy*, London 1962
Kerry, S. S. *Schiller's Writings on Aesthetics*, Manchester 1961
Kindermann, H. *Theatergeschichte der Goethezeit*, Vienna 1948
Knudsen, H. *Deutsche Theatergeschichte*, Stuttgart 1959
Lamport, F. J. *Lessing and the Drama*, Oxford 1981
Lewes, G. H. *The Life and Works of Goethe*, London 1855 (reprinted in Everyman's Library)

Lindenberger, H. *Historical Drama: The Relation of Literature and Reality*, Chicago and London 1975

McInnes, E. *Das deutsche Drama des 19. Jahrhunderts*, Berlin 1983

Mainland, W. F. *Schiller and the Changing Past*, London 1957

Mann, O. *Geschichte des deutschen Dramas*, Stuttgart 1960

Mason, E. C. *Goethe's 'Faust': Its Genesis and Purport*, Berkeley and Los Angeles 1967

Menhennet, A. *Order and Freedom: German Literature and Society, 1720–1805*, London 1973

Musulin, S. *Vienna in the Age of Metternich: From Napoleon to Revolution 1805–1848*, London 1975

Nicholls, R. A. *The Dramas of Christian Dietrich Grabbe*, The Hague 1969

Patterson, M. *Peter Stein: Germany's Leading Theatre Director*, Cambridge 1981

Paulin, R. *Ludwig Tieck: A Literary Biography*, Oxford 1985

Peacock, R. *Goethe's Major Plays*, Manchester 1959

Politzer, H. *Grillparzer oder das abgründige Biedermeier*, Vienna 1972

Prawer, S. S. (ed.) *The Romantic Period in Germany*, London 1970

Prohaska, D. *Raimund and Vienna*, Cambridge 1970

Prudhoe, J. *The Theatre of Goethe and Schiller*, Oxford 1973

Purdie, E. *Friedrich Hebbel: A Study of his Life and Work*, Oxford 1932 (reprinted 1969)

Pütz, P. *Die Leistung der Form. Lessings Dramen*, Frankfurt 1986

Reed, T. J. *The Classical Centre: Goethe and Weimar 1775–1832*, London and New York 1980 (reprinted Oxford 1986)

Robertson, J. G. *Lessing's Dramatic Theory*, Cambridge 1939 (reprinted New York 1965)

Schöne, G. *Tausend Jahre deutsches Theater*, Munich 1962

Sharpe, L. *Schiller and the Historical Character*, Oxford 1982

Silk, M. S. and Stern, J. P. *Nietzsche on Tragedy*, Cambridge 1981

Smeed, J. W. *Faust in Literature*, Oxford 1975

Stahl, E. L. *Friedrich Schiller's Drama: Theory and Practice*, Oxford 1954
*Heinrich von Kleist's Dramas*, Oxford 1960

Steiner, G. *The Death of Tragedy*, London 1961

Sullivan, H. W. *Calderón in the German Lands and the Low Countries: His Reception and Influence, 1654–1980*, Cambridge 1983

Ter-Nedden, G. *Lessings Trauerspiele. Der Ursprung des modernen Dramas aus dem Geist der Kritik*, Stuttgart 1986

Thompson, B. *Franz Grillparzer*, Boston 1981

Trevelyan, H. *Goethe and the Greeks*, Cambridge 1941 (new edn 1981)

Valency, M. J. *The Tragedies of Herod and Mariamne*, New York 1940

# Bibliography

Vaughan, C. E. *Types of Tragic Drama*, London 1908

von Wiese, B. *Die deutsche Tragödie von Lessing bis Hebbel*, Hamburg 1948

Wilkinson, E. M. (ed.) *Goethe Revisited*, New York/London 1983/4

Wilkinson, E. M. and Willoughby, L. A. *Goethe, Poet and Thinker*, London 1962

Williams, J. R. *Goethe's 'Faust'*, London 1987

Yates, W. E. *Grillparzer: A Critical Introduction*, Cambridge 1972
*Nestroy*, Cambridge 1972

# Index

# Index

# Index

# Index

63–4, 67, 82–6, 125, 137, 139, 183,
  201, 211, 228–9n4
Providence, 18–19, 21–3, 28, 56, 72–4,
  76, 208
Prussia, 5, 8, 15, 18–20, 160, 162, 167,
  176, 216

Racine, J., 2–3, 46, 78, 81, 93, 100, 101
Raimund, F., 182, 194
Raupach, E., 210
realism, 15–16, 22–3, 24–5, 27–9, 31,
  37, 39, 48–9, 50, 61–4, 66–7, 69,
  77, 82, 97, 104–5, 115, 119, 121–2,
  123–4, 154, 200, 211–13, 216
Reformation, 5, 43, 110, 132, 149
Renaissance, 1, 4, 127, 146–7, 149, 153,
  154
revolutions of 1848, 181, 183, 185,
  191–2, 207, 213, 215, 218
Romanticism, 32, 43, 90, 119, 122–3,
  147, 151, 158–60, 183
Rousseau, J.-J., 117
Rowe, N., 83

Sachs, H., 6, 49, 83, 134, 154, 210
Sartre, J.-P., 2
Saxony, 8, 15, 18
Schiller, F., 7–8, 35, 36, 39, 45–6, 52–3,
  95, 97–100, 139–41, 145, 150, 154,
  155, 158, 159, 161–3, 166, 181,
  182, 183–4, 208, 209, 214, 217,
  218, 219
  Briefe über die ästhetische Erziehung des
    Menschen, 99, 148
  Demetrius, 130, 210
  Die Braut von Messina, 119–24, 126,
    166
  Die Jungfrau von Orleans, 119–24,
    126, 151, 206, 209
  Die Räuber, 53–8, 62, 63, 103, 104,
    109, 115–16, 128, 165, 183
  Die Verschwörung des Fiesco zu Genua,
    59–61, 62, 63, 64, 67, 79, 115
  Don Carlos, 67–86, 97, 99, 113, 193
  Kabale und Liebe, 61–4, 65, 67, 210,
    213
  Maria Stuart, 106, 115–19, 120, 122,
    126, 165, 174, 176

Über das Erhabene, 116
Über naive und sentimentalische
  Dichtung, 35, 54, 97–8, 122, 128
Wallenstein, 100, 103, 104, 109–15,
  117, 118, 119, 126, 130, 154, 168,
  176, 188, 191, 192–3, 199, 220–1;
  Prologue, 108, 109–10, 142–3, 162
  Wilhelm Tell, 102–3, 128–30, 220–1
Schlegel, A. W., 158–9
Schlegel, F., 84, 158–9
Schlegel, J. E., 13, 28, 82, 85, 109, 158,
  167, 225–6n7
Schnitzler, A., 31
Schönaich, C. von, 210, 230n3
Schopenhauer, A., 36, 184, 209, 229n3
Schreyvogel, J., 181
Schröder, F. L., 28, 37, 48, 50, 89
Schröter, Corona, 68, 88, 216
Schubert, F., 49
Schwerin, 27, 107
Scott, W., 44
Seneca, 1, 4, 14, 17
Seven Years' War, 15, 18–19
Seyler, A., 87
Shakespeare, W., 3–5, 11–13, 29, 34–6,
  37, 39–40, 42, 47, 53, 78–9, 83, 85,
  95, 96, 101, 109, 114–15, 119–20,
  154, 159, 181
  Hamlet, 9, 37–8, 53, 79, 96, 104, 124
  Julius Caesar, 13, 47
  King Lear, 53, 119
  Macbeth, 53, 100, 113, 221
  Measure for Measure, 177, 197
  Richard III, 53, 55, 189–90
  Romeo and Juliet, 197
  The Comedy of Errors, 172
Shaw, G. B., 122
Shelley, P. B., 48, 123, 128
Simon, B., 189
'Singspiel', 49, 216
Sonnleithner, J., 182
Sophocles, 1, 75, 115, 120
Spanish drama, 4–5, 158, 161, 183–4,
  194, 198
stage technology, 2, 37, 101–3, 119–20,
  127–8, 155–7
Stein, Charlotte von, 88, 90, 220
Stein, P., 176–7, 221